Orwell and Empire

Orwell and Empire

DOUGLAS KERR

OXFORD
UNIVERSITY PRESS

Great Clarendon Street, Oxford, OX2 6DP,
United Kingdom

Oxford University Press is a department of the University of Oxford.
It furthers the University's objective of excellence in research, scholarship,
and education by publishing worldwide. Oxford is a registered trade mark of
Oxford University Press in the UK and in certain other countries

First Edition published in 2022

Impression: 1

Published in the United States of America by Oxford University Press
198 Madison Avenue, New York, NY 10016, United States of America

British Library Cataloguing in Publication Data
Data available

Library of Congress Control Number: 2021952783

ISBN 978-0-19-286409-3

DOI: 10.1093/oso/9780192864093.001.0001

Printed and bound in the UK by
Clays Ltd, Elcograf S.P.A.

Acknowledgements

My interest in George Orwell goes back to a childhood reading of *Animal Farm*, but my focus on Orwell and the Orient owes a great deal to the many years I spent in Hong Kong, about half of them in the colony and half, after 1997, in the Special Administrative Region. I have affectionate memories of discussions of Orwell, and much else, with Kelvin Au, Stuart Christie, Chu Man Yin, Wendy Gan, Ian Holliday, Ruth Hung, Chris Hutton, Kendall Johnson, John H. Joseph, Caitlin Vandertop, Zhang Weiliang, and other colleagues and students in Hong Kong, and Henk Vynckier in Taiwan. To Elaine Ho, once again, I owe more than I can say.

Elsewhere I have benefited a lot from talking with distinguished Orwellians, and especially Richard Lance Keeble, Darcy Moore, John Rodden, Dione Venables, and Nathan Waddell. I owe a particular debt to Andrew Glazzard, who was in on the beginning of this project and lent it his critical skills. I am also very grateful to the anonymous readers at Oxford University Press. Finally, this book could not have been written without the scholarly labours of Peter Davison in producing the superb *Complete Works of George Orwell*.

An earlier version of Chapter 2 was published in *Essays in Criticism*, and adumbrations of other parts of the book have appeared over a number of years in *Textual Practice*, *Literature and History*, *Concentric: Literary and Cultural Studies*, *Clio*, and *Law and Literature*. I am grateful to these journals for letting me revisit and reshape some of the ideas first explored in their pages. I wish also to thank the staff of the Hong Kong University Library, the British Library, and the London Library for their courteous help. In the early stages of my research I benefited greatly from a grant from the Hong Kong Research Grants Council.

Contents

Orwell's Writings

George Orwell's writing is collected in the twenty volumes of *The Complete Works of George Orwell*, ed. Peter Davison (London: Secker and Warburg, 1998), and references here are indicated by volume and page number, e.g. 7:103.

The following titles by Orwell are indicated in the Notes by abbreviations:

ACD: A Clergyman's Daughter (*Complete Works*, vol. 3)
AF: Animal Farm (*Complete Works*, vol. 8)
BD: Burmese Days (*Complete Works*, vol. 2)
CUFA: Coming Up for Air (*Complete Works*, vol. 8)
D&O: Down and Out in Paris and London (*Complete Works*, vol. 1)
HTC: Homage to Catalonia (*Complete Works*, vol. 6)
KAF: Keep the Aspidistra Flying (*Complete Works*, vol. 4)
NEF: Nineteen Eighty-Four (*Complete Works*, vol. 9)
RWP: The Road to Wigan Pier (*Complete Works*, vol. 5)

Page numbering in the Penguin Modern Classics (or Penguin Twentieth-Century Classics) editions corresponds to the pagination of the *Complete Works*.

1
Introduction

Anglo-India

Imperialism means India.*

The national beverage of the British, consumed in stately homes and in the shelters of the homeless, and celebrated in a characteristic essay by George Orwell called 'A Nice Cup of Tea',* is brewed from the leaves of a plant that cannot be cultivated in Europe, but grows on the hillsides of India and China. Tea was not the only quintessentially English thing, important to Orwell, that was not English at all. The aspidistra, that hardy and inelegant plant once so common in English middle-class homes that Orwell made it a comic symbol of respectability in *Keep the Aspidistra Flying*, is also a botanical immigrant from the East. In English country gardens, oriental rhododendrons and camellias and peonies flourished under their assumed European names. And, although often unacknowledged, throughout the British way of life a strong oriental subtext ran like the great seams of coal beneath the landscapes of northern England described in *The Road to Wigan Pier*.

The most remarkable, and most naturalized, of oriental imports was one of the foundations of western culture. For a millennium and a half, people in the Christian West thought of the Bible as the sacred book of their own spirituality, although its Old Testament contains not a single European (or American), and Europe is present in the New Testament only in the ambiguous form of imperial and pagan Rome, and the Greek and Greek-speaking cities to which Saint Paul and his friends spread the gospel of Jesus. At school and at home, and in their Anglican and non-conformist places of worship, British children and adults alike, whose feelings towards the Jews who were their contemporaries may not always have been friendly, read or listened to passages of the Bible and thought and sang of themselves as the children of Israel. In Orwell's lifetime, they felt a spiritual ownership of actions like crossing the Jordan, or entering Jerusalem, in a context far removed from the challenges of the British mandate in Palestine (1920–48). They absorbed the history and laws, the genealogies and the teaching, the heroes and ancestors of an oriental tribe and petty kingdom of the Near East as if they were their own. This is a good example of the ubiquity, and yet the weird invisibility, of things oriental in everyday British life. It was an identification so thoroughly naturalized that it seems not to have struck most churchgoers as bizarre, though 'oriental' people in the Bible did very unEnglish things, as Orwell's George Bowling remarks in *Coming Up for Air*—'Sacrificing burnt offerings, walking about in fiery furnaces, getting nailed to crosses, getting swallowed by whales.'* The theological elaborations may have been western, but the origins and spirit of Christendom, as of other monotheisms, were native to Asia, and Christians reading about their patriarch Moses, their prophet Isaiah, and their Messiah Jesus, were doing something oriental.

In the work of George Orwell, as in the national life, there ran a strong oriental theme, sometimes submerged, half-acknowledged, sometimes plain for all to see. Orwell, like Rudyard Kipling, was Asian by birth. Another thing these two had in common was a frustration at the ignorance and incuriosity of their British neighbours about the huge importance of Asia to their own lives. 'And what should they know of England who only England know?' is Kipling's complaint, in his poem 'The English Flag', about what he saw as a national apathy, part wilful and part lazy, towards the profound links that bound his country to the rest of the world through its commitment to a global empire anchored in the Indian subcontinent. (If, in the twenty-first century, the British are not sufficiently aware of the part played by empire in shaping their nation, as many feel,* it is useful to remember that the same complaint was made in empire's heyday.)

For the history of Great Britain in the years between the Battle of Waterloo in 1815 and the Battle of the Marne in 1914 had been more Asian than European. British foreign and military policy was largely determined by the need to protect interests and possessions acquired in the seventeenth and eighteenth centuries by the East India Company, extended in the nineteenth century, and then formalized in 1858 as the British Empire of India. Much of Britain's imperial expansion in that century, in South-East Asia and in East Africa, was undertaken to consolidate British India and protect the trade that flowed to and from it. Britain's entanglements with its European neighbours, like its enormous navy, were motivated by the need to guard this relationship with the East, about which its own citizens seemed to know and care so little, even if they invested their savings, like the Rector in Orwell's *A Clergyman's Daughter*, in far-flung enterprises like Sumatra Tin and United Celanese.*

The liberal economist J. A. Hobson had warned in his book *Imperialism* (1902)* that Britain's economy was so thoroughly geared to its empire that it was starting to lose out to more agile competitors. He argued that the country would be better advised to use the surplus of its industrial wealth to improve the lot of its poorer citizens at home, instead of annexing ever more territory overseas. The slave trade was over, but many British families continued to enjoy enormous wealth made from the processing of materials from the East—cotton from India, timber from Burma, tin from Malaya. The material culture of their kitchens and bedrooms, offices and streets, testified to their country's oriental adventures and tastes, and to the teeming traffic in commodities across the empire. The Orient cluttered bourgeois homes. 'Middle-class domestic space became crammed as never before with furniture, clocks, mirrors, paintings, stuffed animals, ornaments, guns and myriad gewgaws and knickknacks.'* Bourgeois families in England slept in pyjamas on Egyptian cotton sheets, consumed English favourites like kedgeree and rice pudding and drank from teacups with pretty Chinese designs, clad the wheels of their vehicles with rubber from Malaya, donned jodhpurs to compete in gymkhanas, and went to Church on Sundays to pray to an oriental god for the conversion of the heathen in India and China.

In Orwell's lifetime, British culture, like the British economy, was already part-oriental, but in a way that was almost invisible to most people. The immigrations of the second half of the century would bring it into visibility. While many people in Britain paid little attention to their country's actual interactions with the Orient, as Kipling complained, they had had access since childhood to a fund of exotic, stereotypical, exciting, often patronizing or demeaning images and ideas about people and places in the East. These images and ideas belonged to the popular-culture wing of the body of knowledge that Edward W. Said was to critique when he repurposed the word Orientalism—which meant scholarly expertise about oriental languages, geography and so on—to mean a western idea of the East shaped, consciously or not, by European political and economic dominance of the Middle East and Asia in the age of empire.* (In this book an initial capital O will indicate when I am using the words Orientalist and Orientalism in this Saidian sense.) Orwell would have much to say about the 'false map of the world' people carried in their heads from childhood.*

This book puts the powerful oriental dimension in George Orwell's work in the foreground. I am aware of the negative connotation of the word 'oriental' for most modern readers, its association with mastery, selection, and prejudice. But my aim is to show how Orwell struggled all his life, and not with complete success, to exorcise the Orientalism (in Said's sense) which came with his Anglo-Indian patrimony. The argument is that this is absolutely formative to his intellectual and political development. Replacing Orwell in the Orient—and examining the Orient in Orwell—are central to the ambition of this book to rehistoricize him. This makes his case highly relevant to our present-day debates about the legacy of empire, but also, I hope, cautions against the temptation to over-simplify that beguiles the 'Orwell our contemporary' approach.

It is significant that Orwell is one of the touchstones, or heroes, of Paul Gilroy's book *After Empire* (2004). Gilroy argues that conflicts in a multicultural society need to be understood to exist in a context supplied by imperial and colonial history, and that this history should not be whitewashed in order to promote imperial nostalgia, or recruited to endorse new forms of colonial rule. For Gilroy, Orwell is an exemplary figure, in his 'combination of anti-imperialism and patriotic attachment to a uniquely English ecology of belonging'; and he is talking about a man whose formative experience in Burma 'drew him into the humanistic outlook which anchors his impatient universalism and is directed sharply against the injustice and inequality of the Empire's racial domination'.* Gilroy sees that not only Orwell's anti-imperialism, but the humanistic outlook in which it is rooted, were made in the East.

The Britain to which the infant Eric Blair was brought, or brought 'home', in 1904 would be plunged ten years later into a deadly European crisis that was to last his lifetime. But at the same time it was obliged to deal with developments in Asia that would prove equally momentous, a momentum drawing on, by the time of his death in 1950, towards the complete dismantling of the western empires in the East, and later in Africa and the Caribbean. His provenance made George Orwell well placed to understand both these narratives in the context of each other. I will argue that both the socialism towards which he groped in the 1930s, and the patriotism he discovered or rediscovered as his country came under the shadow of fascism, were made in the East. They were formed by his Asian experience, crystallized into an anti-imperialism that emerged from his time in Burma, and informed by his membership of the English imperial service class.

Much of what Orwell wrote has startling applicability to issues and predicaments today, and a great deal of secondary literature is devoted to elucidating this relevance.* However, Orwell is not our contemporary. To approach him as such risks missing much that makes him most specifically himself. Like any other historical figure, to see him clearly involves judging his distance from where we now stand. One thing that makes him foreign to the twenty-first century is his membership of a class which has vanished (as he said it would) from contemporary Britain, but which was crucial to his formation and the way he saw the world. He had both feet in Anglo-India. This may be the part of Orwell's historical and cultural environment which is most remote from modern readers, and consequently useful to recover. Three-quarters of a century after Indian independence, the Anglo-Indians, of whom Orwell was one, have disappeared from view as completely as the Elizabethan apprentice boys or the London Huguenots.

In many British families there were members who had seen service in the East, from the panjandrums of the Indian Civil Service to the ordinary seamen of the merchant navy. What I have called the imperial service class was the officer class, official and civilian, of the Empire. Those whose menfolk served or had served in the Orient were sometimes called Anglo-Indians. This was an important cohort of the upper-middle class, including the 'lower-upper-middle class' to which Orwell famously assigned his own family.* It was a tribe in which he was not at all comfortable. The sahibs and memsahibs who formed it, the Indian army officers, civil servants (like his father), professionals like doctors and surveyors, missionaries and planters, whether ensconced in their tropical bungalows or retired to Cheltenham or the coastal towns of England, had a reputation as florid-faced reactionaries, which was not inaccurate. 'No Anglo-Indian will ever deny that India is going to the dogs,'* Orwell wrote, and most believed the home country was bound for the same destination. You can sometimes hear their Tory accents in Orwell's writing, especially when he is at his most English. A few turned against the empire they had served: Orwell's friend, George Woodcock, in his excellent *Who Killed the British Empire?*, classes Orwell with John Strachey as 'members of old Anglo-Indian families' who 'rejected the service of empire'.* But in any case they were set apart by what they had seen. In their heads they carried a geography, and a history, different from people who took their bearings unquestioningly from the Greenwich meridian.

This extra dimension of experience—not cosmopolitan, but oriental— gave them a perspective that was estranged and eccentric, off-centre. It is celebrated in Kipling's delighted (and show-off) reaction to the prospect of becoming a property-owner in Sussex: 'England is a wonderful land. It is the most marvellous of all foreign countries that I have ever been in.'* For many of them, this perspective that marked them as an outclass produced a harrumphing dissatisfaction, an inability to change, or to reconcile themselves to their own country and what seemed to have become of it. It did not make them popular or admired, by their countrymen or by Indians. Mulk Raj Anand, for example, writing in 1936, found a cluster of them in Bayswater, 'the retired Anglo-Indians who rotted in the boarding-houses of that district, completely out of touch with India and alienated from their own people'.* But in the particular case of George Orwell, his oriental eccentricity of perspective gave him the vision for a body of work now reckoned one of the most significant in the literature of the twentieth century. It is work marked and formed by his off-centredness, his estrangement.

There is nothing more understandable than that a boy who spent four and a half years walking every day in the streets of a Berkshire town in black silk top hat and tail-coat, speaking in the accents of privilege and derided by gangs of working-class boys, should have grown up to become a socialist. What better education than Eton College for an understanding of the English class system? Likewise his years in the Imperial Police in Burma equipped him with a first-hand knowledge, of a kind not available to the domestic British observer, of how political power could be unjustly wielded. The map of the world was different if it was centred not on Greenwich but on Delhi or Mandalay.

But although he became a critic of this business of empire, he had been its willing agent. Nobody forced him into making his career in the East after he left school, or pressured him into applying to join the disciplined services. He chose the Indian Police, and asked to be posted to Burma (which, for administrative purposes, came under the government of India) because of his family's links to that country. When he returned to Europe, he came back as an ex-imperial policeman; he had not resigned from the force before he left, and was presumably expected to return to Burma. But he had accumulated a number of reasons to want to remain in Europe. Among these may have been, as he said later, his feelings about the empire he served.

He mocked the imperial service class, but even as his political views developed, much of his cultural identity remained that of his Anglo-Indian family, and many of its attitudes and values persisted. Orwell loved lists: here is a list of some of his Anglo-Indian attitudes. He disliked London, preferring to live in rural retirement; above all things, he loved gardening.* After working all day in his garden, visitors reported, he insisted on dressing for dinner.* He determined to put his baby son's name down for his old school, Eton, later changing this preference to Westminster.* Many of his closest friends—they included Richard Rees, David Astor, L. H. Myers, Anthony Powell, Cyril Connolly—were old Etonians like himself, and this old-school network was useful throughout his career. He had few friends among the working class. He formed no lasting friendships with Burmese or Indians in Burma. He remained loyal to 'the England I was taught to love so long ago', acknowledging 'the spiritual need for patriotism and the military virtues'.* His manners and conduct were gentlemanly, and so were his clothes, even at his shabbiest. As V. S. Pritchett observed, he was 'one who had been trained for duty and was inured to suffering'.* All his life, he read Kipling, 'a sort of

household god' in middle-class and especially Anglo-Indian families,*
with deep enjoyment. On his walls hung swords brought back from
Burma, and the portrait of an aristocratic eighteenth-century ancestress.
His second wife was, like himself, the India-born child of a colonial official. He abhorred communism. He remained sceptical about the prospect of democracy for Burma, the country he had helped to rule, and
believed it could never achieve true independence.* He enjoyed shooting. He was clumsy with women, and often gauche in the expression of
feeling: when his first wife died unexpectedly, he was devastated,* but
replied to condolences saying, 'Yes, she was a good old stick.'* He was
scornful of homosexuals ('pansies'), and of 'cranks' of all kinds (pacifists,
vegetarians, nudists, Quakers, feminists, etc.).* In the Aragon trenches,
he drank proper English tea ordered from Fortnum and Mason. On the
whole, he despised left-wing people, especially the intellectuals, for what
he called 'their utter ignorance of the way things actually happen.'* In
fact, he had an English mistrust of intellectuals in general, the 'sleek professors' who could twist words to defend, or disguise, the indefensible.*
(They would become the pigs of *Animal Farm*.) He held to a soldierly
belief in plain speaking, and writing. He was anti-Catholic, and steeped
in Anglican culture, and at the end of his life expressed a wish to be
buried according to the rites of the Church of England. Such lifelong
beliefs, habits, and tastes were among the fetishes of his tribe. 'In fact,' he
acknowledged, in a sentence we might be inclined to return to again and
again, 'it is very difficult to escape, culturally, from the class into which
you have been born.'* And like all repatriated Anglo-Indians, he looked
on his homebound fellow-countrymen and women as provincial, in a
global sense, and limited in outlook. What could they know of England,
who only England knew?

   The George Orwell of the present day is often regarded, in Rosinka
Chaudhuri's phrase, as 'a custodian of Englishness'.* But his formation
was so thoroughly English, as has so often been observed—his love of
animals, his enthusiasm for English cookery and pubs and a nice cup of
tea, his admiration of Dickens and *A Shropshire Lad**—as to obscure the
fact that he was really a lifelong immigrant, reporting on England, like
Kipling, as on a foreign land. It is a fact that shaped the way he knew
things, his knowledge of his own education, of the natural world, of

violence, of literature, of manual labour, of home, and much more. Everywhere he went—Spain, and Morocco, for example—he saw with that extra oriental perspective, and these new experiences in turn reflected back on what he knew of the East, and changed it. The essays that follow are about what Orwell knew about the world, and how that knowledge was importantly shaped by his eastern experience.* His writing about the East, and the presence of the East in his writing, is my subject—Orwell and Empire, Orwell and the East.

Here is the story of Orwell, the Empire, and the Orient.

George Orwell's mother was French, his father English. His inheritance was imperial on both sides, and his ancestors had left their fingerprints all over the globe. After the disastrous attempt to found a Scottish colony at Darien, on the Isthmus of Panama, a certain Colonel John Blair (1668–1728), a lowland Scot, had settled in Jamaica in 1699, and made a fortune as a slave-owning man of property. His grandson, Charles Blair, also a plantation owner, amassed further wealth, and married a daughter of the Earl of Westmoreland. The Blair family continued to enjoy the profits from plantations worked by slaves. Charles's son, Thomas Richard Blair, was ordained a deacon of the Anglican church in Calcutta in 1839, and served as a priest in Tasmania. He later returned to England and finished his career as vicar in a parish in Dorset. Slavery had been abolished in 1833, and although slave-owners were generously compensated, the family's circumstances began a slow decline thereafter, due to the consequent loss of revenue. Richard Walmsley Blair, the youngest of Thomas's ten children, born in 1857, belonged, in Darcy Moore's striking words, to 'the first generation of Blairs not to profit financially from slavery since 1699'.* He became a civil servant in India.

The thousand or so top members of the Indian Civil Service, the 'Civilians' so hero-worshipped in Kipling's writing, who ruled the three hundred million inhabitants of the British Raj, were a glittering elite. Beneath them was a larger class of uncovenanted civil servants, both British and Indian, who worked in the forestry, telegraph, educational, and other such services, and in many subordinate administrative positions. Richard Blair became one of these, joining, as Maung Htin Aung has it, 'a "Provincial" Civil Service which was essentially for natives'.*

He entered the Opium Department of the province of Bengal in 1875, as an Assistant Sub-Deputy Opium Agent, his job being to supervise the poppy growers in his district and ensure the efficiency of their work and the quality of the crop. It was not a glamorous appointment. Its consumption being illegal in India, opium was a British monopoly, cultivated in Bengal mostly for export to China, and a very important source of revenue for British India. But the government of China wanted the opium traffic banned, and meanwhile many people in Britain were also asking how their country could justify profiting from selling addictive narcotics to foreigners. W. E. Gladstone's last government set up a Royal Commission on Opium in 1893, but when it reported, the Commission did not recommend ending the trade. The traffic in opium from British India to China continued until 1915, but at least towards the end of Richard Blair's career, the writing must have been visible on the wall.

He retired from the Opium Department in 1912 at the age of 55, with an annual pension of £400, and came home for good. He became secretary of the Henley Golf Club. It had not been a scintillating career. There was a late spasm in 1917, when at the age of 60, he gamely volunteered for active service and became a second lieutenant and probably 'one of the oldest junior officers in the British Army'.* He was sent to France with the 51st (Ranchi) Indian Labour Company, and was later seconded to the Royal Artillery, and was not demobilized until December 1919. He moved his family to Southwold on the Suffolk coast, while the effect of inflation on his pension continued to nibble at the shabby fabric of their gentility. Richard Blair died in 1939. He had embodied much that his son came to despise. They may have had little in common, but, as Darcy Moore has pointed out, 'we have no record of Orwell being embarrassed or concerned by his father's line of work'.* Five years after the old man's death, Orwell named his own son after his father.

In the 1850s, Frank Limouzin, a timber merchant from Limoges in central France, emigrated with his wife and two brothers to Burma. They settled in Moulmein, a thriving port which owed its prosperity to shipbuilding and the timber trade. Timber, particularly Burmese teak, was a valuable export commodity, and its cultivation had been controlled by the British colonial government since the 1840s. Local people, mostly Karens, having been discovered to have no legal title to the forests where they had lived for generations, these were declared Crown property. All the timber in Burma, therefore, belonged to the government. The industry—harvesting, treatment, sale, and shipping—was entirely in the hands of foreign companies, mostly British. Frank Limouzin prospered, as head of Limouzin and Co., timber merchants. When his first wife died, he married again, this time to an Englishwoman. They had eight children, including Ida Mabel, born in England while they were visiting her mother's relatives, and Nellie, who would play an important part in Orwell's adult life.* The children grew up in Moulmein, and in due course Ida took a position as assistant mistress in a boys' school in Nainital, a hill station in north-eastern India, where she met and married Richard Walmsley Blair. This was in 1897. Richard had risen, though not very far, from Assistant Sub-Deputy Opium Agent to Sub-Deputy Opium Agent, fourth class.

Meanwhile in Moulmein, the Limouzin family was in trouble. Frank lost most of his money. Scandalously, his brother William, and one of his sons, also called Frank, both fathered children by Burmese women. The family scattered, most of them ending up in England, but Orwell was to meet his grandmother, Thérèse Limouzin, an old lady deemed eccentric, in Moulmein in 1925. She was said to have 'gone native', and adopted Burmese dress, but though she had lived in the country for forty years, she had never learned Burmese.

Richard Blair took his young bride back to the plains district of Gaya, a centre of Bengal's opium cultivation, where their eldest child, Marjorie, was born. In 1903, promoted now to Sub-Deputy Opium Agent, third class, Richard was transferred north to the more remote Motihari, in the shadow of the Nepalese Himalayas. There their son Eric was born, on 25 June 1903.

Later in the year, Ida took the two children to England, where they were to grow up. A second daughter, Avril, was born in 1908. Richard Blair continued to work in India, and for the first nine years of Eric Blair's life his father was an absence, punctuated by an appearance on long leave in the summer of 1907, when he must have seemed a stranger to his young children. The strangeness of this dislocated family life, by no means unusual in Anglo-Indian families, was a constant reminder that the Blairs were not, in any simple way, at home in England.

'The dirty work of empire' is a phrase Orwell was to use twice: in 'Shooting an Elephant' and *The Road to Wigan Pier.** It is usually supposed to refer to his own involvement in police work in colonial Burma. But the dirty work of empire started much further upstream. His family's fortunes, dwindling though they may have been, were built on it: slavery, opium, the appropriation on a grand scale of other people's natural wealth. He was to make the hero of his first novel a timber merchant like his Limouzin grandfather.

The Blair family's financial position never matched their idea of their own social standing and worth. Nevertheless, with the help of scholarships, Eric Blair was privately educated, at St Cyprian's preparatory school at Eastbourne on the south coast and then at Eton, the pre-eminent English public school and nursery of the governing class. A contemporary at St Cyprian's remembered him as dull and unfriendly, 'unlike the other Anglo-Indian boys at the school.'* Most of his contemporaries went on from Eton to university or the armed forces. Although no militarist, at Eton he had served like everyone else in the Officers' Training Corps for five years, a good preparation for a career in uniform. The idea of colonial service seems to have been always at the back of his mind as a career. 'Blair's destiny apparently lay in the East,' as John Newsinger says, 'remaining loyal to family tradition, hardly the action of a member of the awkward squad.'* Steven Runciman remembered enthusiastic conversations about the mysterious Orient. 'He wanted to go to the East. He had a sort of sentimental side. This nostalgia for the East which he can hardly have remembered.'* And his tutor at Eton, Andrew Gow, recalled later that when they discussed his future, 'Blair was intent on Burma.'* The covenanted Indian Civil Service was for university graduates only, and there was a highly competitive exam. The police was a respectable alternative. 'In actual fact, the Imperial Police was a very prestigious service, second only to the Indian Civil Service, and whereas the "I" in other Imperial services modestly stood for "Indian", the "I" in the Police Service was proudly and openly "Imperial".'* Recruits to the Imperial Police signed a covenant of service directly with the Secretary of State for India.

While most of his Eton friends looked forward to going to university, Eric Blair crammed for and passed the entrance examinations for the Indian Imperial Police, stating a preference to be posted to Burma. He also passed the medical and riding test. Ten months after leaving school he became a Probationary Assistant Superintendent, sailed for Rangoon in October 1922, and joined the Police Training School in Mandalay for a year. He was 19, and it was his first venture abroad. It was a decade of unrest, of a growing Burmese nationalism, and worsening relations between local people and the British. It would culminate, after he had left the country, in a violent uprising in 1930, with bloody reprisals. It was an uncomfortable time to be a British policeman in Burma, and besides, he was chronically homesick for England. Christopher Hollis, though often an unreliable witness, was no doubt right to speculate that Orwell's later writing was stimulated by 'the tang of uncongenial life' in Burma.*

Part of his training involved a month's attachment to a British regiment at the pleasant hill station of Maymyo. Thereafter, he was posted around: to Myaungmya and then Twante in the Irrawaddy delta, to Syriam near the capital Rangoon for nine months, then (promoted to Assistant District Superintendent) to Insein, also near Rangoon, where the main responsibility of the police was to guard the large Burmah Oil Company refinery. His next posting was to the port city of Moulmein, where some of his Limouzin relations still lived. Possibly as a consequence of his having shot an elephant belonging to a British timber company, he was next sent upcountry to Katha at the far end of the Burma railway.*

Katha is the model for the town of Kyauktada in Orwell's novel *Burmese Days*. It was to be his last posting in the country. In July 1927, he left Burma to return to Europe after almost five years, departing a few months ahead of his long-leave date for medical reasons, having contracted dengue fever in Katha. He had not resigned from the police and if, as he later asserted, he was now thoroughly disaffected with the regime he served, he appears to have kept these feelings to himself: people who knew him in Burma seem to have regarded his opinions as blamelessly orthodox.* He would never return. But he was about to begin the rest of his life as an ex-colonial official.

The five years spent in Burma would be a lifelong point of reference, and became the paradigm for his idea of political injustice. But the country haunted him in other ways too, and Burmese landscapes and faces continued to visit his dreams. Memories of the Orient are to be found in all his books, as we shall see, but it is directly present in his writing only intermittently. He came back from Burma with a handful of poems, and some preliminary workings on a novel, inspired by his experience there. While living in Paris in 1928–29, he made some money from journalism, and one of four articles on political and social themes translated into French and published in the newspaper *Le Progrès Civique* is 'How a Nation is Exploited: The British Empire in Burma'. It explains how Burma was colonized for purposes of resource extraction, particularly of the country's wealth of timber, metals, gems, oil, and rice. The British government of Burma is essentially despotic, the argument continues: the local inhabitants are being shamelessly robbed and pilfered by foreigners, though they hardly notice it. 'Their country is so rich, their population so scattered, their needs, like those of all Orientals, so slight that they are not conscious of being exploited.'* Some two years after leaving the East, and already generalizing rather patronizingly about 'all Orientals' with the confidence of a true Anglo-Indian, the author of this article, E. A. Blair, now writes as a convinced anti-imperialist.

Two of his most famous short narratives, 'A Hanging' (1931) and 'Shooting an Elephant' (1936), return to his Burmese experience, with a more complex psychological and emotional plot. The first of these appears over the name Eric A. Blair, but by the time of the second, he is writing as George Orwell, a name adopted, in a last-minute decision, for *Down and Out in Paris and London*. These two pieces are self-consciously literary productions, and both have a quantum of fictionality which is difficult to determine. This is equally the case with longer works like *Down and Out* and *The Road to Wigan Pier*. Between 'A Hanging' and 'Shooting an Elephant' comes *Burmese Days*, a novel set entirely in Upper Burma and its author's most extensive treatment of oriental subject-matter.

Throughout the 1930s and into the 1940s, when he was a prolific reviewer of books, editors who knew of his interest and experience in the East sent him for review books of all sorts, novels and memoirs and political studies, about Burma, India, and other Asian countries. His reputation in journalistic circles as someone knowledgeable about the Orient was responsible for his being offered a job, in December 1937, writing for the *Pioneer*, a newspaper in Lucknow, India. He was tempted, thinking that the job might give him 'a clearer idea of political and social conditions in India'.* He wondered if his now left-wing views might be an impediment; but in the end it was probably his precarious state of health that meant that this opportunity came to nothing.

When war with Germany came in 1939, Orwell was medically unfit for service (though he did join the Home Guard), and he could not find other war work. He spent many months moping about, doing journalistic writing and reviewing plays and films for *Time and Tide*. At one point, as imminent invasion threatened in 1940, he found himself in the theatre reviewing the fantasy Orientalism of the popular musical play *Chu Chin Chow*. This was something of a nadir. Things seemed to be looking up in August 1941 when he began work as Talks Assistant (later Talks Producer) in the Indian Section of the Eastern Service of the British Broadcasting Corporation. He stayed with the BBC until November 1943, writing features and regular newsletters, and producing programmes, for an English-speaking audience in India consisting, he hoped, largely of students. The remit of the Eastern Service was to provide a link, through the airwaves, to distant India from the imperial centre. Its aim was to foster Indian interest in the English language and its culture, and to encourage Indians' loyalty to Britain and the empire at a time when this was directly threatened by Japanese military successes in Asia, as well as by a powerful nationalist movement demanding that the British quit India. Orwell was a supporter of Indian independence, but he also felt Britain and the Allies first needed the help of India to win the war. This interesting dilemma underlies his broadcast commentaries on the progress of the war, in which he strives to adopt an Indian point of view, as well as other editorial activities such as his promotion of Indian writers in English, such as his nationalist friend, Mulk Raj Anand.

Orwell left the BBC towards the end of 1943, taking up the literary editorship of the left-wing *Tribune*, for which he wrote a regular column. With the late successes of *Animal Farm* (1945) and *Nineteen Eighty-Four* (1949), he became at last a famous author. Though exhausted and critically ill, in his final months he began drafting his next novel, tentatively given the Maughamesque title, *A Smoking-Room Story*. In his imagination he was returning for a last time to the East.

This study of Orwell's writing reads it as a complex network, in which the individual nodes—novel, essay, review, diary entry, and so on—are richly interconnected. One of the pleasures of reading Orwell is this movement across the face of his writing, and the discovery of congruences, contrasts, and dialogue between and among different moments of expression. It is in the whole of his work that Orwell and the Orient takes shape.

One context for this book is the current set of debates about how to deal with Britain's imperial past, and its shaping of questions of race, justice, and identity in the present. Orwell wrestled all his life with these questions. An anti-imperialist whose involvement with empire was direct, personal, and acknowledged, he was and remains essential reading, not least for people who believe that the legacy of empire is an issue for other people. To help to understand him, this book replaces him in his oriental story, and historicizes this writer who struggled all his life with his own history.

In what follows, I have tried as far as possible to allow Orwell to speak for himself. The chapters themselves are designed to be relatively free-standing, so that they do not need to be read in order. However, they do have an overall architecture. I find my entry point in a subject, animals, that has deep roots in Orwell's childhood experience, and which was in many ways formative, as he himself recognized. He was a lifelong animal writer, and it was not only in *Animal Farm* that he recruited animals to help him talk about human beings. The theme of animals then broadens out to the natural environment. The earlier chapters are quite closely focused on Orwell's Burma, and what he wrote about it. He may have been Indian-born, but Burma was the theatre of his direct oriental experience, and this finds its fullest expression in the early novel *Burmese Days.*

His return to Europe sees his engagement with the issue of class, which was largely in abeyance during his time in the East. The chapters on empire and geography watch him constructing a global picture shaped by the activities of imperialism and, to some extent, its discontents. In the chapter on women particularly, we can understand how hard it was for him to leave behind his Anglo-Indian patrimony and prejudices. The same is true of the question of race, which follows: nobody starts from nowhere, and Orwell is at his most vulnerable when struggling to overcome the sort of preconceptions that inhibited the clear and fair view of the world that was his intellectual objective. These issues recur throughout his writing, and not just when his attention is fixed on the East. The sections about the police and the law go together. They return us to the Burmese experience, but both subjects are carried forward from there, through their permutations in England and Catalonia, to their projections into the powerful imaginary worlds of *Animal Farm* and *Nineteen Eighty-Four*. In the last chapter, I foreground what has been my topic all along: Orwell the writer. There the argument is made that the writerly Orwell is the eastward-facing Orwell, poised between the Anglo-Indian Rudyard Kipling and the Indo-Anglian Mulk Raj Anand.

2
Animals

It begins with animals. The world in which George Orwell (as Eric Blair) grew up was alive with them. His fiction teems with them, from the buffalo in *Burmese Days* to the rats of *Nineteen Eighty-Four*. In his youth, he thought he remembered, 'most middle-class boys grew up within sight of a farm, and naturally it was the picturesque side of farm life that appealed to them'.* His most popular book would tell a story about animals, and there are animals in all his novels. As soon as he was old enough, the young Eric was kitted out with equipment for exploring and subduing the natural world: he had his own bicycle, fishing rod, and gun. He was a middle-class boy, and his upbringing at home and school encouraged a sometimes proprietorial and predatory interest in nature. The 'lower-upper-middle class' to which he belonged had assumed some of the gentry's absorption in matters of land and livestock, though their ownership of these things might amount to no more than a suburban garden and a cat. Wherever this was possible, even in Burma and Morocco, in adult life, Orwell kept livestock on a small scale. His diaries keep a scrupulous record of the egg-laying achievements of his hens, and his neighbours in Wallington were treated to the sight of the writer and his wife taking their goats for a walk on the common in the evening. Animals were there from the first in his writing too. At the age of 4 or 5, his first poem—appropriately, for an Anglo-Indian child—had been about a tiger (it had 'chair-like teeth').*

For him, animals would remain a good way of thinking about human beings. In *Burmese Days*, almost every character, local or European, has some animal characteristic, as Rosinka Chaudhuri points out.* U Po Kyin resembles a crocodile, his wife has a brown simian face. The two Eurasians corner Flory like a pair of dogs looking for a game. A Chinese baby crawls around like a large yellow frog. The club butler has eyes like those of a dog. Verrall has a face like a rabbit, MacGregor looks like a saurian monster, Maxwell brings to mind a carthorse colt, Mrs Lackersteen has the hands of a newt, and so on. These notations were no doubt an aid to visualization, but also usually pointed to character. So did people's attitudes and behaviour towards animals. Elizabeth Lackersteen is horrified by the Burmese. 'So *coarse*-looking; like some kind of animal.'*

He was not sentimental about animals. From his boyhood days in the Thames valley, Eric Blair had been a great slaughterer of rabbits, and on the island of Jura the cruelty with which he slit open the body of a live snake disturbed one friend, an ex-soldier.* But animals were always important in his life. He never wrote an autobiography, and it is often impossible to verify objectively the things he said about himself, and particularly his young self. Cyril Connolly, for example, who had been to school with him, remembered his rebelliousness at St Cyprian's but not the misery he described so bitterly in later life.* Jacinta Buddicom, a childhood friend, remembered him as an ordinarily 'happy, smiling schoolboy'.* By his own account, however, particularly in the essay 'Such, Such Were the Joys', his childhood was unhappy, self-conscious, and self-loathing, emotionally withdrawn and lonely.* He was quite convinced he was ugly. Uncomfortable in his body and awkward in his social surroundings, he sought emotionally enriching experience where he could find it. 'Most of the good memories of my childhood,' he recalled, 'and up to the age of about twenty, are in some way connected with animals.'*

Later in life, though he was sociable and loved to talk, he seems to have remained awkward and often clumsy with both men and women. But you knew where you were with animals. In the spring of 1946, he wrote an essay for *Tribune* saluting the emergence of the common toad from hibernation in springtime, and noting unexpectedly that the toad has the most beautiful eye of any living creature. 'I think that by retaining one's childhood love of such things as trees, fishes, butterflies and— to return to my first instance—toads, one makes a peaceful and decent future a little more probable,' he wrote, a startling claim to make, in a political magazine, in the aftermath of a catastrophic world war.*

Animals could be fascinating, useful, enjoyable, and exciting. A love for the natural world, beginning in childhood, was the basis for a respect for one's surroundings which might help to restrain competitive and destructive behaviour. But in Orwell's case, it went beyond this. In his mature writing, and especially in the Burmese material, the world of nature—of animals, and growing things, and the landscape—becomes a way of seeing and talking about what it was hard to see and talk about in simply human terms. It is not merely a matter of nature supplying 'good memories' and nourishing the life of feeling, which human contact does not satisfy. Burmese nature was just as capable of terrifying as consoling, and the story it told could as soon turn into a nightmare as an idyll. In 'A Hanging' and the novel *Burmese Days*, as obviously in 'Shooting an Elephant', there is an animal plot that clarifies the issues of the human world. What happens is that the natural world, and animals in particular, become a sort of code in which things can be made articulate both to characters and to a narrator. And, above all, the natural world is a way for people to see Burma who are not able, for one reason or another, to see the Burmese.

In colonial history, the elephant gun and the butterfly net followed, and sometimes preceded, the flag. And when that history expressed itself in stories and pictures, mastery over places often took the form of possession and mastery of animals. 'There is the usual photograph of Mr Relton sitting rifle in hand on a dead tiger,' Orwell wrote in a review of a book about travels in the East. 'I never see one of these without wanting to see a photo of a tiger sitting on a big-game hunter.'* There is an allegory of this mastery in the person of Mowgli in Rudyard Kipling's *Jungle Books*, where the authority—the natural authority—of the human child over the jungle beasts is proved, not only by his superior cleverness, but by the command of his gaze: none of the other animals dare look him in the eye. Even so, Kipling's animals, even the anthropomorphized beasts of the *Just So Stories*, can have a life more independent of human activity than Orwell's usually enjoy. For Orwell's animals, there is nearly always a human being nearby, to domesticate, hunt, or just observe them.

In the skirts of the expanding European empires of the later nineteenth century came plenty of Social Darwinists and anthropological skull-measurers ready to explain that non-European 'natives' were several rungs down on creation's ladder, and *ipso facto* closer to the animal state.

This bizarre doctrine was canvassed by its proponents with impressive measurings of differences of geography, climate, and anatomy, but was simply accepted as a scientifically proven fact, well into the twentieth century, by many people further down the knowledge hierarchy. The fact in turn served both to explain and to justify the subjection of one kind of people to another. The first thing Orwell says he saw in the British empire in Asia, in the Colombo docks, was a white policeman kicking a coolie. Watching Europeans made no protest. 'They were white, and the coolie was black. In other words he was sub-human, a different kind of animal.'* If 'natives' were close to animals, it was all right to treat them as you might treat an animal. The relation between humans and animals had become tangled up in the relation between rulers and ruled.

Orwell had no difficulty in seeing these nasty racialist fantasies for what they were, and he attributes some of them to the most repulsive of his European characters in *Burmese Days*. His own feelings about western myths of biological supremacy can be gauged from a 1944 piece where he talks about the sola topi, the famous pith helmet once considered an essential part of the kit of Europeans in the tropics:

> Till recently the Europeans in India had an essentially superstitious attitude towards heat apoplexy, or sunstroke as it is usually called. It was supposed to be something dangerous to Europeans but not to Asiatics. When I was in Burma I was assured that the Indian sun, even at its coolest, had a peculiar deadliness which could only be warded off by wearing a helmet of cork or pith. 'Natives,' their skulls being thicker, had no need of these helmets, but for a European even a double felt hat was not a reliable protection.*

(This is 1944: he has learned to enclose the word 'natives' in inverted commas.) The pith helmet was thought to be needed to protect the thinner European skull from the rays of the sun, which were stronger nearer the equator. Somewhere beneath this nonsense is a version of a Lamarckian theory about the adaptation of species to environment, later given a new explanation by natural selection: white people in the tropics were vulnerable because they were outside their natural habitat. They were different from the local people, and, Orwell explains, an endless emphasis on the differences between races was one of the necessary props of imperialism:

> You can only rule over a subject race, especially when you are in a small minority, if you honestly believe yourself to be racially superior, and it helps towards this if you can believe that the subject race is *biologically* different. There were quite a number of ways in which Europeans in India used to believe, without any evidence, that Asiatic bodies differed from their own. Even quite considerable anatomical differences were supposed to exist. But this nonsense about Europeans being subject to sunstroke, and orientals not, was the most cherished superstition of all. The thin skull was the mark of racial superiority, and the pith topi was a sort of emblem of imperialism.*

Racism rests on the belief that different groups belong to different, and unequal, orders of nature.

This will bring us back to Orwell and animals, but not in a straight line. Trained from childhood as an observer of the natural world, when he travelled to distant places, he was used to paying attention to the environment and its non-human inhabitants. But to turn to these things was not a way of averting his gaze from the human reality of the imperialism he served and, he said, soon came to despise. One clue to the focus on nature in Orwell's Burmese writing is to be found in an apparently remote context, the essay 'Marrakech', written early in 1939 while he was spending half a year in French Morocco, after a serious breakdown in health. It was here, anomalously, that he wrote *Coming Up for Air*, his most English novel, about a man trying to recover the pleasures and simplicity of the landscape of his rural childhood. In French Morocco, Orwell for the first time was seeing somebody else's empire. (Nominally a sovereign state, Morocco was a French protectorate ruled by a colonial administration.)

There is an often-remarked upon tendency of European explorers to see and report on the land they were discovering as unpeopled and without history. A description or sketch of an inviting broad new landscape, devoid of signs of human habitation, is a familiar trope of exploration narratives.* On a larger scale, Australia, for example, was declared *terra nullius*, nobody's land, a principle used in international law to justify its acquisition and occupation by British settlers, even though the continent had an indigenous population of very long standing. Orwell in Marrakesh offers a valuable insight into a similar blindness of his own. 'In a tropical landscape,' he says, 'one's eye takes in everything except the human beings.'* For several weeks after his arrival, he did not really see the file of ancient women who passed his house every day, bent double under loads of firewood. 'Firewood was passing—that was how I saw it.'* Poverty and colour weave a cloak of invisibility. But he saw the donkeys. In fact, he had not been five minutes on Moroccan soil, he says, before he noticed the overloading of the donkeys, and was infuriated. 'People with brown skins are next door to invisible. Anyone can be sorry for the donkey with its galled back, but it is generally owing to some kind of accident if one even notices the old woman under her load of sticks.'*

The indignation of the English at foreigners' ill treatment of animals was something of a cliché: there is a comic example in Evelyn Waugh's novel *Black Mischief* (1932). Something more interesting is happening here. The wounded animals at first obscured the observer's vision of the miserable humans, but when written up in 'Marrakech', the tactical juxtaposition of donkeys and old women makes the latter sharply visible; the image of the old women is developed, as it were, from the negative of the donkeys. If he noticed the donkeys, why hadn't he noticed the old women?

Something similar happens in Orwell's Burmese writings. Animals first distract from, and then make visible, the indigenous human. It is a strange kind of acknowledgement, or repurposing, of the kinship between local people and animals that festered underneath the imperial theory of race, which said that people of colour belonged to a different and lower order of being from people who were white. And so there is a pattern, in which the local human is seen and not seen—or seen and not noticed—as the eye attends instead to features of the animal life and landscape of the other place, or else the local human appears as a feature of that animal life or an exotic element in the landscape. But then there may be an unexpected turn. From within the animal life or landscape, the disregarded or denied human face can be found staring back at the observer, like the faces which haunted Orwell's dreams. This leads to a Romantic confession of the observer's own secret life, his isolation, inadequacy, cruelty, and guilt.

We can watch this pattern unfold in the Burmese writing, but there are two other instances in the 'Marrakech' essay. Orwell has been feeding one of the gazelles in the public gardens, when an Arab navvy, a municipal employee who had been working nearby, sidles up and asks shyly if he could have some bread too. This unexpected replacement of the animal by a hungry human is left to speak for itself. There is a more complicated moment at the end of 'Marrakech'. The visiting Englishman has been observing Africa: now Africa looks back. He describes watching a column of Senegalese infantry marching by, and among these colonial troops he notices a young soldier of powerful physique who gives him a 'shy, wide-eyed Negro look, which actually is a look of profound respect'—proof, thinks Orwell to his discomfort, that the young man 'has been taught that the white race are his masters, and he still believes it'.* A look is exchanged, but no words pass between the apparently reverent black conscript and the embarrassed white socialist ex-policeman. The young African soldier here is essentialized. Orwell is struggling to make a point against racism and empire, but the moment is saturated in racist assumptions. Who really knows what meaning, if any, that look contained? The soldier's look is a 'Negro look', which can only mean a look often seen on the faces of black people, and Orwell translates it confidently (this is entirely his own interpretation) as expressing respect for those the young man believes to be his masters—including the man who is looking at him. No words are exchanged, but the silence has the shape of an unuttered question:

> But there is one thought which every white man (and in this connection it doesn't matter twopence if he calls himself a Socialist) thinks when he sees a black army marching past. 'How much longer can we go on kidding these people? How long before they turn their guns in the other direction?'*

Every white man, the French officers and NCOs, and the onlookers, has this thought stowed somewhere in his head, Orwell concludes. A trick has been played on colonized people. 'It was a kind of secret which we all knew and were too clever to tell; only the negroes didn't know it.'* It is the look on the soldier's face that delivers an uncomfortable insight into the white observer himself, but the insight is not given to the Africans as they march away under white men's orders, and are last seen as part not of the human but of the natural scenery. 'And really it was almost like watching a flock of cattle to see the long column, a mile or two miles of armed men, flowing peacefully up the road, while the great white birds drifted over them in the opposite direction, glittering like scraps of paper.'*

What, after all, is the difference between a human being and an animal? The answer is simple. Animals (or so we suppose) do not know how to think for and of themselves. Beyond a very rudimentary bodily self-consciousness, they have no subjectivity. In *Animal Farm* the pigs, who are the thinkers of the revolution, do not long remain animals. One of the first signs of the ominous kinship between pigs and people is not only the pigs' readiness to interpret and change the world but also a concomitant ability to keep things to themselves, to nurse a secret mental life of their own, illegible to the entirely outward-oriented and merely bodily horses and sheep and hens. It is worth thinking of the little drama of the Senegalese soldier and the European observers, with their secret complicity, in the light of this difference.

There is a direct link in Orwell's imagination, as *Animal Farm* makes perfectly clear, between animals and the poor. His experience as a *plongeur* (dishwasher) in Paris, and among tramps in England, convinced him that the life of the underclass was, like that of animals, essentially bodily and mindless. Antonio Gramsci believed optimistically that a life of repetitive drudgery actually gave people plenty of time to think revolutionary thoughts, but Orwell's view was different. Thought was a luxury a dishwasher could not afford, and this was what kept him or her a dishwasher. 'If *plongeurs* thought at all, they would long ago have formed a union and gone on strike for better treatment. But they do not think, because they have no leisure for it; their life has made slaves of them.'* Interestingly, this confinement to the life of the body both animalizes and orientalizes them, and Orwell goes on immediately to compare the *plongeurs* of Paris to rickshaw-pullers and gharry-ponies in the East, human and animal beasts of draught. In *Nineteen Eighty-Four*, the animality of the proles is merely a cliché, and even Winston Smith, who sees in the proles the only hope for the resistance, can only imagine that the resistance will prevail by behaving like animals—not ideas, but 'the animal instinct', the life of the body, will defeat the Party, or so he hopes.*

This is Winston Smith, of course, not George Orwell. But in characterizing the lower classes as incompletely human, Orwell was no doubt drawing on memories of his boyhood, when to children of families like his own, he remembered, '"common" people seemed almost sub-human' with their 'coarse faces, hideous accents and gross manners'.* To analyse such habits of mind, as he does in *The Road to Wigan Pier*, as part of an 'emotional attitude' inherited from social class, was an honourable achievement. But to analyse them was not to exorcise or relinquish them. All Orwell's career was a struggle to stop being the person he was, and to become someone better. This had been the project since his return from Burma. There were successes in this campaign, but also backslidings and pockets of resistance. Throughout his career, a passionate belief in equality is at war with an ineradicable disbelief in it, so that his most eloquent statements of the right of all people to be treated equally, as human beings, are haunted by the suspicion that some human beings are more human than others.

So it is the life of the unthinking body that provided Orwell with the metaphorical link between the oppressed (and from his arrival in the East, this included the colonized) and the animals, a metaphor which he was to extend in *Animal Farm*. Orwell described the genesis of his story in this way, in the preface he wrote in 1947 for the Ukrainian edition of his fable:

> [T]he actual details of the story did not come to me for some time until one day (I was then living in a small village) I saw a little boy, perhaps ten years old, driving a huge cart-horse along a narrow path, whipping it whenever it tried to turn. It struck me that if only such animals became aware of their strength we should have no power over them, and that men exploit animals in much the same way as the rich exploit the proletariat.
>
> I proceeded to analyse Marx's theory from the animals' point of view.*

Orwell lived in the village of Wallington before and after his months in Morocco, but it is not important whether this incident took place before or after he saw the Senegalese soldier, or indeed if either event actually happened. In effect, they tell the same story. A dumb (silent, and slow-witted) creature is held in subjection by a weaker master, through simple unawareness of his powers. The Senegalese soldiers, with their 'splendid bodies' and 'curiously sensitive faces', lack that within— just as the cart-horse does—which could free them. They don't know their own strength. 'It was a kind of secret which we all knew and were too clever to tell; only the Negroes didn't know it.'

In finding a likeness, however sympathetically, between the oppressed and animals, Orwell showed himself to be the true child of an imperial class brought up to see its task in terms of the functions of an older elite, the husbandry of estates, and the management of animals. He knew what it was like to think in this way, because that is how people of his background—with his family history of service in the empire, the plan-tation owners, and the clergy and, of course, the government opium agent—were used to think, unflatteringly, of the non-European people among whom they lived and worked. To make a subject of this way of thinking, to try to free himself from it, was to acknowledge that it was part of him, a kind of genetic inheritance. It was part of the Orient in Orwell.

And yet it remains a problem. To see the fate of oppressed and bullied human beings as or through the condition of animals was a way for Orwell to express his compassion. But who wants to be compassionated as if they were an animal? For all its good intentions, is it not an extraor-dinarily patronizing attitude? It was a problem that would not go away, except once. That was when Orwell wrote a book about suffering that really *was* about animals: *Animal Farm*. Their animal simplicity, and their intellectual limitations, explain the helplessness of the citizens of Animal Farm before the manipulation and cruelty of their oppressors. Unsentimentally as they are portrayed, it is Orwell's most indignant and heart-breaking book, and perhaps his best.

The relation between humans and animals remains his favourite fig-ure of political authority, all the way through to *Nineteen Eighty-Four*, in which 'the Party taught that the proles were natural inferiors who must be kept in subjection, like animals,* and a contempt for their human worth is expressed in the cynical Party slogan: 'Proles and animals are free.'* But though he usually thinks of animal existence as merely bodily, and the inner life as something that belongs uniquely to humans, there are jolting moments when this taxonomy is upset: in what had seemed animal, unthinking and bodily, capable only of ignorant suffering, something else is revealed, and becomes an instance of a kind of epiphany. Some such revelation of the truth was promised to the Senegalese soldier, but at some unspecified future time. A more familiar instance, in which the oppressed *look back*, is recorded in this famous vignette in *The Road to Wigan Pier*.

> She had a round pale face, the usual exhausted face of the slum girl who is twenty-five and looks forty, thanks to miscarriages and drudgery; and it wore, for the second in which I saw it, the most desolate, hopeless expression I have ever seen. It struck me then that we are mistaken when we say that 'it isn't the same for them as it would be for us,' and that people bred in the slums can imagine nothing but the slums. For what I saw in her face was not the ignorant suffering of an animal. She knew well enough what was happening to her—understood as well as I did how dreadful a destiny it was to be kneeling there in the bitter cold, on the slimy stones of a slum backyard, poking a stick up a foul drainpipe.*

In this passage you can see the singular first-person pronoun (I) trying to emancipate itself from the plural first-person pronoun (We, the author and his readers), and express a kinship, however awkward and compromised, with the other person in the story (She). The expression on her face shows him that 'we' are wrong to assume that she isn't capable of imagining that life might be better. He starts by assuming that he has to do her thinking for her, to humanize her by filling out her unthinking vacancy with self-consciousness (as indeed he was to do with the characters of *Animal Farm*).* However, her expression shows that she needs no passing bourgeois sentimentalist to make her aware of her misery. She is no dumb animal: 'we' would be mistaken to think so. She may be on all fours, kneeling on the greasy stones of the yard, but it is insulting to suppose she doesn't know what is happening to her. (It needs to be added that Orwell granted no such self-awareness to the Senegalese soldier in 'Marrakech'; he interprets the black man's gaze as meaning that he really *doesn't* know what is happening to him.)

The story tells you as much about the observer as about the woman he was too ready to patronize and demean. *The Road to Wigan Pier* is full of such moments when he embarrasses himself with snobbish attitudes as hard to shake off as the accent which badges him immediately in his class. Incidentally, in the diary Orwell kept at the time, he says he saw the woman while 'passing up a horrible squalid side-alley'.* But in retelling the story in the book, he moves the point of view, saying he saw her through the window of the train which was bearing him away from 'the monstrous scenery' of the industrial town.* 'She looked up as the train passed': as if to emphasize his insensitivity, he has placed himself above her, at a distance, and leaving her behind.

This is a pattern too. There are moments of similar epiphany in the Burmese writing, where what had seemed merely bodily and animal can confront the observer with his own lack of humanity. The woman at the drainpipe looks up as a subject, not just an object, and makes a claim on him which he cannot ignore. But to glimpse this human bond between them is also to be reminded that it is a kinship that has been violated and lost.

A complicated drama of this kind gets enacted in 'A Hanging' (1931), an early piece apparently based on Orwell's experience in the Burma police. It describes the execution of a Hindu, in a Burmese prison yard. The narrator is a member of the party—warders, the superintendent of the prison, 'magistrates and the like'—who escort the condemned man to the scaffold, listen as he calls upon his god, see him die, and go off together, in a mood of jocular relief, to have a drink afterwards. But what about the strange case of the dog?

The narrative gets down to business with an air of efficiency, and a tendency to count and measure distances and time (there are thirty-five numbers in this five-page story). In the prison yard, the Indian warders crowd close round the condemned man, while the officials, including the narrator, keep their distance, and stand 'five yards away' to see him die. There is a proper way of doing these things, and the ritual makes the event formal and predictable. Then 'a dreadful thing' happens, and the procession to the gallows is interrupted, by a dog:

> It came bounding among us with a loud volley of barks, and leapt round us wagging its whole body, wild with glee at finding so many human beings together. It was a large woolly dog, half Airedale, half pariah. For a moment it pranced round us, and then, before anyone could stop it, it had made a dash for the prisoner, and jumping up tried to lick his face. Everyone stood aghast, too taken aback even to grab at the dog.*

The dog does not know its place. Noisy, promiscuous, alarming, and gleeful, it has blundered into this occasion like a clown at a funeral. Itself a cross-breed, it disrupts the carefully observed distinctions between the people in front and the people behind, the breaker and the enforcers of the law. For a while it succeeds in turning the solemn march to the scaffold into a carnival procession, barking, bounding, and leaping about, confounding distance and measurement by keeping just out of reach of its pursuers and dodging the stones they throw. The unruly life of the body disrupts the hierarchical performance of rule.

In time, nature is subdued by culture, the dog is caught, and the procession resumes. But its interruption has altered the vision of the narrator, as he paces behind the prisoner. The animal makes the human visible. The narrator's English eye, trained from an early age to pay attention to what animals do but not always so ready to take note of people different from himself, now finds itself drawn back to the prisoner as a human being, by the dog's precedent. Abundantly alive in its physical senses, but politically illiterate, the dog had looked at the procession and seen, simply, 'many human beings together'. That was not the way the narrator saw things.

For him, the occasion could only be understood and justified by a radical difference, an actual and political distance between himself and the condemned man, and between himself and the Asian functionaries— the Eurasian jailer, the Indian warders, and so on. The ideology of empire itself, as we have seen Orwell suggesting, rested on such a faith in such categorical differences as a fact of nature. But when he looks now at the prisoner, as he steps slightly aside to avoid a puddle, the narrator sees as it were through the skin, the ethnic difference, to a man like himself, one of the 'many humans beings together' which the dog had responded to:

> This man was not dying, he was alive just as we were alive. All the organs of his body were working—bowels digesting food, skin renewing itself, nails growing, tissues forming—all toiling away in solemn foolery. His nails would still be growing when he stood on the drop, when he was falling through the air with a tenth of a second to live. His eyes saw the yellow gravel and the grey walls, and his brain still remembered, foresaw, reasoned—reasoned even about puddles. He and we were a party of men walking together, seeing, hearing, feeling, understanding the same world; and in two minutes, with a sudden snap, one of us would be gone—one mind less, one world less.*

Here is a different way of looking at the 'native' as animal. This glimpse into the bodily, animal life of the prisoner is an admission of kinship. The secret physiological workings of the man's body are also tokens of human interiority, the consciousness, and the inner life that bind him into the same community as the observer, who now paraphrases the dog's perception of that community as 'a party of men walking together'. The dog was the prophet of this insight: the narrator, and the condemned man, and the others are the same animal.*

This epiphany, however, makes nothing happen. The procession resumes. Soon enough, the insight has faded, the prisoner into whose heart the narrator had seemed to see for a moment has become opaque again, a 'lashed, hooded man on the drop', making an incomprehensible noise as he calls on his god. 'There was a clanking noise, then dead silence. The prisoner had vanished, and the rope was twisting on itself.'* The dog, having seen enough, slinks away.

The rest of the story performs a sort of cover-up, and the servants of empire return to normal life. But what normal life! The kind of society which has been made safe by the liquidation of the deviant (we never learn his crime) is a dreadful parody of community, built on violence, repression, anxiety, and segregation. The narrator turns, to watch what seems to him 'a homely, jolly scene, after the hanging',* the breakfast of the other convicts, where the men eat squatting in long rows, served rice out of a bucket under the eye of warders armed with lathis. With much nervous laughter and relieved chatter, like conspirators, the officials go off to drink whisky together, their own differences temporarily forgotten. The end of the story is a nasty imperial utopia that parodies Kipling's dream of an empire of co-operation between faithful natives and authoritative white men with the common touch: 'We all had a drink together, native and European alike, quite amicably. The dead man was a hundred yards away.'*

Animals figure prominently in the novel *Burmese Days*, which I will discuss in Chapter 3. The most famous of Orwell's oriental beasts is to be found in 'Shooting an Elephant', a piece written for John Lehmann's *New Writing* in 1936, two years after the publication of the novel. It is a first-personal account of the shooting of a working elephant which has gone 'must' and killed a coolie—another animal encounter, with striking echoes of these earlier scenes.

'In Moulmein, in Lower Burma, I was hated by large numbers of people.'* The Burmese in this story feature as an undifferentiated and hostile crowd in a town where anti-European feeling is very bitter; but although the thrust of the story is anti-imperial, it is far from unambiguously pro-Burmese. The local people are shown to be hopelessly incapable of mounting a real resistance to the masters, or of doing anything with their resentment, except standing around and jeering at the Europeans. Local people do not make things happen: Burmese history is colonial history, and the British are the people who do things, to and for the Burmese. When an elephant goes out of control, a British police officer is sent for, for the local population have no weapons (the story does not mention that since the early colonial days, the Burmese were forbidden to bear arms) and are helpless against it; their only function is as spectators of a show of masterly force. The passive aggression of the crowd earns the contempt of the policeman telling the story, for it seems to make them an ineffectual herd, less than fully human, and parasitic on the work of Europeans for both their safety and their entertainment. They seem both useless and hostile. This ambivalence expresses itself, not surprisingly, in an uncertainty as to whether the Burmese have anything inside them. 'No one had the guts to raise a riot';* on the other hand, 'I thought that the greatest joy in the world would be to drive a bayonet into a Buddhist priest's guts.'*

'All I knew was that I was stuck between my hatred for the empire I served and my rage against the evil-spirited little beasts who tried to make my job impossible.'* In this unresolved state of mind the narrator is summoned to 'do something' about a great beast, the rampaging elephant. The story, he promises, will offer a glimpse of 'the real nature of imperialism—the real motives for which despotic governments act'.* At the heart of this animal story, we can expect a revelation.

'Must' or mhust in male elephants is a state of aggressive behaviour accompanied by a hormonal surge. It is temporary, and by the time this elephant is located, its attack of 'must' is over and it is no longer dangerous. The policeman narrator knows it ought not to be shot. But it is at this moment that it is borne in upon him that his own judgements and feelings are of no consequence here. He thinks he should not shoot the elephant. He also thinks the British Raj is a tyranny. But these thoughts, kept to himself, count equally for nothing because he is already caught in the current of the drama that he and the watching crowd are enacting. He is entangled in a cliché of oriental adventure. Marching fearlessly down the hill to meet his antagonist, the mighty beast, a lone white man with a rifle over his shoulder at the head of an Asian crowd it is his duty to protect, the imperial policeman is part of a myth of such momentum that he is not a free agent. Once again, imperial power has to be enacted in the form of dominance over the natural world. All his fragile prestige is invested in the promise of violence which will confirm his rank in nature's order. There must be a performance of superiority, over both the now harmless elephant, and the unarmed local crowd, who would certainly mock him if, by not shooting, he proved himself as innocuous as themselves. The elephant has to die. This is the revelation we were asked to wait for. 'I perceived in this moment that when the white man turns tyrant it is his own freedom that he destroys.'*

He has no choice. The elephant's frightening natural force, first heard about in confused and unreliable reports, is a challenge to the law and order the policeman serves. It is a menacing counter-attack of nature against civilization, a tamed animal that has reverted to destructive wildness, and thus an embodiment of colonial anxieties about colonized nature. The man goes to meet the beast in conditions of extreme antagonism. The elephant is a killer, the policeman carries a murderous weapon. But once in sight, the animal offers no danger, standing harmless and dignified in a field, peacefully eating, and paying no attention to the excited crowd. Again, there is a flash of Romantic kinship, as there was in 'A Hanging' between the observer and the condemned man going to his death, but this time expressed in ethical terms. 'It seemed to me that it would be murder to shoot him.'* But again, that Romantic kinship changes nothing. It is over-ruled by a stronger imperial imperative. The power the policeman serves has brought him here not as a Romantic naturalist but as an executioner, and now he is going to have to use his gun to assert imperial prestige, by violating the body of Burmese nature. Imperial policeman and colonized crowd are going to be complicit in the shooting, which is in effect a political murder. And, once again, the observer, in betraying his own Romantic insight as he did in 'A Hanging', is left alienated from himself—he has acted against his better nature—and given over to self-pity and guilty isolation. From the hanged man, from the Senegalese soldier, from the woman on all fours at the drain-pipe, now from the elephant, the last move will be to distance himself. 'In the end I could not stand it any longer and went away.'*

'A sahib has got to act like a sahib.'* Not acting—in the sense of both drama and agency—is not an option open to a policeman of the empire. The consequence in this case is the extraordinary self-pity of the core insight—'suddenly I realised'—that 'when the white man turns tyrant it is his own freedom that he destroys'. It looks as if the heart of the story is the suffering of the white man. But the reading experience, I think, belies this. There is another heart to the story, and for this we have to look to what is said about the body of the elephant itself.

After the frightening rumours about his destructive progress through the village, the elephant, when actually seen, does not look like an apocalyptic beast, but is anticlimactic in his ordinariness, a familiar and banal sight, a tame animal in a field, eating grass. Yet at the moment of the triumph over the natural world by violence—the moment of the shot—the great beast seems to undergo a metamorphosis into something tragic and unknowable:

In that instant, in too short a time, one would have thought, even for the bullet to get there, a mysterious, terrible change had come over the elephant. He neither stirred nor fell, but every line of his body had altered. He looked suddenly stricken, shrunken, immensely old, as though the frightful impact of the bullet had paralysed him without knocking him down.*

'One could have imagined him a thousand years old.' The moment the bullet penetrates the animal's body, the moment of a literal and violent entry into his interiority, is also the moment when he is realized to be untouchable, out of range, possessed of an unfathomable history of his own, which puts him beyond the policeman's instruments of measure-ment and control, even as he is framed in the precision sights and the shot goes home. He has become free, like the condemned man on the scaffold who cried out so incomprehensibly on his god from some point beyond the reach of his executioners.

The stricken animals falls, and his killer comes close and literally looks into him, into his gaping mouth and 'far down into caverns of pale pink throat'. What is inside him? Even in his abjection, the animal in some sense escapes his murderer, for the elephant is dying in his own time, 'in some world remote from me', and shot after shot 'poured…into his heart and down his throat' is unable to find where his life is, and end it. The beast's life is possessed by the policeman's power, but it baffles and defeats his knowledge. He will only yield up the secrets of his body after his killer has left the scene, to the Burmese crowd who will take possession of it and strip it almost to the bones. The policeman mean-while returns to bad community, to the company of the Europeans who are his own kind, to 'endless discussions' about the propriety of what he has done, and to share again in their callous language as he cynically professes himself glad that the elephant had killed a coolie because 'it put me legally in the right and it gave me a sufficient pretext for shooting the elephant'.* In the end, the narrator does not shield himself from his own brutality. The unnatural history of empire could not be illustrated more succinctly.

3

Environment

Burmese Days

Burmese Days is a novel, that is, a work of fiction. What about writings
such as 'A Hanging', 'Shooting an Elephant', and 'Marrakech'? Are they
essays, short stories, autobiographical fragments? Are they reportage?
Are they, perhaps, what used to be called *belles lettres*? Although they all
undoubtedly draw on personal experience, they all have a strong literary
quality, and are written with an eye to their rhetorical effect on the
reader, in their vivid sensuous descriptions, their drama, their irony,
their movement between narrative and ideas. Then what about *Down
and Out in Paris and London*, what about *The Road to Wigan Pier*, what
about *Homage to Catalonia*? There seems to be more at stake in these
awovedly documentary works. Do they tell the truth? We have already
seen Orwell move the point of view of the observer of the woman at the
drainpipe in Wigan. Was he being false to the original experience (if
there was an original experience), or finding a way to be more true to it?

For *The Road to Wigan Pier*, he consulted the notes he had kept on his
travels. 'Words are such feeble things. What is the use of a brief phrase
like "roof leaks" or "four beds for eight people"? It is the kind of thing
your eyes slide over, registering nothing.'* And so he had to find the language to render these things in bright light, to catch the eye—the writer's
task, as Joseph Conrad wrote, is 'to make you *see*'.* To do this, Orwell
used the resources of literature, although literature is rarely interested in
the unvarnished literal truth. His non-fictional work is full of memorable
sketches: the condemned man stepping aside at a puddle, the policeman
at Colombo kicking a coolie, the Wigan miner buried in three successive
rockfalls, the handshake of the Italian militiaman at the Lenin Barracks
in Barcelona. Did these things actually happen, and happen like that?

There was once a long-running argument among Orwell scholars over whether or not he had really shot an elephant. In the end, it matters less whether Eric Blair really did and saw these things, than that George Orwell wrote about them. But Orwell's blurring of the lines between fiction and non-fiction does raise a lingering question, especially given his fear, expressed in 'Looking Back on the Spanish War', that with so many lies being propagated, 'the very concept of objective truth is fading out of the world.'*

Burmese Days, however, is a novel. What is it about? 'In all novels about the East,' Orwell says in *The Road to Wigan Pier*, 'the scenery is the real subject-matter.'* In talking of 'scenery', he is thinking about the natural environment and particularly the landscape of Burma, but there is also a suggestion of 'scenery' in the theatrical sense, the usually painted stage background against which a dramatic action is performed. Novels of this kind, he is saying, are back to front. What ought to be in the background unexpectedly moves up to occupy the foreground, and becomes the centre of attention. Novels about the East are really about the scenery; their centre of gravity is not so much in their action, as in the environment in which the action is set.

It is an unexpected observation in more than one sense. The first half of *The Road to Wigan Pier* is about what Orwell saw in the north of England. The second half is autobiographical: this is where you can find his most extended discussion of his service in Burma. But this passage about the scenery of his Burmese novel comes in the first half, the Burmese material erupting prematurely into the descriptions of life in the north. He has been talking about the ugliness of the English industrial landscape, but then concedes that from a purely aesthetic standpoint, it may have a certain macabre appeal. He goes on:

> I find that anything outrageously strange generally ends by fascinating me even when I abominate it. The landscapes of Burma, which, when I was among them, so appalled me as to assume the qualities of nightmare, afterwards stayed so hauntingly in my mind that I was obliged to write a novel about them to get rid of them. (In all novels about the East the scenery is the real subject-matter.)*

Back in Europe, the landscapes of Burma haunted him, like a ghost. *Burmese Days*, then, is a kind of attempted exorcism. It is a way of dealing with what is not only strange but outrageously so.

The natural world and its 'scenery' had been very much linked with literature and the other arts, especially for the English, since the Romantic revolution in the early days of industrialization had undertaken to restore the bond, or deplore the rift, between humans and habitat. The best-known English Romantic artists, Constable and Turner, were specialists in landscape. Schoolchildren were taught that modern English poetry had started with Wordsworth, seen largely as a sentimental rural moralist. The natural (i.e., rural) landscape, very strongly identified with the nation itself, remained the stock-in-trade of the more traditional poets Orwell knew while he was growing up. Nature seemed to be implicated in the literary vocation; English writers habitually wrote about the natural world, the countryside and what grew and lived there, its beauties, and its heartbreaks. The poetry of the young Orwell's favourite poet, A. E. Housman, was not separable from the Shropshire landscape in which it was set. In Orwell's youth, the doyen of English novelists was Thomas Hardy, who set all his stories in the south-west of England; the Wessex Edition of his novels came with a map. Hardy is behind the young Orwell's ambition to write 'enormous naturalistic novels with unhappy endings, full of detailed descriptions and arresting similes, and also full of purple passages in which words were used partly for the sake of their sound', and he added that *Burmese Days*, his first completed novel, 'is rather that kind of book'.*

Not only was there a general bond between English domestic literature and what is called natural history. There was also a particular connection between the literature of colonialism—and the lives of colonialists—and the collection, description, and appreciation of what was to be found in the natural habitats of distant places. There is something of the naturalist, as well as of the ethnographer, in every colonial writer. One of the functions of the traveller was to observe nature, and one of the functions of the writer was to describe it. Evocations of the natural world had an important part to play in the writing in all genres—scientific, geographical, narrative, and picturesque—in which western readers were informed about the East. And accounts of foreign nature, as we have seen with the case of animals, have a tendency to find expression in tropes of possession and control. Also, the foreign eye is drawn to things that are different. There are sparrows and green pigeons in Burma, but there are no sparrows in *Burmese Days*, because sparrows are commonplace in London. The natural history of a strange land is *strange*: this is an important word for Orwell. And the strange nature of foreign places cannot always be subdued and owned. Sometimes it is beyond control. This is when it evokes the emotions that Romantic writers associated with the sublime—wonder and terror. This is the language Orwell is using when he describes his reaction to the 'outrageously strange' scenery of Burma, which fascinated and so appalled him as to assume the qualities of nightmare.

The point of view of *Burmese Days* is thoroughly Eurocentric. It is a novel of colonial life squarely centred on the experiences of an English timber merchant, John Flory, a member of a small European community in Kyauktada, an upcountry town in Burma. It rarely enters the private life or the consciousness of local people. Flory has a Burmese mistress, an Indian friend, and a Burmese enemy, but virtually all the novel's action is focused through his European consciousness, and it is largely through his perceptions too that the novel engages with the 'scenery', the natural environment of Upper Burma.

Against the landscape of Kyauktada, the colonial presence is foregrounded as a series of bursts of clarity and meaning—the dazzling white bungalows, the white-walled cemetery, the 'spiritual citadel' of the European whites-only Club. These features stand out against the obscure, indistinct and shapeless background of the khaki-coloured maidan (an open public space), the ochreous Irrawaddy river, and the native town hidden from sight in green groves of peepul trees.* The contrast between clarity and obscurity might remind us of the distinction made later in 'Shooting an Elephant', with its complaint that stories in the East are always vague and indefinite.* But we might also remember the warning, in *The Road to Wigan Pier*, that in books about the East, the background is the real story.

The Club itself centres the plot of *Burmese Days* and it centres the geography of Kyauktada. It is a rock of tawdry European culture in a Burmese sea, the refuge of the English, and the aspiration of the rivals U Po Kyin and Dr Veraswami. From their legal system to their railway terminus, the British have laid a commanding grid of discipline over a sluggish and unruly landscape. Flory cynically imagines some future triumph of empire in which all local variety—forests, villages, monasteries, pagodas—will have been replaced by an orderly reproduction suburbia measured out with 'pink villas fifty yards apart'.* In his habitual arguments with his friend Dr Veraswami, it is the 'oriental' doctor who keeps putting the case for the empire as a project of selfless aid and progress, and Flory who sees the designs of empire on the colony as basically hostile and denaturing. Flory's own job (not that we see him doing any work) involves converting the jungle trees into a saleable commodity, an industrial process of chopping timber, dispatching it (no doubt by river) and replanting.

Flory cynically, and Veraswami naively, in their regular conversations together, both see imperialism as a force contending against the resistance of the given natural world in Burma, with designs either to transform it or to despoil it. Empire brings modernity. That is why Veraswami approves of it and Flory does not. Veraswami is sorry to see the British resisted by a naturally recalcitrant and backward local population. Flory is sorry to see the British triumphing, inevitably, over local ways of living and the diversity of the Burmese natural environment. It is empire against nature.

In one of his first published articles, about the British empire in Burma, Orwell describes the geography of the country. 'If we add that the Burmese countryside is exceptionally beautiful, with broad rivers, high mountains, eternally green forests, brightly coloured flowers, exotic fruits, the phrase "earthly paradise" naturally springs to mind'.* This hardly sounds like a nightmare environment. And despite his claim that he had to write his novel in order to exorcise the memory of the landscapes of Burma, there is actually not much description of 'scenery' in *Burmese Days*—except the jungle.

There are two places in the novel: the town and the jungle. The town is basically the site of European life. It is the jungle that is authentically Burmese, a metonym for Burma itself. The employee of a timber company, Flory's work involves him in the industrialization of the jungle. But at other times he can see Burma and Burmese nature with different eyes, and is able to imagine a relationship with the place which is not one of plunder and violence (trees chopped down for timber), but rather of integration, kinship, and pleasure. And in the way the jungle is experienced in *Burmese Days*, we can find again the pattern identified, in Chapter 2, in the representation of animals, or of people seen through the prism of animals.

There are three phases or movements to this pattern. First, estrangement: what is Burmese is seen as grotesque and outlandish—'outrageously strange'. Then identification: a Romantic epiphany reveals a creaturely kinship between the (male) observer and the object of observation, and seems to offer the chance of a Romantic integration into a kindly and unalienated natural life—an integration of the kind yearned for by Wordsworth between the poet and the natural environment and the simple folk who inhabited it. But for Orwell's observers, to glimpse this utopian possibility is also to see that it can never be realized. So this is the third phase: alienation. The roles provided for the observer by his place in the imperial project, by his race and his gender, his class and his job, distance him and drive him away into postures of antagonism, indifference, or violence. The distance and antagonism return him to his earlier estrangement, this time not only from the creature or the natural scene but also from himself, because his betrayal of the glimpsed relationship is also a betrayal of himself and of (as we say) his own better nature. This is the drama of the observation of the condemned man, the woman on all fours at the drainpipe, the dying elephant. It is also the drama of the jungle in *Burmese Days*.

But we should start where the novel starts, in the town of Kyauktada. When we first see John Flory, he is in no Wordsworthian mood, as he steps out of the sanctuary of his house into the glare of Burmese day. In the garden of his house close to the edge of the jungle, Burmese nature seems to retaliate against the invader, causing the English flowers planted there to overflow their borders in a riot of vast size and richness. 'The clash of colours hurt one's eyes in the glare', where native trees and bushes sprawl in grotesque super-abundance across what should be the lawn, wildness reclaiming the garden as 'a jungle of flowers'.* This political imagery (the violated borders, the rioting, the blood-colours), in a place of European cultivation precariously won from the jungle, suggests that the English in the Club are right to feel embattled and insecure as they do, for a teeming nature seems bent on overwhelming the place they have cleared for themselves in this hostile environment.

The obliteration of culture by the jungle—of history by natural history—is one of colonial literature's recurrent and most interesting tropes.* Human habitations succumb to the jungle (to give some examples) in Kipling's story, 'The Judgement of Dungara', and in two tales in *The Jungle Books*, 'The King's Ankus' and 'Letting in the Jungle', as well as in Leonard Woolf's novel about Ceylon, *The Village in the Jungle*, and in Hugh Clifford's Malayan story 'The Skulls in the Forest'.* For the Europeans in *Burmese Days*, the jungle is unfriendly, an alien and unruly place of discomfort and danger, incorrigibly foreign, lacking restraint. A rebellion against the British is fomented in the jungle. Maxwell, a Divisional Forest Officer, is killed there. Lackersteen, a suburban Mr Kurtz, goes to the dogs in the forest unsupervised by his shrewish wife. It is a perilous place. 'The more you are in jungle', Leonard Woolf remembered, 'particularly if you are alone, the more one tends to feel it personified, something or some-one hostile, dangerous.'* In Somerset Maugham's disturbing story, 'Neil MacAdam', an Englishwoman is abandoned in the jungle and never heard of again.* She simply disappears off the map of the narrative, lapsing from history into nature, rejoining the life of the beasts.

But Flory's relationship with the jungle singles him out from the other Europeans in *Burmese Days*, and represents (as do his dealings with his mistress Ma Hla May) an important truth about his feelings towards Burma. Indeed, his unusual enjoyment of nature—it would be accurate to describe him as an amateur naturalist—is in line with other unsound proclivities of his, which seem to threaten the usual prohibitions about too close an involvement with native life. He goes to the jungle for pleasure. As a timber company man, he spends weeks on end about his business in the forest, but the novel never follows him there on one of these working treks. We first see him enter the jungle in the fourth chapter, seeking escape from the awfulness of the town, full of self-disgust after an encounter with Ma Hla May and unable to face the only social alternative, an evening at the club with people he dislikes. He sets out for a solitary walk with his dog, Flo.

At first, the jungle is ugly and unwelcoming, dried-up and lifeless, with its stunted bushes, turpentiny fruits, and poisonous smells. A bird cries with 'a lonely, hollow sound like the echo of a laugh'.* But as he moves alone into the interior, along a track few human beings ever follow, Flory is rewarded by a quite different view of his environment, as a place not of mocking hostility, but of benediction, not of estrangement, but of belonging. Coming to a clear pool where the roots of a peepul tree make a natural cavern, he strips and steps into the water, accompanied by the dog. The disarming vulnerability of his action is important, in view of the state of hostilities that has been seen to obtain between humans—and especially western men—and the jungle. Flory becomes like an infant, or even an unborn child floating in its amniotic element. Unarmed, unclothed, even unmoving, he sits in the cool water as shoals of silvery fish come nosing and nibbling at his body. Naked and as near as he can come to a state of nature, he is ready for a lesson in natural history:

> There was a stirring high up in the peepul tree, and a bubbling noise like pots boiling. A flock of green pigeons were up there, eating the berries. Flory gazed up into the great green dome of the tree, trying to distinguish the birds; they were invisible, they matched the leaves so perfectly, and yet the whole tree was alive with them, shimmering, as though the ghosts of birds were shaking it. Flo rested herself against the roots and growled up at the invisible creatures. Then a single green pigeon fluttered down and perched on a lower branch. It did not know that it was being watched. It was a tender thing, smaller than a tame dove, with jade-green back as smooth as velvet, and neck and breast of iridescent colours. Its legs were like the pink wax that dentists use.*

In this sylvan cathedral, an epiphany is given to Flory only after he has laid aside his clothes, his agency, even his identity, meeting the jungle as a naked animal, a creature not of the colonial history the British were making in Burma, but of natural history. He and the jungle surrender to each other and Flory sees into its heart; something invisible, ghostly, is made manifest to him, in a moment of communion. The overtones of natural piety and the Romantic afflatus show that, though it is an exotic and entirely unEnglish scene, this passage could only have been written by someone familiar with the way Wordsworth in solitude found a kind of sacredness in the natural environment. Flory's is a moment related to the innocent enjoyment of a Mowgli or a Kim, Kipling's privileged children in the Indian scene. Time stops; and for once in his clumsy life, it is natural for Flory to be where he is, as integral a part of a scene of nature as the birds whose colour matches the leaves. He seems for a moment of stillness as perfectly adapted as they are to the environment of which tree, water, birds, and man together are the constituents.

He is no longer defined *against* the scenery of the East, but blends into it, and the formerly alien forest is now experienced as a habitat, a place where he belongs. But if this moment is as Romantic as Tintern Abbey, its aftermath is as Romantic as the Ancient Mariner. For time resumes. Flory is jolted back into chronic estrangement and insufficiency. 'Alone, alone, the bitterness of being alone!', he actually says (or thinks) to himself.* Self-consciousness returns, and brings a self-pitying awareness that he has no one to share the beauty of his vision. Even his pleasure at having seen it reminds him, and us, of how different his experience has been from more normal encounters between Western men and Burmese birds. Flory thinks:

> One does not often see green pigeons so closely when they are alive. They are high-flying birds, living in the treetops, and they do not come to the ground, or only to drink. When one shoots them, if they are not killed outright, they cling to the branch until they die, and drop long after one has given up waiting and gone away.*

The second estrangement, and the distancing. Flory cannot linger at the jungle pool. And indeed, it is part of the novel's pattern of betrayals that he will later be seen slaughtering green pigeons with his gun, and even coaching Elizabeth Lackersteen as she unsportingly shoots one on the branch of a suspiciously similar peepul tree.* (The naturalist was also a hunter, as we have noted. Jacinta Buddicom writes disapprovingly of the teenaged Eric and her brother shooting garden birds in the nesting season.)* Yet Flory's jungle pastoral under the great green dome of the tree plays a strategic part in the novel's thinking about the Orient. For it establishes a friendly and even innocent relation between western subject and eastern place, and if this seems a modest enough achievement, it never happens in Orwell's Burmese writings outside this chapter. To be sure, this important revelation is given in a scene of natural description that contains no Burmese people. However, Flory's sharing of the inner life of the jungle is replayed in social terms soon afterwards. He and his dog lose their way in the forest. A Burmese with a bullock-cart takes them to a jungle village, where he is welcomed as a stranger. Courteous conversation is exchanged (in Burmese), Flory is given refreshment, and sent on his way with a conventional blessing.

The little scene is remarkable in being the one social contact in the novel that is unproblematic for Flory. By losing his bearings, a worrying experience as Woolf and Maugham testified, he has stumbled into the inner human life of the jungle, and shared it for a while. The village itself is off the colonial map and therefore untroubled by change, living in the traditional timelessness of idyll. This is why Flory is able to enter and enjoy it, in what is for him literally an excursion, while the narrative of Burmese days gives way to the idyll of Burmese place, history ceding to natural history. The excursion in the jungle is another insight, the glimpse of a possible non-colonial (pre- or postcolonial) place for Flory in an Orient which he need neither fear nor control. It is poignant because it depends on his forgetting or escaping from the colonial present and his own part as an agent, beneficiary, and victim of colonial history. But the alienation, and the turning away, follow inevitably. Flory's Burma soon has to be reconfigured as a European-centred space. For he has to go back, of course, to Kyauktada, to his Burmese servant who 'hated to see his master behave differently from other white men,'* his Burmese mistress who has gone gambling with the money he gave her for sexual services, and to a communal life which consists of playing bridge and getting drunk every night in the racially exclusive Club, where nobody likes him.

But the excursion shows that Flory is a man who is able to find, however briefly, a place for himself in the natural world which is beautiful, simple, and good—a pastoral scene, in literary and art-historical terms, and much to be preferred to the spiteful and soulless civilities of the European club, and the murky dangers of Kyauktada politics. He is unusual, and, to his fellow-Europeans, suspect, in seeking to overcome his estrangement from Burma and its natural environment. Much more typical, it seems, is Elizabeth Lackersteen, the English girl he falls in love with.

If Flory's jungle is at least temporarily Rousseauesque, to Elizabeth Lackersteen, Burmese nature seems Hobbesian, monstrous and chaotic. Her first utterance is a terrified scream, as she is discovered, just inside the fringe of the jungle, cowering before a huge buffalo that seems to menace her with its crescent-shaped horns. Flory has no difficulty in rescuing her from this harmless beast. This debut performance of colonial panic fixes Elizabeth, fresh from Europe, as a type of Orientalist prejudice. The mild-faced and unmoving water-buffalo offers her no harm, but she has come out East equipped with a quasi-paranoid theory of natural history, and of colonial history, so that she assumes humankind and nature to be forever at war, just as she assumes the relationship between West and East to be always one of natural antagonism. To her, the buffalo looks like a killer, as surely as the Burmese look like criminals ('I remember reading something in a magazine about the shape of people's heads'), or animals ('So coarse-looking').*

To Elizabeth, Burmese people and the Burmese natural environment are beastly. It is worth dwelling for a moment on this little word, which is one of her favourites. She uses it for everything in her life that is cheap, low, shabby, and laborious: the 'cheap, beastly schools' she attended, then life with her slatternly mother in straitened circumstances in Paris, where she is pestered by predatory men.* Art and ideas are beastly, because associated in her mind with poverty. Now she finds herself in the beastly Orient, and Flory is trying to get her to like it. 'He did not realize that this constant striving to interest her in Oriental things struck her only as perverse, ungentlemanly, a deliberate seeking after the squalid and the "beastly".'* 'Beastly' is a pejorative adjective for 'animal'. Though in everyday usage, it is almost bleached of its original force, it indicates something or someone low, ugly, and brutish, at the opposite end of the spectrum from the civilized, comfortable, and comely.

No wonder Elizabeth finds Burma beastly. The word sounds quaint to modern ears, but was once widely used among the English middle classes. Indeed, it seems to have been the first word little Eric Blair learned to say,* and it occurs in all Orwell's books except *Animal Farm*.

Flory too uses it frequently; he complains to Veraswami about 'our [British] beastliness to the natives'* but sometimes, in Elizabeth's presence, he uses it to refer to Burma and Burmese life. But he has another word for the place, when allowing himself to dream of a future with Elizabeth. 'What fun they would have together in this alien yet kindly land!'* 'Kindly' too is a word that has shed much of its original force and now means not much more than benevolent, but its earlier meaning was 'natural'. Dame Kind was a name for Mother Nature: 'kind' meant nature in the abstract, and also the given nature of a creature (as in mankind), and so 'kindly' means both good-natured and seemly. In these two words, the Elizabethan 'beastly' and the Florian 'kindly', we find two attitudes to Burma, and two theories of the relation between humans and the natural environment.

Elizabeth treats Burma itself as a dangerous beast, keeping it always at arm's or gun's length, and never reaching beyond the phase of estrangement in which she first set foot in the country. She shows no curiosity about the place, and is only roused to enthusiasm by the prospect of a hunting expedition in the jungle. On this hunting trip, she and Flory shoot a number of doves, and, on hearing that there is a leopard nearby, they seek it out and kill it. This hunting scene is exciting, and probably draws on Orwell's own experience, but now the jungle environment has become the stage for sporting tourism, the opposite of an innocent enjoyment of nature. Flory, the harmless swimmer and wanderer of the earlier chapter, finds himself performing for Elizabeth's benefit the stereotype of the white hunter, a drama which casts them both as trophy-hunting predators, destructive, and acquisitive. When Flory puts a freshly killed pigeon, limp and warm, into Elizabeth's hands, it is clear that he has proved himself the man of her dreams:

> She could hardly give it up, the feel of it so ravished her. She could have kissed it, hugged it to her breast. All the men, Flory and Ko S'la and the beaters, smiled at one another to see her fondling the dead bird. Reluctantly, she gave it to Ko S'la to put in the bag. She was conscious of an extraordinary desire to fling her arms round Flory's neck and kiss him; and in some way it was the killing of the pigeon that made her feel this.*

Her delight over the dead bird stands in emblematic contrast to Flory's delight over the living bird at the forest pool (might it be the same creature?). These two moments belong to different orders of nature. The natural world excites Elizabeth because she is not part of it. Here, her understanding of Burma is exactly congruent with her understanding of wild nature. Both are dangerous, potentially overwhelming (the leopard hunt is certainly high-risk), but in their grotesque and barbaric difference, they are there to be triumphed over and controlled.

This violent estrangement goes against Flory's own conventionally Romantic feelings for his natural surroundings. His attempt to make a garden and its odd hybrid results, his affection for the dog Flo, his inability to shoot a pariah dog in the compound, his enjoyment of the forest, are all tokens of goodwill towards what he finds in Burma. The perfect adaptation of the green pigeons to their jungle foliage is beyond his reach, and he is doomed in any case—as his unsightly birthmark indicates without much subtlety—to a Romantic outsider's fate. Still, he is unique among the British in the novel in making an effort to belong, and his attempts at integration show that he can at least imagine a peaceful and decent future in Burma, a place—and a home—for himself in this land which he thinks of as 'alien yet kindly'.* His ability to see the 'kindly' within the 'alien'—to see through estrangement to kinship—recognizes his own place in a shared order of nature, and is similar to the insights at the centre of 'A Hanging' and 'Shooting an Elephant'.

But none of these insights can have any practical effect unless they can be propagated and shared, and in none of the stories does this happen. So long as he is alone, Flory's Romantic intimations of the natural life only fuel his feelings of melancholy, solitude, and self-pity. And the moment he is in the company of his own kind, his utopian glimpses of a natural relationship and innocuous interaction with the oriental environment are doomed. The whole of colonial culture, its institutions, and language, cast a European in Orwell's Burma in the roles of domination and possession. Inescapably, the East is a stage for the performance of white power. Flory's weak liberal insights into the possibility of Burmese life as an environment and even a society that could be belonged to, rather than governed, wither in the harsh atmosphere of colonialism understood as exploitation by force. Flory the naturalist is elbowed out of the way by Flory the aggressive imperialist, blazing away (like the French warship in Conrad's *Heart of Darkness*) into a jungle which becomes more alien with every shot.

This is the story of which 'the scenery is the real subject-matter' in *Burmese Days*, and it is a tragic one. It is curious that it came to his mind again when he was writing *The Road to Wigan Pier*, and thinking about the blighted industrial landscape of Sheffield, which 'could justly claim to be called the ugliest town in the Old World'.* Would it be possible to see through the ugliness and strangeness? 'I find that anything outrageously strange generally ends by fascinating me even when I abominate it. The landscapes of Burma...'.* So could the landscapes of the North yield a kind of beauty, as the Burmese jungle did for Flory before everything went wrong? After all, Orwell thinks, Arnold Bennett in his novels extracted a sort of beauty from the blackness of industrial towns, and one could easily imagine Baudelaire writing a poem about a slag-heap. But this is not the point. As empire came between Flory and the natural scene in Burma, what must come between the observer and a redemptive view of the North of England is not its ugliness but its injustice. 'It is important to remember this, because there is always the temptation to think that industrialism is harmless so long as it is clean and orderly.'*

But probably the closest analogue in Orwell's fiction will be *Coming Up for Air*. George Bowling, middle-aged and estranged from the scenery of his childhood, makes an attempt to rediscover and rejoin the innocence of his first world. It is an attempt at ecological reintegration, as well as a search for a lost organic community.* Hopeless, of course: too much history has intervened. The only real paradise is paradise lost, and for all his goodwill, Bowling finds the gates of a natural life slammed violently in his face. But he is following a path trodden by John Flory and perhaps by Eric Blair. Empire, the injustices of class, history: Orwell's work was exploring ways in which these things could be understood as radically inter-related.

4

Class

'The road from Mandalay to Wigan is a long one and the reasons for taking it are not immediately clear.'* This clumsy sentence marks the moment when *The Road to Wigan Pier* becomes Orwell's strangest book. Its first half is a report on the writer's experiences on a visit to Wigan, Barnsley, and Sheffield in the months of February and March 1936. By late 1934, he had become 'familiar with Marx's major works', according to Stephen Ingle, 'and with the arguments and ambitions of mainstream British socialism, but he did not formally become a socialist of any sort'.* However much or little he had read Marx, he was well aware of the work of British communist writers, several of whom were his friends.* Now he had been commissioned by the publisher Victor Gollancz to report on conditions in the industrial towns of the North of England, where unemployment was rife. This he did in the first half of *The Road to Wigan Pier*. Then without preparation or explanation, in the second half of the book he embarks on an essay-memoir, akin to the English Protestant genre of the spiritual autobiography, a narrative of conversion like Bunyan's *Grace Abounding*. It deals with his background and schooling, his service in Burma, and the story of his intellectual and political formation.

The road from Mandalay to Wigan was the road to a kind of socialism, although a kind that some socialists found dismaying and inauthentic. And the second part of *The Road to Wigan Pier* contains also a kind of Romantic autobiography—the genre which finds fictional form in *Jane Eyre*, for example, or *David Copperfield*—in that it traces the organic development of its protagonist to the point where he is ready to begin to write the book: he has become what he is. He wants to show the patterns and connections of a life that had seemed to him, at least until recently, directionless and a failure. He makes sense of his life by analysing it in terms of class. He then turns the optic of class upon socialism itself.

The discovery that class was a heuristic, a method of explaining things, hardly made him unique in his generation. After the Great War and the Russian Revolution, and after the rise of authoritarian right-wing governments in western Europe, very large numbers of young people were attracted to Marx's analysis of history in terms of the struggle between classes, and Marx's proposals for the redistribution of wealth and common ownership of production. They allied themselves to socialist parties and movements, and in some cases to left-wing activism. Many of these new socialists were from the working class, but others came, like Orwell, from advantaged backgrounds. These found themselves opposed to the privileges and traditions in which they had been brought up: for example, a theme in Christopher Isherwood's or Stephen Spender's writing about the 1930s is rentier guilt, the discomfort of a person who has had the unfair advantage of unearned income.

Orwell had been educated in single-sex, fee-paying, boarding schools in the affluent South of England, and then spent his early adult life as a police officer in the East. When he came back to England in 1927, he brought with him a fund of knowledge and experience unknown to most of his countrymen, but he was quite unusually ignorant of how people lived in his own country. His political ideas were fairly unformed; it would be more accurate to speak of his political emotions. Five years in Burma, as the servant of an 'evil despotism',* had left him with a bad conscience, and having been an oppressor, he now wanted to get down among the oppressed:

> It was in this way that my thoughts turned towards the English work-ing class. It was the first time that I had ever been really aware of the working class, and to begin with it was only because they supplied an analogy. They were the symbolic victims of injustice, playing the same part in England as the Burmese played in Burma.*

This is a crucial moment in the story of Orwell and empire, because it explicitly states a link between his Burmese experience and his developing socialism. But how useful, actually, was his imperial experience to an understanding of class injustice in England? Crablike, he sidled up to the class system by way of the empire. In Burma, the issue had seemed quite simple:

> The whites were up and the blacks were down, and therefore as a matter of course one's sympathy was with the blacks. I now realised that there was no need to go as far as Burma to find tyranny and exploitation. Here in England, down under one's feet, were the submerged working class, suffering miseries which in their different way were as bad as any an oriental ever knows.*

But what did he know about this submerged class, here in England? The poverty and injustice he had seen in Burma would remain a benchmark, even if the structures of inequality in Europe were different from those in the colonial East. The 'analogy' he seized on between injustices in the East and in England may have contributed to the passion but also the simplification of his analysis of English poverty and unemployment, an instance of what David Dwan calls Orwell's habitual 'naïve sense of certitude'.*

A consciousness of class had been with him almost from the very beginning: he had an extremely sensitive nose for it.* Much of this sensitivity to class matters derives from his own position in the Anglo-Indian lower-upper-middle class—his family's history, and his own as a prematurely repatriated colonial official. When they retired to England, these people had had to come down in the world, relinquishing the pomp of their racial prestige, the comforts of their colonial privilege, and the habits of command, while retaining the manners of the bungalow and club. Families like the Blairs, in genteel but reduced circumstances, struggled hard to keep up appearances. Hence their acute class consciousness. Its components were many: their history of rule abroad, with a feeling of belonging to the governing class, the *sahiblog*, and their diminishing status at home; a nostalgic affection for working people who knew their place (as for loyal 'natives'), inherited from the *noblesse oblige* of earlier generations, and an ingrained conviction that the workers were the 'lower orders'; their constant need to look in the rear-view mirror at neighbours of dubious manners who seemed to be overtaking.

If he is to be believed, families like George Orwell's considered the working class as hostile and dangerous. As a small child, Eric Blair had looked with admiration on people like fishermen and blacksmiths and farm labourers, and had played with their children. But from about the age of 6, he learned that such people were 'common' and coarse, and smelled bad, and furthermore that they resented and hated everyone that was not like themselves. 'So, very early, the working class ceased to be a race of friendly and wonderful beings and became a race of enemies.'* This may be the first instance of the pattern in which a friendly closeness gives way to paranoid distance and alienation.

By attending Eton, Eric Blair had immediately secured for himself one of the premier credentials of the governing class. But his had been an insecure position, a scholarship boy surrounded by others richer and more confident than himself, most of whom glided on apparently effortlessly to Oxford or Cambridge. When he arrived in Burma, aged 19, to serve in the Indian Police, he felt that he was socially some way above most of his fellow colonials, who, he reported with some satisfaction, were 'not of the type who in England would be called "gentlemen"'.* There was a name for people of this sort, a term which arose during the Great War when the army's professional officer corps was swollen by men of lesser social distinction with provincial accents, on temporary commissions for the duration of the war: these temporary officers were referred to, behind their backs, as temporary gentlemen. In colonial Burma, Blair found himself mixing with British people, officials and civilians, who enjoyed the privileges of the upper class, especially plentiful household servants, who would not have had access to such amenities back home. In his descriptions of the ghastly members of the Kyauktada Club in *Burmese Days*, Orwell does not disguise his disdain. (Some of this sardonic observation of colonial types he gets from Somerset Maugham, but not from Kipling, who was many things but not, *pace* Orwell, a snob.)

In 1927, he returned to England and to the bosom of the middle class, specifically the repatriated Anglo-Indian lower-upper-middle class. He remained an ex-colonial official even as he embarked on his strange social experiment among dossers and tramps, the first of several forays in his life and writing to get down among 'the lost people, the underground people', as Gordon Comstock calls them in *Keep the Aspidistra*

Flying.* This was motivated sincerely by a need to mortify his privilege, purge his Burmese guilt, and 'go to the dogs', even if between excursions he was able to return to sanctuaries of comfort (where he had left his good clothes), including the parental home in bourgeois Southwold. 'In fact it is very difficult to escape, culturally, from the class into which you have been born.'* Incidentally, these were journeys of self-discovery. He realized all his ideas were 'essentially middle-class notions',* and '[i]t is only when you meet someone of a different culture from yourself that you begin to realise what your own beliefs really are'.* There is something a little comic, as well as admirable, in the prospect of Orwell on the road, with his scruffy clothes and his Etonian accent. Of course, he was not a real tramp, but for many reasons adopting the tramp's life was not an easy thing to do, even temporarily, and the loss of dignity was real enough. 'Dressed in a tramp's clothes it is very difficult, at any rate for the first day, not to feel that you are genuinely degraded.'*

He did not have much of a chance of convincing either tramps or officials that he was working class. As soon as he shuffled into a casual ward in his shabby clothes, the supervisor clocked him: 'You are a gentleman?'.* More interestingly, he says he found that his fellow tramps were not actually interested in social origins, his or anybody else's. Besides, the decayed toff, fallen on hard times and often an alcoholic, was a recognized figure of the social economy of the down-and-outs in England, as of the bohemian substratum in Paris. In squalid lodging houses ('Good Beds for Single Men'),* in casual wards, and on the road, (though not in the hop-picking, which was a traditional seasonal occupation for the London proletariat), he was associating not with the workers but with people who had actually fallen out of the class system—people who had lost their place on the social map. Tramps were monstered in public opinion, by people who knew little about them, but '[t]his tramp-monster is no truer to life than the sinister Chinaman of the magazine stories'.* A tramp is not a typically working-class person, and 'you do not solve the class problem by making friends with tramps'.* Orwell was becoming a professional writer, and no doubt he was on the look-out for good copy. But more importantly, he was trying to unlearn superiority, and to see things from the underside.

He writes about 'the strangeness of being at last down there among "the lowest of the low" '.* It was strange, but not unsympathetic, and not quite unfamiliar. This estranged vision was the principal gain from his days on the road, though its origins are probably to be found in his own five years overseas in the East. He knew what it was to be a stranger, and perhaps thinking as a stranger, as Paul Gilroy says of the Montesquieu of *Persian Letters*, 'might instructively be linked to actually becoming estranged from the cultural habits one is born to'.* Orwell had now undertaken this strange journey as a way of purging himself of guilt, but what it accomplished was something different, the beginnings of a liberation from unthinking, from prejudice and its pernicious expressions, the stereotype and the cliché. If you remember, he says, that 'a tramp is only an Englishman out of work', then 'the tramp-monster vanishes'.* This is an authentically Orwellian estrangement. It defamiliarizes the tramp as a scary figure, and refamiliarizes him as an example of an unemployed man.

When he went to Paris, he lived in a poor quarter of the city and took some menial jobs, but he had little contact with the French *ouvriers*. He went as a bohemian intellectual, to write books, belatedly joining a substantial and later famous generation of expatriate artists, and mixing with a crowd of penniless exiles and eccentrics, few of whom seem to have been French. The Parisian experiences in *Down and Out* are derived from his last couple of months in the city. When in *Down and Out* he describes his time as a dishwasher in a big Paris hotel, almost all of the people he names are migrant workers, the waiters mostly Italians and Germans, the *plongeurs* 'of every race in Europe, besides Arabs and negroes'.* Again, the East provided an analogy: poverty was a kind of Orient. The *plongeur* was like an 'oriental', or a draught animal, a rickshaw-puller or a gharry-pony, permanently exhausted, worked into an early grave to provide luxury services for others.* Inevitably, the life of a *plongeur* was 'beastly',* but at the end of the day it had the compensations of the animal life, 'a sort of heavy contentment, the contentment a well-fed beast might feel, in a life which had become so simple'.* Here again is the recurring suspicion that the oppressed are merely bodily, and have no interesting mental life. While he may have shared their sufferings, this is not a man writing about his equals. The *plongeurs*, as far as Orwell could see, had little in the way of inner life, and still less political consciousness. Manual labour kept them in a kind of slavery. After all, if they thought at all (he says loftily), they would surely have done something to improve their condition.*

This is patronizing, for all his good intentions. His sympathy with the downtrodden is admirable, as is his determination to try to share some of their experience. But in the case of the *plongeurs*, as often with the 'oriental' people he met and remembered, it can be mixed with a sometimes condescending tone, a disbelief in their capacity to understand or solve their own problems. It is certain that this awkward combination of feeling derives from Orwell's experience as an imperial official in a relatively under-developed country. Readers today may find it disconcerting and disappointing. But (to repeat) Orwell is not our contemporary. The values of the twenty-first century did not all pertain in the past, and he was under political and cultural pressures different from ours, and not entirely clear even to him. Historicizing Orwell, replacing him as far as possible in the context of his time, is our best hope for understanding how it was that, for all his undoubted intelligence and thoughtfulness, he nonetheless felt, believed, and said some things that make us profoundly uneasy.

His eastern experience, and a developing socialism with its attention to class struggle, were part of the intellectual equipment he took on his tour of inspection to the North of England in 1936. Inspection and report: these were among the professional functions of the officer. But although he was to insist that his political consciousness was born out of his service in Burma, how useful was this for his investigation of the working class in England? If you were going to take the road to Wigan Pier, would you start in Mandalay?

The Road to Wigan Pier opens in the Brookers' tripe shop and lodging house, where the observer stays for several days, sharing a bedroom with three others. Mr and Mrs Brooker are slovenly, dishonest, and dirty, and life in the crowded and filthy boarding house is an affront to each of the senses. 'On the day when there was a full chamber-pot under the breakfast table I decided to leave. The place was beginning to depress me.'* As a description of working-class life, this was not flattering. As a matter of fact, the Brookers' house was not the first place Orwell stayed in Wigan, and yet in the book he places it in the foreground of his picture, as if he needs to vent once and for all his feelings of revulsion at the dirt, the squalor, the ugliness, and of course the smell, that sometimes accompany the life of the poor.

When we turn to the other end of the first part of the book, we find, in architectural symmetry, a quite different picture of a working-class interior.* If the Brooker house was the infernal version, this one is nothing short of paradisal, as Orwell evokes a home with 'a warm, decent, deeply human atmosphere', where domestic life has 'a sane and comely shape'.* The place sustains a happiness only possible, he points out, if the father is in work. Two more points are worth making about this cosy scene. First, it is not only an idealized picture, but a generic one ('Father, in shirt-sleeves, sits in the rocking-chair at one side of the fire'),* and is as literary—all Orwell's paradises are literary*—as Robert Burns's warmly sentimental 'The Cotter's Saturday Night'. And, second, although he claims such scenes are still to be found, they are increasingly rare; he is remembering something more distant than Wigan, 'the memory of working-class interiors—especially as I sometimes saw them in my childhood before the war, when England was still prosperous'.* It is a good place to be, he says, 'provided that you can be not only in it but sufficiently *of* it to be taken for granted'*—when you are in the scene, in other words, but not feeling out of place. It is an innocent vision in more senses than one, from before the Great War, but also from before the burden of class-consciousness, a working-class interior seen by a child who did not know that was what it was.

Between these two contrasting, almost allegorical pictures, comes Orwell's report on working-class life in a time of mass unemployment. With its statistics, its meticulous social detail, and its verbatim talk, it is in the documentary mode so important in the decade of John Grierson's films and the Mass Observation project. It is an impressive, even brilliant, piece of reporting. He establishes his credentials as a knowledgeable social investigator by invoking his eastern experience, which is useful to him in a number of ways. On the 'caravan colonies' he visited in Wigan, he reports that he had never seen such squalor except in 'the filthy kennels in which I have seen Indian coolies living in Burma', adding that the coolies did not have the cold and damp of English winter to contend with.* He half-recognized such conditions—that was the benefit of his experience—but to see them in England was a shock. He had seen nothing of unemployment before he went abroad, and in Burma, unemployment had been only a word. So in Wigan his perspective was that of an exile, informed by his lack of acclimatization to British socio-economic conditions. No doubt the long-term residents had got used to the foul smell of the Brooker house by repeated exposure, but to one coming in from outside, it made one catch one's breath. Not only had Orwell been out of the country, but his outsider's perspective enabled him to defamiliarize what he described. It became vivid because it was strange. 'I find that anything outrageously strange generally ends by fascinating me even when I abominate it.'* He had been describing the 'macabre appeal' of industrial landscapes.

But at the heart of the first part of *The Road to Wigan Pier* is coalmining, and the justly famous description of his descent, or rather descents, to the coalface. This is a journalistic investigation, but also the latest and most severe of many attempts to assuage the need he felt, on returning to Europe, to expiate his feelings of guilt by going under, burying himself in suffering and abjection. There are many examples of this descent in his writing: the squalid 'spikes' and rooming-houses of the tramp world, the revolting sculleries of the Paris hotel, and in fictional form the midnight degradation of Dorothy Hare in a Dantesque tangle of bodies in *A Clergyman's Daughter*, Gordon Comstock's wilful surrender to failure and penury in *Keep the Aspidistra Flying*. Orwell's voluntary exile to the trenches of Aragon is another iteration, waiting in the future of the following year, with *Nineteen Eighty-Four* and the cells of the Ministry of Love yet further ahead. But his descent to the coalface is perhaps the most vivid.

With his height and his unfitness, he is a foreigner to this underground world, which the nimble miners themselves negotiate as if native to the place. Here we have an interior of a different kind. Earlier epiphanic moments had revealed to Orwell the interior of the condemned convict (the bowels digesting, the tissues forming), the unfathomable depths of the dying elephant (with his caverns of pale pink throat), and the unexpected inner life of the woman at the drainpipe. Now, with breaking back and tortured muscles, it is his turn to traverse the tunnels of a coalmine, the literal interior of working-class England. As before, what is revealed is a kind of kinship, though a compromised one.

> More than anyone else, perhaps, the miner can stand as the type of the manual worker, not only because his work is so exaggeratedly awful, but also because it is so vitally necessary and yet so remote from our experience, so invisible, as it were, that we are capable of forgetting it as we forget the blood in our veins.*

He has discovered a hitherto invisible world inside the life of the country, a dark Lawrentian unconscious, intimate and essential as the blood itself. In a similar way he would talk about the comforts and amenities of the British at home being dependent on the equally invisible labour of differently coloured people in remote places, a 'coolie empire',* out of sight and out of mind.

Here the analogy between empire and class fits closely. Still, he could not quite leave behind a certain disappointment with these exploited people. If the middle classes were ignorant about the life of the workers, working people themselves often took little notice of the world outside. Orwell had earlier written about the 'political apathy' of the people of Burma,* and the apolitical sluggishness of the Parisian *plongeur*. It sometimes seemed a pity that the English working class too did not take a more lively interest in things that concerned them vitally. In April 1941, he recollected a time in March 1936, during his time in the North, when the Germans re-occupied the Rhineland:

> I was in Barnsley at the time. I went into a pub just after the news had come through and remarked at random, 'The German army has crossed the Rhine'. With a vague air of remembering something someone murmured 'Parley-voo'. No more response than that…So also at every moment of crisis from 1931 onwards. You have all the time the sensation of kicking against an impenetrable wall of stupidity. But of course at times their stupidity has stood them in good stead. Any European nation situated as we are would have been squealing for peace long ago.*

In Winston Smith's visit to the pub in the prole quarter in *Nineteen Eighty-Four*, we can find another example, satirized this time, of the exasperation of the intellectual at the bovine unwillingness of blue-collar (or collarless) people to rise to the occasion. Orwell's grumble about the workers in Barnsley is not all that far removed from Bertolt Brecht's dark joke about the need to dissolve the people and elect a new one.* Even so, Orwell concedes that in wartime this boneheadedness could translate into stubborn resistance. (And in any case, how stupid was the remark? 'Parley-voo' is the chorus of an obscene soldiers' song, 'Three German Officers Crossed the Rhine', about a gang rape. It was a pretty appropriate comment on Hitler's foreign policy.)

The second part of *The Road to Wigan Pier* turns its attention from working people to two different tribes of the middle class, both treated with hostility. Orwell's own middle-class upbringing made him a snob and his schooling made him a miserable one, burdening him with a kind of self-hatred as well as with a whole gamut of prejudices about people different from himself. These were the things it was needful for him to unlearn if he was to become the person he wanted to be, but his claim that he had now 'got rid of [his] class-prejudice', after his time in Burma, was premature.*

A naval officer and a grocer might have the same income, but were not of the same class. Class, he wrote, was determined by economic status, but was 'also interpenetrated by a sort of shadowy caste-system; rather like a jerry-built modern bungalow haunted by medieval ghosts'.* The strata of this oddly Gothic-sounding caste system were exclusive kindreds whose rites, beliefs, habits, tastes, language, and memories were a badge of their prestige, and guaranteed their sense of their own identity. The Anglo-Indians were an example Orwell knew a great deal about, and they crop up all over his work, in *Burmese Days* and *Keep the Aspidistra Flying* and *Coming Up for Air* as well as in *The Road to Wigan Pier* and intermittently in his non-fiction writing. In their overseas service, he was prepared to admit, they were 'at any rate people who did things',* but his focus in *The Road to Wigan Pier* is on Anglo-Indian families in England like his own—'colonial repatriates' as Sathnam Sanghera calls them.* Here they formed a sept of the larger tribe of the shabby-genteel upper-middle class, which included most clergymen, army and navy officers, schoolmasters, a sprinkling of professionals and artists, and (an Orwell obsession) old ladies in Bournemouth or Cheltenham living off the income from dividends. 'In such circumstances you have got to cling to your gentility because it is the only thing you have.'* These people had a genteel culture, but not the affluence to go with it; this is what made them, and made Eric Blair, so painfully sensitive to the signs of class.

In *Coming Up for Air*, George Bowling visits his wife's family, who for generations have been 'soldiers, sailors, clergymen, Anglo-Indian officials and that kind of thing' (an exact description of the Blair heritage).* When Orwell is most confident of his material, he generates lists. 'The carved teak furniture, the brass trays, the dusty tiger-skulls on the wall, the Trichinopoly cigars, the red-hot pickles, the yellow photographs of chaps in sun-helmets, the Hindustani words that you're expected to know the meaning of...';* this could go on and on. Hilda Bowling's family are hard up, but ignorant and snobbish about business ('trade'). 'I looked on them as my social and intellectual superiors,' says Bowling, 'while they on the other hand mistook me for a rising young business man who before long would be pulling down the big dough.'* Orwell was expert at reading these signs of the cultural capital—the beliefs and way of life, the tastes and speech and material possessions—that badge particular classes and sub-classes: if he had not determined to mortify his snobbishness, he might have been a satirist like Evelyn Waugh.

These—Bowling calls them 'the poverty-stricken officer class' and 'the officer-rentier-clergyman class'* (he also calls them 'these decayed throwouts')*—were Orwell's own people. *The Road to Wigan Pier* shows, in sometimes ungainly ways, how he was trying to shake off their prejudices with their culture, and how difficult that actually was. At the same time he looked forward to a future in which they would give up their painful pretensions and distinctions, and relapse without further struggle into the working class where they belonged, 'for, after all, we have nothing to lose but our aitches'.* It was one of his less accurate predictions.

Meanwhile his nose, and ear, for the culture that defined a particular group were turned, in the latter part of the book, towards another English tribe. He had lambasted the Anglo-Indians of the lower-upper-middle class among whom he grew up, and now he turned his guns on the group he had recently joined: bourgeois socialist intellectuals.

Socialism, with its ideals of cooperation, liberty, and justice, was elementary common sense, offering a way out of modern problems; so why wasn't everybody a socialist? The problem, he could see, was the socialists themselves. As with Christianity, 'the worst advertisement for Socialism is its adherents'.*

We meet few blue-collar socialists in the first part of *The Road to Wigan Pier*, and on the whole Orwell presents the working class as victims, and makes 'virtually invisible' the network of political activists in northern towns on whose help he relied during his tour of inspection.* In the second half of the book, he insists that the typical socialist is bourgeois and 'book-trained'.* These are usually, he says with relish, 'unsatisfactory or even inhuman types', 'all that dreary tribe of high-minded women and sandal-wearers and bearded fruit-juice drinkers who come flocking towards the smell of "progress" like bluebottles to a dead cat'.* Many individual socialists, he adds frankly, sounding like a eugenicist, are 'inferior people'.* And they are ugly.

> One day this summer I was riding through Letchworth when the bus stopped and two dreadful-looking old men got onto it. They were both about sixty, both very short, pink and chubby, and both hatless. One of them was obscenely bald, the other had long grey hair bobbed in the Lloyd George style. They were dressed in pistachio-coloured shirts and khaki shorts into which their huge bottoms were crammed so tightly that you could study every dimple. Their appearance created a mild stir of horror on the top of the bus. The man next to me, a commercial traveller I should say, glanced at me, at them, and back again at me, and murmured, 'Socialists', as who should say, 'Red Indians'.*

Whatever this brilliant vignette is, it is not a political debate, for or against socialism. As John Newsinger says, here Orwell is 'substituting a prejudice for an argument'.* The passage uses the kind of descriptive rhetoric Orwell was developing to talk about social class—in this case, a sub-group of the educated bourgeoisie—in terms of its culture, the signs of its styles and manners. It was to provide much of the comedy in his next novel, *Coming Up for Air*. The second part of *The Road to Wigan Pier* has little to say about the left-wing ideas Orwell had espoused (workers, he said, were never interested in ideology anyway), but it goes on at length about the ghastliness of socialists. Having started this hare, Orwell is unable to let it go. There is something here of the snobbery he was trying to put behind him. He repeats that 'the manners and traditions learned by each class in childhood' generally persist from birth to death,* and he instances H. G. Wells and Arnold Bennett, who never shook off 'their lower-middle-class Nonconformist prejudices'.* In his attacks on ugly and ludicrous socialists, Orwell could be said to be displaying the kind of tribalism, the habit of categorizing and disparaging groups perceived as inferior, which was part of his own awkward Blair patrimony.

The book's publisher, Victor Gollancz, was horrified, and wrote a Foreword to the Left Book Club edition in which he distanced himself, and the Left Book Club, from some of its contents. He has been derided for what might seem an act of moral cowardice—Richard Hoggart called the Foreword 'a striking example of much Orwell was attacking'*—but for all its bluster and half-truths, it does make some creditable points.* Gollancz is right to point out that Orwell seems to suggest that every Socialist is a crank, and that a crank appears to be anyone holding opinions not held by the majority.* He congratulates his author on exposing 'the shameful way in which he was brought up to think of large numbers of his fellow men', but adds that Orwell has not really left this habit of mind behind, and that there may remain in him a compulsion 'to conform to the mental habits of his class'.* Orwell could hardly disagree, having said as much several times himself in the book.

He was not, however, finished with these two sub-sections of the middle class, to both of which he belonged. In 1941, in *The Lion and the Unicorn*, at a time when he believed in the possibility of revolutionary change in Britain, he returned to attack them again, and bury them side by side. He now wanted to point out that the military and imperialist middle class, in wartime nicknamed the Blimps, and the left-wing intelligentsia, were actually close kin to each other. They were still ugly.

These two seemingly hostile types, symbolic opposites—the halfpay colonel with his bull neck and diminutive brain, like a dinosaur, the highbrow with his domed forehead and stalk-like neck—are mentally linked together and constantly interact upon one another; in any case they are born to a considerable extent into the same families.*

Both groups have been rendered redundant in the people's war against Hitler, he argues, ending his quarrel with them by consigning both to the dustbin of history. 'The Bloomsbury highbrow, with his mechanical snigger, is as out of date as the cavalry colonel. A modern nation cannot afford either of them.'*

His portrayal in *The Road to Wigan Pier* of these different classes and sub-classes—the workers of northern England, the Anglo-Indian tribe in which he was brought up, the middle-class socialists whom he had awkwardly joined—is fraught in various ways by the modality of his own prejudices and identity. He was both nervous of the working class, and admiring. He was indignant about the officer-rentier-clergyman class, while acknowledging it as his own. And he attacked bourgeois left-ists with some violence, without saying much at all about the beliefs he shared with them. His best writing about social class was to come in *Coming Up for Air*, three years later, in the creation, and voice, of George Bowling. Here was an English figure from the solid, non-intellectual, politically apathetic, commercial middle class, a group in which Orwell had no personal stake. Giving due attention to the culture of this class as well as to its economic history, to Bowling's cheerful philistinism as well as to his loyalty to place and his good sense, it is a subject Orwell was able to approach confidently and without snobbery. Perhaps the ungainly, self-questioning gymnastics of *The Road to Wigan Pier* helped him to see his way through to this clarity. It is a matter of more than curiosity that *Coming Up for Air* is the only one of his novels which he chose to narrate in the first person.

Meanwhile, with its dispiriting class system, England remained 'a family with the wrong members in control', as he put it famously in *The Lion and the Unicorn*.* But he allowed himself the utopian hope that the war might precipitate a kind of revolution in England and sweep the sys-tem away. (He is inclined to call his country England; perhaps Britain in his mind was too closely identified with the noun phrase the British Empire. England for him is usually the name of a culture.) In the end, only a democratic revolution would allow England at last to be herself.

She is not being true to herself while the refugees who have sought our shores are penned up in concentration camps, and company directors work out subtle schemes to dodge their Excess Profits Tax. It is good-bye to the *Tatler* and the *Bystander*, and farewell to the lady in the Rolls-Royce car. The heirs of Nelson and of Cromwell are not in the House of Lords. They are in the fields and the streets, in the factories and the armed forces, in the four-ale bar and the suburban back garden; and at present they are still kept under by a generation of ghosts. Compared with the task of bringing the real England to the surface, even the winning of the war, necessary though it is, is secondary. By revolution we become more ourselves, not less.*

Even this stirring peroration is haunted by its own history. For the ancestors of the true English of the classless future, Orwell chooses two military men. While Nelson was more a brilliant naval strategist than an imperialist (though he fought in imperialist wars), it is not possible to think of Oliver Cromwell without reflecting on his genocidal subjugation of Ireland and the colonial settlement that followed. And so Orwell's generous hopes for a truly democratic future for his country, even as they are expressed, remain entangled in the impossibility of leaving the past behind.

5

Empire

An English timber merchant pays a call on an Indian medical doctor in his bungalow between the European club and the hospital in Kyauktada, Upper Burma. The Englishman is Flory, the doctor Veraswami, and the scene comes early in the novel *Burmese Days*. The two have been good friends for two years, and their conversation soon settles on their favourite subject, the British Empire. This is the 1920s, and the Montagu-Chelmsford reforms, introducing a measure of self-government in British India in response to a growing Indian nationalist movement, are a frequent topic of conversation among the English in the Club—'these dreadful Reforms', Mrs Lackersteen calls them.* Unexpectedly, however—an example of Orwell's estranging or defamiliarizing procedures—in the doctor's house it is the Indian, Veraswami, who is full of praise for the Raj, while the Englishman, Flory, puts the case against.

Veraswami puts the classic auto-Orientalist side of the argument. He admires British justice and the Pax Britannica. He maintains that British officials are 'civilising us, elevating us to their level, from pure public spirit'.* What have the British ever done for the East? He lists the benefits of British rule, including the provision of roads, irrigation, famine relief, education, hospitals, and so on. His imperialism is complemented by his conviction that 'orientals', being corrupt and degenerate, are unfit to govern themselves.

The doctor self-identifies as an 'oriental', but is not Burmese. He is part of a significant and unpopular Indian minority in Burma. There were Indian labourers, and Indian professionals like Veraswami (who as the doctor in charge of the hospital is a government official), but also many of the merchants and most of the money-lenders in Burma were Indians. Veraswami lumps the non-British together as 'orientals'. Many of the British in turn lazily termed all non-British throughout the empire as natives, or blacks; here Flory refers, though not out loud, to Veraswami's 'black skin'.* Throughout his writing career we can watch Orwell trying to purge his own language, including the language of this novel in a later edition, of disparaging racial terms, including 'Chinaman' and 'native'.* The doctor, the only unequivocally decent character in *Burmese Days*, is fanatically loyal to the British and believes that, as an 'oriental', he himself 'belonged to an inferior and degenerate race'.*

In their conversation, Flory's attack on empire is close to the arguments Orwell made elsewhere. Since he has just come from the European club, Flory's first complaints are about his fellow Anglo-Indians: they are boring, philistine, above all racist, he tells the doctor. They hate the Burmese, and each other, and are only in the country to make money, whatever 'the slimy white man's burden humbug', 'the lie that we're here to uplift our poor black brothers instead of robbing them'.* Rudyard Kipling's poem, 'The White Man's Burden: The United States and the Philippine Islands' (1899) was an appeal to the government of the United States to step up and assume its racial destiny as an imperial power alongside Britain. In the poem, empire is presented as a noble and tragic vocation, and a kind of welfare project. It is the responsibility of the white races to look after, educate, and improve the lot of backward peoples, patiently expending labour and even lives for the benefit of their uncooperative and ungrateful subjects. Humbug, according to Flory. The British are in the East for their own profit and nothing else. Their racism is convenient, if sincere: their economic and educational policies keep the local people under, and the poverty and ignorance of the local people justify the policies. Orwell's belief was that you can only rule over a subject race, 'if you honestly believe yourself to be racially superior'.* It was obvious to him that race and empire were not to be separated. (It would not have surprised him to see the postcolonial critique of empire in the twentieth century evolve into a critique of race in the twenty-first, when imperialism, in its formal phase, is long dead.)

'The official holds the Burman down while the businessman goes through his pockets,' says Flory.* He mentions his own timber company, and the oil companies, the miners, and planters and traders, and the Rice Ring, to whose monopolizing activities the British government turned a blind eye.* Veraswami counters by saying that the Burmese would be incapable of running these industries for themselves, but Flory's point is that the British have crushed local enterprises and made sure that local people will never get their hands on the management of their own resources. They are educated, at best, to be clerks for European companies, and are not even taught useful manual trades. 'Now, after we've been in India a hundred and fifty years, you can't make so much as a brass cartridge case in the whole continent.'*

Meanwhile, Flory goes on, the Pax Britannica protects the money-lender and lawyer (not a tactful point to make to an Indian in Burma), and only ensures the building of more banks and more prisons. The European empires brought modernization to the East (as Marx had acknowledged). But in Flory's eyes, modernization was wrecking the national Burmese culture and trashing the environment—'forests, villages, monasteries, pagodas all vanished', to be replaced by 'pink villas fifty yards apart; all over those hills, as far as you can see, villa after villa, with all the gramophones playing the same tune.'*

Flory's indictment of empire as a combination of racism and exploitation is one that Orwell spent the next fifteen years elaborating, but he never really deviated from it. Its terms were already worked out in the article 'How a Nation is Exploited: The British Empire in Burma', which he published in May 1929 when he was living in Paris, five years before *Burmese Days* appeared.* We cannot know how fully he had reached this anti-imperialist position when he returned to England on home leave in August 1927, or whether it was behind his decision to resign from the Indian Imperial Police the following month. (It is possible that his radicalization really belongs to friendships formed in his time in Paris, still under-explored by scholars.) He complained more than once that the great weakness of Kipling's portrayal of the Raj was his total blindness to its commercial motives. Kipling was interested in British officials, and soldiers, and in Indians, but very little in the European planters and traders, the civilian businessmen making their profits in India. Orwell, by contrast, never took his eye off the economic basis of British imperialism. Indeed, he may have exaggerated, or at least simplified, the economic predations of empire. In a chapter called 'Dirty Money' in his book *Empireland*, Sathnam Sanghera lists plenty of instances of rapacity, but adds that 'the territories of empire were not routinely or uniformly profitable, for individuals or for the British government.'*

Curiously, Orwell seems to speak as a lone voice in his critique of empire. One gets little sense that he was aware of being part of a long tradition of English critics of imperialism that included both earlier anti-colonial figures like Adam Smith and Jeremy Bentham, and contemporaries such as Leonard Woolf. It is possible that his antipathy to Bloomsbury prevented him from seeing how much he had in common with Woolf, just as his suspicion of communism stood in the way of his giving due weight to indigenous anti-colonial movements around the world (including South-East Asia) in which communists often played a leading role.

India was huge and complicated. Some Caribbean and African colonies did not present rich pickings. But Burma, with its cornucopia of natural resources, was an immensely rich country, 'one of the richest in the world' in Orwell's opinion.* Its conquest in a series of nineteenth-century wars had no credible strategic motive but was frankly acquisitive, and its twentieth-century economy was entirely dominated by foreigners. In Burma, the economic motive of modern empire was hard to miss. And if empire was inseparable from capitalism, that meant that capitalism was inseparable from empire. Orwell's quarrel with empire is the basis of his quarrel with capitalism. He was not very interested in political economy, but this was to remain the immovable point of his understanding of economics, and so of socialism. It is present in his earliest journalistic writings. It is behind his frequent exasperation with leftist intellectuals, and with the Labour Party, who, he felt, never paid it enough attention. It is still there in *Nineteen Eighty-Four*.

Orwell knew about the economics of empire because his duties as a policeman took him into all corners of Burmese life, and all regions of the country. To the character John Flory, the commercial side of empire is also a given, since he works for a timber company. It is nugatory to wish a fictional work to be other than it is, but it is perhaps a pity, especially after his lively argument with Veraswami early in the story, that we do not see more in *Burmese Days* about Flory's work. He spends three weeks of every month in his logging camp in the jungle, a day's march from the town of Kyauktada, but in the whole book there is just one paragraph describing this place,* and we never learn anything about his employers or colleagues.

In the three novels of English life that followed *Burmese Days*, we can see Orwell keeping an eye on the imperial theme. It is Gordon Comstock, the moth-eaten poet of *Keep the Aspidistra Flying*, who, in some ways, is Orwell's most genuine radical, indignant witness to the degradation of society, nature, and language. His gospel of failure may seem (indeed, it is) peevish and adolescent. But it is nothing less than a quixotic war on the Money-God, lord of a world-system centred on a seedy late-imperial London, its fetish the aspidistra. Gordon Comstock's critique, more startling in its way than anything in *Nineteen Eighty-Four*, sees money and empire as different names for the same thing, a system that reaches from the trade routes of the earth to the daily and intimate lives of its inhabitants.

> He had a vision of London, of the western world; he saw a thousand million slaves toiling and grovelling about the throne of money. The earth is ploughed, ships sail, miners sweat in dripping tunnels underground, clerks hurry for the eight-fifteen with the fear of the boss eating at their vitals. And even in bed with their wives they tremble and obey. Obey whom? The money-priesthood, the pink-faced masters of the world.*

It will do us good to remember that, a decade before he started *Nineteen Eighty-Four*, Orwell's first formulation of a vast unconquerable tyranny has the form not of a political system, but an economic one. Empire is a form of global capitalism—the highest stage of capitalism, as Lenin had titled it in 1917*—and the tentacles of this world-system are everywhere, in the exploitation of nature, in trade, labour, and the social and private lives of many millions. At the far end of the scale from Gordon's global vision sits his pathetic Aunt Angela, in her miserable little semi-detached house in Highgate, comforting her spinster heart with dark brown tea, 'both Flowery Orange and Pekoe Points, which the small-bearded sons of Coromandel have ferried to her across the wine-dark sea'.* All Orwell's writing is thoroughly lubricated with tea, that imperial brew, preferably Indian or Ceylonese; he called it 'one of the mainstays of civilization in this country'.*

Then there is Dorothy Hare's horrible father in *A Clergyman's Daughter*, a familiar type of shabby-genteel snob, grandson of a baronet, whose declining fortunes are due to his stupid investments in United Celanese and Sumatra Tin and 'numberless other remote and dimly imagined companies' in the far-flung Orient.* It is election week in Knype Hill (modelled on Southwold in Suffolk where the Blairs lived), and a vast banner inscribed 'Blifil-Gordon and the Empire' is stretched across the street from the roof of the Dog and Bottle to the roof of the Conservative Club, from whose window floats an enormous Union Jack.* Blifil-Gordon is duly elected. In contrast, George Bowling in *Coming Up for Air* remembers growing up before the Great War in a Liberal constituency, and has a childhood memory of fierce arguments between his father and Uncle Ezekiel, a cobbler and a pro-Boer. 'Them and their far-flung Empire! Can't fling it too far for me,' opines this old Gladstonian, while George remembers his father countering with 'the white man's burden and our dooty to the pore blacks'.*

The Boer War, which divided people and even families in Britain into mostly conservative pro-war ('jingo') and mostly liberal anti-war ('little Englander') parties, was an important imperial crisis a few years before Orwell was born. For him, however, the empire was always largely an oriental phenomenon, centred in British India and its administrative pendant, Burma. 'Under the capitalist system, in order that England may live in comparative comfort, a hundred million Indians must live on the verge of starvation.'* He keeps coming back to this, as if unable to understand why no one is listening. Britain's eastern possessions, their resources plundered, their people deliberately kept in pre-industrial stagnation, represent a vast pool of labour. 'We all live by robbing Asiatic coolies,'* and anyone who steps into a taxi or eats a bowl of strawberries and cream is a beneficiary of this state of affairs, including those, particularly on the left, who profess to deplore it. The British and French empires, with their six hundred million disenfranchised human beings, are nothing but mechanisms for exploiting cheap coloured labour. At the end of the 1930s, he points out, the per capita annual income in England was something over £80, and in India about £7. 'What we always forget is that the overwhelming bulk of the British proletariat does not live in Britain, but in Asia and Africa.'*

This was the analogy between people in the East and the industrial poor in England. 'Orientals' were the poor of the world. Orwell felt it was a pity that the working class in England and France had absolutely no feeling of solidarity with 'the coloured working class'.* But then, the working class in England did not appear to know that the empire existed,* and besides, if the empire was ever dismantled, the English poor would suffer a blow to their standard of living like everybody else. Even so, it would be a necessary catharsis, however painful. It remained Orwell's great theme: until it purged itself of its empire—'the only large scale decent action that is possible in the world at this moment', in 1943*—his country could not become a modern nation.

Burmese Days is a novel about corruption, a corruption that nobody escapes. Veraswami, the doctor, is perhaps an exception, but he is brought down by the corruption around him, embodied by his wily enemy U Po Kyin, the magistrate. In the novel, their virtually unlimited power and privilege in Burma give licence to the worst side of the British, the cruelty and violence of Ellis and Verrall, the mediocrity of Macgregor, the coarseness of the men and the spite and prejudice of the women. Orwell knew about the free hand given to white men in the East. He had been its beneficiary. He remembered lashing out at servants and coolies with impunity, adding in a worrying parenthesis that 'nearly everyone does these things in the East, at any rate occasionally: orientals can be very provoking'.* (Ironic or not, this aside is one of those moments when he gives expression to the attitude he condemns. Uprooting his own Orientalism was an ongoing project.)

It is Flory in whom we can observe the workings of this corruption most closely, because he is aware of it. His life in Burma has been a long story of prevarications, betrayals, and bad faith. No modern man, Orwell thought, really believes that it can be right to invade a foreign country and hold the population down by force, and consequently every Anglo-Indian is haunted by a secret sense of guilt.* This does not seem to apply to the members of the Kyauktada Club. But Flory, though not an official but a civilian, feels keenly that he is complicit in something unforgivable. He is an imperial conformist and a secret dissident (except with Veraswami), his sense of isolation and self-hatred increasing from year to year, for 'it is a corrupting thing to live one's real life in secret'.* He knows he has been spoilt (over-indulged, and vitiated) by Burma.

The rest of the English in the novel are less fastidious. For all their power and privilege, the Europeans in Kyauktada feel embattled. Their stronghold—literally so, later in the story—is their Club, which is also the centre of the novel's plot, which revolves around the question of who belongs and who does not. Every European in town is automatically a member, but the Kyauktada Club is one of the last in Burma to exclude all local people. Now Macgregor, the Deputy Commissioner, has proposed that they elect an 'oriental' to membership. The proposal precipitates a crisis among the members, most of whom are fiercely opposed to the idea. Even a 'good native' member, entering their space and sharing their status, seems an intolerable threat to what they think themselves to be.

Though the club is flyblown and depressing and it is hard to imagine anyone wanting to join it, the question is of great symbolic importance because of the prestige that would attach to a local who became a member. This is a late-imperial squabble, a spasm of self-importance among colonial personnel quick to circle the wagons because they suspect British authority and prestige are beginning to weaken in the East after the First World War, the groundswell of Indian nationalism, the Amritsar massacre, and the reforming Government of India Act. Their racism has a hysterical edge. They are desperate to cling on to the way of life they enjoy (if that is the right word), and the political and racial inequality that sustains it. The social atmosphere in the club is over-ripe and fetid. It was Orwell's opinion that there was not much good writing about the tropical East because no one capable of describing the atmosphere there was willing to stay long enough to absorb it.*

There is an anecdote in *The Road to Wigan Pier* where Orwell remembers an overnight train journey in Burma, in the company of a sympathetic stranger in the Educational Service, in which the two of them spend the whole night denouncing the British Empire 'from the inside', but then 'in the haggard morning light when the train crawled into Mandalay, we parted as guiltily as any adulterous couple'.* But if Orwell was right when he said that all over India there were Englishmen who secretly loathed the system of which they were part, Flory seems to be the only one in fictional Kyauktada, and his rebellion is isolated and mostly silent, besides being ineffectual. It is a secret that inhibits and sickens him, going, as we have seen, against his better nature, so that his eventual suicide has an inevitability in retrospect. Like Winston Smith, he is up against an enemy of disproportionate size and power, which is also, incidentally, his employer and benefactor. Orwell seems to have envisaged it as a machine: he writes of 'the actual machinery of despotism,'* and of colonial magistrates serving 'a huge machine which exists to protect British interests'.* This too looks forward to *Nineteen Eighty-Four.**

'The distinctive feature of Orwell's analysis,' writes Philip Bounds, 'was his belief that imperialism always ends up dehumanising the colonisers themselves.'* In fact, this idea goes back to Bartolomé de las Casas in the 1500s, and was one of the main arguments made by Edmund Burke in the trial of Warren Hastings two and half centuries later. It was, however, a belief that could express itself in something like self-pity. 'Shooting an Elephant' had inadvertently suggested that it was the British who were the victims and prisoners of empire. 'I perceived in that moment that when the white man turns tyrant it is his own freedom that he destroys.'* *Burmese Days*, however, shows the corruption of empire's injustice spreading out to local people. The most spectacular and pathetic victim of this spoliation is Ma Hla May, Flory's Burmese mistress, who is bought, debauched, alienated from her family, cruelly discarded by Flory, and exploited in turn by U Po Kyin. She ends the story working in a brothel in Mandalay. Her looks are gone, her clients pay her only four annas and sometimes beat her.

Before continuing with this catalogue of corruption and debasement, an observation by the historian Jürgen Osterhammel should be considered:

> Classical critics in the decolonization period were right to describe colonial relations as generally productive of deformations. By the measure of a fictitious normal condition, the ideal-typical colonizer and colonized both suffered damage to their personalities. However, we would be reinforcing the colonizer's fantasies of omnipotence if we were to see the whole of life in a colonial space as built upon heteronomy and coercion.*

The damaging effect of colonization was profound, but it was not uniform, and it was not responsible for absolutely everything.

To resume. The magistrate U Po Kyin is not just corrupt in himself but the cause of corruption in others. Slothful in appearance, he has the zest of a Dickens villain. He is by far the cleverest character in the story. He takes bribes, suborns witnesses, writes anonymous letters; he even foments an insurrection in the jungle, so as to gain the credit for suppressing it. As a result of his machinations, Flory dies, Veraswami is demoted, and Po Kyin himself becomes the first 'oriental' member of the club. But this is not motiveless villainy. It has an origin. His earliest memory was of watching the British troops march victorious into Mandalay (this was in 1885), 'great beef-fed men, red-faced and red-coated'; the Burmese child understands that his own people are no match for this race of giants, and so his ruling ambition is formed, to fight on the side of the British, 'to become a parasite upon them'.* The machinery of empire becomes his own instrument of corruption, and he wields it throughout his career to promote and enrich himself and his clients. He will never be found out.

Philip Bounds has made the argument that the main function of the magistrate Po Kyin in the story is to discredit the idea of 'progressive imperialism', embodied in the Montagu-Chelmsford reforms, in which local people were to be invited to make a limited contribution to the governance of their country.* This is right. In the novel, no form of imperialism is shown to be acceptable. But there is no credible anti-imperialism either.

Burmese Days is a powerful indictment of empire in the East. An argument could be made for Orwell as a postcolonial writer *avant la lettre*, except that his work lacks one element that plays a vital part in postcolonialism, the resistance of colonized peoples against their oppression. The case against empire is made strongly in *Burmese Days*, through the disaffection of Flory and in the narrative, but it is not made credibly by local people.* The anti-British *Burmese Patriot* is not much more than a scandal sheet. U Po Kyin's moves to discredit Veraswami and Flory are mere cynical ploys to advance his own interests. He aims to profit from the empire, not to overthrow it. While they alarm the British, the rebellion in the jungle and the riot in Kyauktada are easily dealt with. In 'Shooting an Elephant', the Burmese crowd are hostile to the European officer, but only in a passive-aggressive way. For them, his confrontation with the elephant is a kind of theatre; he feels they would enjoy seeing him make a fool of himself.

In 1931, when Orwell started to work on *Burmese Days* in England, a two-year peasant revolt in the north, led by Saya San, was still going on. Many of the rebels were ignorant and superstitious, but the uprising was worrying enough to cause the authorities in Rangoon to ask for emergency powers (which the government of India did not grant). There is no mention of this episode in *Burmese Days* or elsewhere in Orwell's surviving writing.* He did not think the Burmese capable of mounting a serious challenge to British power. 'And after all,' he told his French readers of *Le Progrès Civique* in 1929, 'the Burmese are mere peasants, occupied in cultivating the land. They have not yet reached that stage of intellectual development which makes for nationalists.'* Yet he had been an imperial police officer, and very well aware that anti-colonial feeling was widespread in Burma when he was there. He experienced it—the jeering of school students, the hostility of Buddhist priests—as something more chronically exasperating than formidable.

There seems a bad fit between his indictments of empire and his disparaging of local resistance to it, for he must have seen that the end of empire could only be brought about by the colonized, not the colonizers. His later championing of independence for India has to be set alongside his lack of enthusiasm for the Congress leaders, and his antipathy to Gandhi. (And was Gandhi not another middle-class, sandal-wearing, pacifist vegetarian?) But there was another issue here. Empire was unacceptable, but Orwell was unhappy that the alternative, and resistance, to empire took the form of nationalism, which was unacceptable too.* His writing engages powerfully in the cultural work of anti-imperialism, not so much by supporting the forces of liberation, as by undermining his own people's belief in empire, their own or anybody else's.

The other European empires impressed him even less than the British. During his stay in Morocco in 1938–39, he found the French who lived there 'dull and stodgy beyond all measure, far worse than Anglo-Indians'.* They were of a lower class than most of the British in the East, and there were more of them, but at least they had less colour-prejudice.* But the French were ruthlessly squeezing the country dry, poverty was worse than in Burma, and Moroccans living anywhere near a town were similarly corrupted, being 'utterly debauched by the tourist racket and their poverty combined, which turn them into a race of beggars and curio-sellers'.* As for the Italians in nearby Libya, he had heard they treated their Arab subjects atrociously.* In the East Indies, the Dutch had faced a serious insurrection in their colonial war of 1900–12, and had behaved brutally. This was the logic of colonialism: 'When a subject population rises in revolt you have got to suppress it, and you can only do so by methods which make nonsense of any claim for the superiority of Western civilization. In order to rule over barbarians, you have got to become a barbarian yourself.'*

There were two other empires at least potentially on the map. Reading *Mein Kampf* in 1940, Orwell could see plainly that Hitler's vision for the future was of 'a horrible brainless empire in which, essentially, nothing ever happens except the training of young men for war and the endless breeding of fresh cannon-fodder'.* The Nazis gloried in a doctrine of racial supremacy which the British were beginning (1940 again) to be ashamed of. 'Hitler is only the ghost of our own past rising against us.'* Orwell was not alone in equating colonialism and Nazism. The same point is eloquently argued by the Martinican poet and politician Aimé Césaire, who said that Hitler 'applied to Europe colonialist procedures which until then had been reserved exclusively for the Arabs of Algeria, the coolies of India, and the blacks of Africa'.* German fascism or British imperialism? In 1943, Orwell wrote a review of a book by his friend Mulk Raj Anand, in the form of a letter to the author:

> Either we all live in a decent world, or nobody does. It is so obvious, is it not, that the British worker as well as the Indian peasant stands to gain by the ending of capitalist exploitation, and that Indian independence is a lost cause if the Fascist nations are allowed to dominate the world. Quite manifestly the battle against Amery [Leo Amery, Secretary of State for India and Burma in Churchill's wartime ministry] and the battle against Hitler are the same.*

It was a startling claim. But it was not Germany that posed an imminent threat to India in 1943. There was another empire, and another emperor, in the East. In his time working for the Eastern Service of the BBC (1941–43), Orwell played a small part in a propaganda war between Britain and Japan for the hearts and minds of Indians. With a string of brilliant military victories behind them, the Japanese were sitting on India's Burmese doorstep, and were offering to free India from its colonial shackles, in the name of Asian solidarity. As we will see in Chapter 6, it fell to Orwell to help to persuade Indians to be loyal to the British empire, so as to prevent India being consumed by the Japanese empire, beguilingly named the Greater East Asia Co-Prosperity Sphere. The irony of this task did not escape him. In 1944, reviewing a book by Konni Zilliacus attacking imperialism and power politics, he notes Zilliacus' argument that Britain went to war in 1914 to prevent Germany becoming master of all Europe, and being strong enough to help herself to British colonies, but adds laconically: 'Why else did we go to war this time?'.*

How could empire end? Most empires fell in the end to military defeat. British India did not open its gates to the armies of Japan, but Orwell watched as the Second World War strengthened the hand of Indian nationalism. Could the British be persuaded to part with their empire, a process which must begin with India? The Labour government under Clement Attlee came to power in 1945 with a commitment to self-government for India, and would no doubt have agreed with Orwell that Britain could not become a genuinely socialist country while continuing to plunder Asia and Africa.*

Orwell gave his support to Attlee's government, but he was afraid Indian independence was not at the top of their agenda. Did they really believe in it? In a cynical moment he had declared that 'every revolutionary opinion draws part of its strength from a secret conviction that nothing can be changed'.* He never joined the Labour Party, but he had strong links with the much smaller and more radical Independent Labour Party (ILP), and was actually a member for about a year in 1938–39, one of the few times he joined anything.* The ILP were active in support of the Spanish Republic, and it was through contacts with the party that he went to Barcelona in 1936 and joined the POUM (the Workers' Party of Marxist Unification). But Orwell was drawn to the ILP because they were the British political party most committed to the abolition of empire, arguing, like Orwell himself, that opposition to Fascism must entail opposition to British imperialism.* His frequent attacks on those who, under the guise of defending Britain against Fascism, wanted to perpetuate the status quo of empire, were echoed in articles by ILP stalwarts like James Maxton and Fenner Brockway.* *New Leader*, their newspaper, gave a platform to prominent colonial leftists and advocates of independence like George Padmore, C.L.R. James, and Jomo Kenyatta.

In some ways, the Attlee years were the worst time to think of dismantling the empire. India would have to work out its own postcolonial plans, but for the British, relinquishing the empire would mean giving up the immediate economic advantages of colonial exploitation, and after six years of war, Britain was already more or less bankrupt. But Orwell's view had always been that the economic price was worth paying in the long term, to end a relationship that was toxic on both sides. 'Once check that stream of dividends that flows from the bodies of Indian coolies to the banking accounts of old ladies in Cheltenham, and the whole sahib-native nexus, with its haughty ignorance on one side and envy and servility on the other, can come to an end.'* To make his argument, he was apt to cast women as the domestic beneficiaries of empire. In an essay in 1946, he imagined putting before 'the average woman in the fish queue' a choice between liberating India and having extra sugar.* It was actually the imperial centre, not the periphery, that was in a state of dependency. The British would need to break their addiction to empire, whether or not they were aware of it.

Against Orwell's expectations, independence for India and Pakistan came about rapidly. It was achieved on 15 August 1947, and followed by massive population exchanges, with great loss of life, in consequence of partition into the two new nation states. Orwell was on Jura, struggling to write the book that would become *Nineteen Eighty-Four*, and India goes unmentioned in his writing that month, or indeed for the rest of that year. He confessed in 1948 that, even five years before, he would never have predicted Gandhi's success in getting the British out of India peacefully, even if he was not able to prevent the fighting between Moslems and Hindus.*

As for Burma, its independence came in the first week of 1948. This event too is not marked in Orwell's writing. But a year earlier, he had written that what concerned him was the welfare of minority ethnic groups in an independent nationalist Burma, which he feared would not be properly safeguarded. (He was to say that most of his political predictions were wrong; unfortunately, in this case, not so.) What would become of the Karens, the Kachins, the Shans, not to mention the many Indians and Eurasians in Burma? The desire of some minority groups for autonomy was genuine, but could not realistically be met. Could they even expect fair treatment in the new dispensation? And what about 'the Jews, the Balts, the Indonesians, the expelled Germans, the Sudanese, the Indian Untouchables and the South African Kaffirs'?*

What about the Biafrans, the Tuareg, the Tutsi, the Sri Lankan Tamils, the Chechens, the Kurds, the Amazonian indigenes? What about the Rohingya? As the postcolonial theorist Robert Young has it, 'empire's structure of government was necessarily organized around the accommodation of diversity, albeit according to an imperial hierarchy'.* The tragic flaw of the nationalism that replaced it was an often intolerant principle of autonomous homogeneity, which tended sooner or later to imperil minorities. In the 1940s, Orwell welcomed the fact that the age of formal imperialism was coming to an end around the world. But he could foresee that this great human triumph bequeathed a problem that would go on to haunt the postcolonial age. 'The fact is,' he wrote, 'that the question of minorities is literally insoluble so long as nationalism remains a real force.'*

6
Geography

George Orwell's first known (but unfortunately lost) literary output, that poem about a tiger with chair-like teeth,* testifies to the way the Orient had already set up camp in his childish imagination. Later in life he was fascinated by the way distant lands and people exist for us in the form of images, built up from books, popular culture, and a kind of rumour, which may bear little relation to what they are actually like:

> The books one reads in childhood...create in one's mind a sort of false map of the world, a series of fabulous countries into which one can retreat at odd moments throughout the rest of life, and which in some cases can even survive a visit to the real countries which they are supposed to represent.*

We might want to add that material can be fed into these false maps in adult life from other sources, such as the cinema, journalism, the internet, and political propaganda. We had better also leave aside the question of whether there can ever be an absolutely true map. Nonetheless, these false maps are part of the soft end of Orientalism, as Edward Said described it, not a western scholarly discourse, but a reservoir of simplified ideas about the East as exotic, essentially different, and peripheral, more colourful perhaps, but inadequate in itself, less strong, less knowledgeable, and less modern than the West.

How was this geographic knowledge disseminated? It started in the nursery and schoolroom. When poor Dorothy Hare, in *A Clergyman's Daughter*, starts work as a teacher in Mrs Creevy's Academy for Girls, she finds her pupils supplied with a reader, dated 1863, which includes 'Nature Notes'. 'The Elephant is a sagacious beast. He rejoices in the shade of Palm Trees, and though stronger than six horses he will allow a little child to lead him. His food is bananas.'* Orwell was a great collector: it is likely this description is not his own invention. Later, he came across a child's illustrated alphabet with entries like these:

> J for the Junk which the Chinaman finds
> Is useful for carrying goods of all kinds.
> N for the Native from Africa's land.
> He looks very fierce with his spear in his hand.
> U for the Union Jacks Pam and John carry
> While out for a hike with their nice Uncle Harry.*

The 'Native' in the illustration was a Zulu dressed only in some bracelets and a fragment of leopard skin, while the Chinese appeared to be wearing pigtails. The book in which they appeared was published in 1947, the year of Indian independence. Its unconsciously patronizing attitude, said Orwell, was learned in childhood and then passed on to a new generation of children.

You could also learn about geography in church. The English hymnal is full of missionary hymns. The ice cupboard in the Hotel X, in *Down and Out*, gave Orwell a sudden memory of 'From Greenland's icy mountains',* which was written in 1819 by the prolific Reginald Heber shortly before he was appointed Bishop of Calcutta. Here are the first three stanzas:

> From Greenland's icy mountains,
> from India's coral strand;
> Where Afric's sunny fountains
> roll down their golden sand:
> From many an ancient river,
> from many a palmy plain,
> They call us to deliver
> their land from error's chain.
>
> What though the spicy breezes
> blow soft o'er Ceylon's isle;
> Though every prospect pleases,
> and only man is vile?
> In vain with lavish kindness
> the gifts of God are strown;

The heathen in his blindness
bows down to wood and stone.

Shall we, whose souls are lighted
with wisdom from on high,
Shall we to those benighted
the lamp of life deny?
Salvation! O salvation!
The joyful sound proclaim,
Till earth's remotest nation
has learned Messiah's Name.*

No wonder this lodged in Orwell's memory: in its genre, it is writing of high quality. It is, however, Orientalist in its assumption that other lands must remain unfulfilled without intervention from the Christian West. 'They' need 'us' to send missionaries: they call us to deliver their land from error's chain (a clever recruitment of the language of the abolitionist movement). In fact, 'we' have been *invited* to intervene. This is like Kipling's 'Mandalay' (1890), where the temple bells are interpreted, on doubtful evidence, to be begging the British soldier to come back to Mandalay. It is an attitude also related to Kipling's more serious apologia, in 'The White Man's Burden', for empire as a vocation to service to the disadvantaged of the Earth.

The Orient could also be the site of glamorous adventure in tales that appealed to boys, often set in imperial badlands like the North-West frontier of India, or the upper Nile.* Popular adventure stories, such as Talbot Mundy's *King of the Khyber Rifles* and A. E. W. Mason's *The Four Feathers*, would have circulated among the boys at St Cyprian's and Eton. Among other 'good bad books', Orwell remembered with affection R. Austin Freeman's *The Eye of Osiris* and Guy Boothby's Tibetan thriller *Dr Nikola*, exercises in imperial Gothic that no doubt contributed to his own false map of the Orient.* There is a kind of knowledge that 'everybody knows'. Everybody knew the Orient was exotic, but dangerous. It was backward, but mysterious and spiritual. Its ways were immemorial and changeless, at least until the Europeans came.

But for the son of an Anglo-Indian family, the East was potentially a destination, a place where he might make a career ('The East is a career,'

says Coningsby in Benjamin Disraeli's novel, *Tancred*),* and put his
talents to use. Anglo-Indians were focused on those parts of the Orient
that were shaded pink in the atlas, the colour of British possessions.
The British empire had three components. There were the mostly white
dominions: Australia and New Zealand, Canada, and South Africa.
There was the Empire of India, which included Burma (until 1937 when
it became a separately administered colony). And there was a collection
of other territories, in South-East Asia, Africa, and the Caribbean and
further afield, mostly Crown Colonies, but each with its own administrative uniqueness, reflecting the ad hoc nature of their acquisition. For
the Blair and Limouzin families, the East was British India, and when he
was a schoolboy considering a career, that was where Eric Blair wanted to
go. He joined the Indian Police, and was posted to Burma. In later writing,
when talking about life in Burma, he sometimes refers to it as India.

In the article, 'How a Nation is Exploited' (to which I so often return)
of 1929, its author E. A. Blair introduces Burma as a country three times
the size of England and Wales. It has a population of fourteen million, of
whom nine million are Burmese, the rest being made up of countless
tribes who have emigrated from Central Asia, and Indians who have
arrived since the British occupation. In Burma, there are 120 languages.
It is, he says, one of the richest countries in the world, abounding in
natural resources, and with one of the healthiest climates in the tropics.
'If we add that the Burmese countryside is exceptionally beautiful, with
broad rivers, high mountains, eternally green forests, brightly coloured
flowers, exotic fruits, the phrase "earthly paradise" springs naturally to
mind.'* Educated Burmese (he explains), and foreigners, like the Indians,
tend to live in the towns and may be recruited by the British for lower-
grade government jobs. But the overwhelming bulk of the Burmese are
peasants, and they live in poverty.

Why was it that, as everybody knew, poverty was widespread in the
East? There were geographical theories about this. One was erected on a
north-south antithesis. In *The Road to Wigan Pier*, Orwell reports coming across a cult of Northernness, which amused him:

When nationalism first became a religion, the English looked at the
map, and, noticing that their island lay very high in the Northern

Hemisphere, evolved the pleasing theory that the further north you live the more virtuous you become. The histories I was given when I was a little boy generally started off by explaining in the naïvest way that a cold climate made people energetic while a hot one made them lazy, and hence the defeat of the Spanish Armada. This nonsense about the superior energy of the English (actually the laziest people in Europe) has been current for at least a hundred years.*

The theory, he points out, was never pushed to its logical end, which would mean assuming the finest people in the world were the Eskimos. But it did help to explain to the British why Mediterranean people like the Spanish, the Greeks, and the Moroccan Arabs appeared to be backward, disorganized, and hopeless. It was also a convenient piece of knowledge for a nation whose empire (if you didn't count Canada) lay entirely to the south, in warmer climes. Southerners were 'sly, cowardly and licentious'.* It was the climate. They were also known to be lazy unless supervised. An influential study of Orientalist stereotyping is entitled *The Myth of the Lazy Native.** It was another case of the idea justifying the empire, and the empire seeming to prove the truth of the idea.

Burma and India lay to the east of Britain as well as to the south. There was a geographical theory about this too. In his *Lectures on the Philosophy of World History* (admittedly, not required reading for Anglo-Indians), Hegel had declared that history had a design and purpose, a *telos*, which was the working out of the spirit's consciousness of its freedom. 'Oriental' peoples had little sense of this freedom, and their natural mode was despotism. 'World history travels from East to West; for Europe is the absolute end of history, just as Asia is the beginning.'* Oriental civilizations and belief systems had risen, climaxed, and declined. Now it was the turn of the West to move history along towards its goal. Even if you did not follow Hegel's metaphysical argument, history seemed to be teaching a lesson that *something* was travelling across the globe, from East to West. You might call it historical initiative, or understanding of the world, or success, or just modernity. After all, the great oriental empires belonged to the past. Now the West was in the driving seat and the East was a passenger.

Orwell had his own version of this historico-geographical determin-
ism, at least as it concerned his own people. He keeps coming back to
the idea of the decay of the English middle class after the Great War, no
longer the makers of history as they had been in Victorian times.
Something (to adapt Philip Larkin) is pushing them to the side of their
own lives. As their economic situation worsens, they seem to be overtaken by a lassitude which can be defeatist, or a kind of denial. Hilda
Bowling's Anglo-Indian family has sunk into a kind of torpor, unable to
pull themselves up out of the slough of their own decline. In *Keep the
Aspidistra Flying*, Gordon Comstock's family is an even better example,
having so completely lost their initiative that '*nothing ever happened* in
the Comstock family'.* They have fallen out of narrative, and are literally
dying out. This English inertia is generalized in the last pages of *Homage
to Catalonia* to cover the entire nation. It might not be pleasant, but,
in Spain, history was being made. But when Orwell returns home from
Barcelona, he finds a country outside narrative, living its immemorial
ways, perilously unaware of what is going on in the world, 'sleeping the
deep, deep sleep of England'.* It would take a war to wake it up.

Weak countries, like weak people, lacked agency. They were unable to
change the conditions in which they lived. If Orwell had a theory of the
relative backwardness of the hot countries he characterized, in a useful
phrase, as 'anywhere south of Gibraltar or east of Suez',* it was not that it
was natural, or inevitable. It was a man-made condition. It was the
intention of the British to keep Burma, for example, as it was. It was a
country of natural riches and human poverty because its resources were
not in the hands of Burmese people. Profits from that natural abundance
were raked off to go overseas (dividend income, perhaps, for those old
ladies in Cheltenham), and in the meantime the British had given free
entry to 'veritable hordes of Indians', who would work for next to nothing,
undercutting local labour.* For the Raj, this policy killed two birds with
one stone (underemployed workers in India, labour costs in Burma),
and was popular with foreign-owned companies. But it worsened both
poverty and racial tensions in Burma. Raw materials were harvested in
abundance—timber, rice, oil, tin, gemstones—but the British, for all their
pious talk of progress and improvement, were not interested in developing local industries. 'We Anglo-Indians could be almost bearable,' Flory

tells Veraswami in *Burmese Days*, 'if we'd only admit that we're thieves and go on thieving without any humbug.'*

Most English people might be, as Orwell complained, constitutionally incapable of believing that anything would ever change.* *Burmese Days* itself is full of anger about the set-up of British Burma, but seems unable to envisage the possibility of things ever being different. But as the 1930s progressed (and, you can't help feeling, speeded up), the map of the world was becoming dynamic. Fascism had taken hold in Italy and Germany, a militaristic Japan had seized Manchuria and was advancing further into China, Italy invaded Ethiopia, and, in Spain too, a kind of Fascism was likely to prevail. In England, probably in 1938, George Bowling looked at the paper, 'but there wasn't much news. Down in Spain and over in China they were murdering each other as usual.'* Hardly a very sophisticated comment, but the inclusion of Spain and China in the same sentence was perhaps a straw in the wind. Something was happening across the world, in the East and the West. A new geography lesson was on the way. To follow it, we need to turn to Orwell's work for the BBC.

When war came in 1939, Orwell was unfit for active service. He soon joined the Home Guard, which he took seriously, but he struggled to find meaningful war work. (Reviewing productions like *Chu Chin Chow* did not count.) So when it came, he welcomed an invitation to apply to join the BBC. From August 1941 until November 1943, he worked as a Talks Assistant, later Talks Producer, in the Indian section of the BBC's Eastern Service. It was his involvement as a writer with Asia that recommended him to the BBC. He was a celebrity, in a small way, and there was a possibility that his name might be known to Indian listeners. The fact that *Burmese Days* was banned in India was not considered a problem, and indeed it may have been thought that someone like Orwell, a critic of the Raj, would appeal to the Indian public at a time of much animosity and distrust between Britain and the subcontinent.

The attack on Pearl Harbor in December 1941 brought the British Empire into a state of war with Japan, and immediately placed all of Britain's eastern possessions under military threat. There were swift British defeats in Hong Kong, Malaya, Singapore, and Burma, and American reverses in the Pacific and the Philippines. The British position with regard to India was now a precarious one. While the leaders of the

Indian National Congress stepped up their demands that the British quit India, British policy was that now of all times, this was out of the question, since the withdrawal of imperial forces from the subcontinent would leave it vulnerable to the approaching Japanese, and in effect would cast all of Asia, and the outcome of the Second World War, into jeopardy. But at the same time, it was felt that Britain could not afford to antagonize the Indians, denying their long-term demands, and driving them into the arms of the Japanese with the same effect. In these circumstances, Britain had to be careful what it was going to say to India.

The BBC was a publicly funded corporation, not a government department, and had a reputation for the relative impartiality and reliability of its news services. Still, nobody seriously believed or argued that in wartime the corporation would be independent of the government. Policy directives were issued to the BBC from time to time by the Ministry of Information, directed by the interestingly initialled Brendan Bracken, and the corporation was charged with censoring its own output in conformity with government requirements. Every broadcast script was vetted in advance, twice, once for Policy and once for Security.* The BBC did not broadcast hard propaganda or outright lies, and late in 1942 Orwell was able to say that the weekly news commentaries he wrote for broadcast to Asia 'in fact have contained very little that I would not sign with my own name'.*

Orwell was responsible for a lot of interesting programmes for the BBC, but it is in these weekly news commentaries (also called newsletters or reviews) that he develops something like a new map of the world. The commentaries he wrote were read out on air by his superior, the distinguished broadcaster Zulfaqar Ali Bokhari, until November 1942 when, after a change in policy, Orwell began reading his own scripts. (It appears that no recording of his voice survives.) A memorandum from the Assistant Controller of Overseas Programmes in February 1942 spells out that the primary purpose of the weekly commentaries was propaganda; they should be a vehicle 'to "put across" the British view of the news, without sacrificing the reputation that has been carefully built up for veracity and objectivity in news presentation'.* Orwell's own stated view, that 'our rule in India [was] just as bad as German Fascism, though outwardly it may be less irritating',* was hardly compatible with the official British view of the news. But he had secured the BBC's agreement that he could take 'an anti-fascist rather than imperialist standpoint' in his commentaries.* And he really did believe that India should remain loyal to the British and the Allies, until the Japanese threat was over. The war must be won. Afterwards, Indians should decide their own future.*

To convince the people of Asia that they have common cause with the Allies, Orwell embarks on what is essentially a narrative combining history and geography. In commentary after commentary, week by week, he tells the unfolding story of the war. Or rather, he retells it, processing its events in a way intended to enable Indians to see and possess it as their own story. Japanese propaganda depicted the European empires as fighting to cling on to their eastern possessions. Obviously, the war that Orwell interprets to Indians is not an imperialist struggle (except on the part of the Japanese), but a global conflict in which all peoples have a stake. He is always careful not to give the patronizing impression of exporting the view from London. Instead, a favourite trope of the newsletters is to ask listeners to imagine the globe itself, or a map of the world, so as to be able to see the big picture. And it is not a map with London (or Greenwich) at its centre. The newsletters themselves move like a restless searchlight easily across the face of the Earth, reporting news from the Pacific and Russia, Mexico and North Africa, in the space of a few paragraphs. Their aim is to help listeners to emancipate themselves from provincial short-sightedness, and see the whole picture:

But in order to follow the events of this war, it is more than ever necessary to study the map of the world, and in addition to remember that the world is round. When we hear of those early successes of the Japanese in the Pacific, we may be inclined to think that they offset the defeats which the Germans have received in Russia and Libya. But when we look at the map, we see a different picture, and we see one immense advantage which the democratic powers have over the Fascists. This is that they can communicate with one another.*

Placing the map in the hands, or the minds, of the Indian listeners was a sort of liberal empowerment, designed to help them to share the strategic vision. In his commentaries Orwell constantly used pictorial and cartographic tropes. And if the globe, and the cause, he invokes are interconnected, they are also interdependent. His Indian listeners had to be reminded that this was their war too, like it or not, and the way to remind them was to insist on seeing the struggle 'in its true perspective', he says, looking at 'the whole picture and not merely one corner of it'.* It was (to revert to an earlier theme) an estranged perspective, not just the narrow view you could see from your home. This global picture—the view from space—was a favourite image of the writing of the 1930s, but its most familiar instance was the turning globe, emitting radio waves, which many people saw every week in the cinema at the start of Universal and RKO movies. With this shift in angle, Orwell's commentaries attempt to clarify India's own interests and global obligations. It is a remarkable and sustained piece of rhetoric. For all that, it is still an imperial one. It seeks to represent India's position and interests to itself, while the all-seeing but invisible metropolitan observer fulfils what has been called 'the ambition of regimes of colonial representation: to see [and to make others see] without being seen'.*

The Japanese, needless to say, were using a different map. The propaganda war was essentially a war of pictures or world-views, and their own propagandists were busy persuading Asians that Japan was their neighbourly liberator from the alien empires of Europe. Orwell warned his listeners against this attempt to sell them 'the picture of a war of Asia against Europe';* they must be helped to see things as they really were. A fine example comes in a newsletter broadcast in May 1942. With India at this point 'within measurable distance of invasion', Orwell asks his listeners to look again:

When we look at the history of this war, which has now gone on for two and a half years, we see that something which started as a localised struggle has become definitely worldwide, and that a meaning and purpose which were not apparent at the beginning have gradually become clear. More than that, we see that this war is not an isolated event, but part of a worldwide process which began more than ten years ago. It started, properly speaking, in 1931, when the Japanese invaded Manchuria, and the League of Nations failed to take action.

From then onwards, we have seen a long series of aggressions, first of all unresisted, then resisted unsuccessfully, then resisted more success-fully, until finally the whole picture becomes clear as the struggle of free peoples who see before them the chance of a fuller and happier existence, against comparatively small cliques who are not interested in the general development of humanity but only in advancing their individual power. One country after another is sucked into the strug-gle, and they are sucked in not purely for reasons of geography, and not purely for economic motives, but primarily for what are called ideological reasons—that is to say, they are practically compelled to take one side or the other, according as their national philosophy is a democratic one or the contrary.*

Thus, Indians, interpellated in phrases like 'we look' and 'we see', are put in the picture, in both senses, and it is a picture that speaks for itself. He goes on to argue that India 'finds itself inescapably on the democratic side, and this fact is not really altered by the ancient grievances which India may feel against Britain'. India is compelled to be with Britain, because victory for the Axis would postpone Indian independence much longer that any British government would be able to do. 'Willy-nilly, India is already in the struggle; and the outcome of the war—and therefore India's independence—may be determined to a very great extent by the efforts that Indians themselves now make.*

That last move was one that Orwell had been building up for some time. The global perspective not only enabled Indians to understand the war as a necessary passage to a post-colonial world. It also reconfigured the map of the world as Indocentric. India was not only involved, it was the key player. Now, in the war, subaltern India was promoted to the highest importance, holding in its hand not only its own future as a nation but the very outcome of the world war. India had become 'immensely more important' after the loss of Singapore, Orwell had written for broadcast in February; in this crisis, 'India becomes for the time being the centre of the war, one might say the centre of the world.'*

The world was turned not only upside down but inside out, and the imperial margin turned into the global centre. This (literal) revolution and orientation of the world map are another significant moment in the story of Orwell and empire. Its geography is not only post-colonial but redemptive. India can save the world, and secure its own freedom, this newsletter concludes; for if India has the will to resist, its enemies can never prevail. 'The thing that will defeat them is the same thing that has defeated the Japanese assault on China and the German assault on Russia—the resolution and obstinacy of the common people.'*

It was indeed the map of a brave new world. Orwell's rallying cry for a geographical utopia, however, seems to have been in vain. Laurence Brander, Intelligence Officer of the BBC, was sent to India in 1942 on a six-month fact-finding tour, and told Orwell on his return in October that 'our broadcasts are utterly useless because nobody listens to them.'* It was depressing news, and Orwell, who was always inclined to disparage his own work, felt that his efforts at the BBC had been futile. By early 1943, Orwell told his listeners (if there were any) that 'the defences of India have been so strengthened that no attempted invasion is now likely.'* He went on dutifully writing newsletters, but for the remainder of his time at the corporation, his main energies went into the cultural and educational programmes which had always been the other part of his brief as a producer in the Eastern Service. That is another story.

Meanwhile, elsewhere, another map was being imagined. Orwell left the BBC on 25 November 1943. Three days later, in Tehran in Persia, three old men met to look at a map of the world. The Tehran Conference, attended by Joseph Stalin, Winston Churchill, and Franklin D. Roosevelt, was one of a series of summit meetings of the Allied leaders, held to decide the direction of the war and to discuss a post-war settlement. These meetings were served up to the public of the allied nations as examples of strategic cooperation. To Orwell, who wrote about 'the sordid bargain that appears to have been driven at Teheran',* they presented a spectacle of three Great Powers carving up the world to their own advantage. From these tripartite summit meetings of wartime allies—chiefly Tehran, Yalta, and Potsdam—emerged the post-war spheres of influence and ultimately the geography of what Orwell was to christen the 'cold war'.

That phrase occurs for the first time in 1945 in a short essay, 'You and the Atom Bomb', in which he looks forward to a dangerous future. 'More and more obviously the surface of the earth is being parcelled off into three great empires, each self-contained and cut off from contact with the outer world, and each ruled, under one disguise or another, by a self-elected oligarchy.'* He had decided soon after returning from Spain that Nazism and Stalinism were moving towards a common form of tyranny, which he called 'oligarchical collectivism'.* But it is notable that he did not make an exception for the western democracies, but foresaw a similar political convergence looming in *all three* great empires which he thought would dominate the post-war world. This, he thought, was the shape of things to come in the second half of the twentieth century, as cooked up in those wartime allied summits, with one important exception: he foresaw that a weakened Britain would soon lose its place at the geopolitical table, to be replaced by a new player, 'East Asia, dominated by China'.* There is thus a straight line from the Tehran Conference to the geography of *Nineteen Eighty-Four*, with its three super-states of Oceania, Eurasia, and Eastasia.

Oceania covers the Americas, the British Isles, southern Africa, and Australasia. Its rivals are both Asian. Eurasia is the equivalent of the Soviet Union after its conquest of continental Europe. Eastasia comprises China, Japan, and most of the Middle East. In the dystopian future of the novel, the populations of all three super-states are locked down in a kind of slavery, while perpetual war exists between shifting combinations of two of these superpowers against the third. That leaves, in the middle of the world map, a quadrilateral of unaligned territory, with its four corners at Tangier, Brazzaville, Darwin, and Hong Kong. (This is close to Orwell's formulation, 'anywhere south of Gibraltar or east of Suez',* which roughly corresponds to what would later be christened the Third World.) The quadrilateral (which contains, of course, India and Burma, and most of Britain's South-East Asian and African colonies) is a huge reservoir of labour, over which the super-states perpetually war.

The quadrilateral is constantly robbed of its labour. But it is not subject to absolute authority and surveillance. In this sense, the quadrilateral in the middle of the globe is the equivalent of the proles in Winston Smith's London, the urban working class who seem to present no threat to the ruling Party in Oceania. They live sequestered in their own part of the city (equivalent to a 'native quarter' in a colonial town), and are even more invisible than the Burmese in *Burmese Days*. The Party despises the proles, but does not bother to police them closely. 'Proles and animals are free.'*

Winston Smith, a Party functionary, knows from the start that his own rebellion against Big Brother cannot succeed. If there is hope, he thinks, it lies in the proles. 'If there was hope, it *must* lie in the proles, because only there, in those swarming disregarded masses, 85 per cent of the population of Oceania, could the force to destroy the Party ever be generated.'* If only made aware of their own strength, the proles can overthrow tyranny. The same must be true, on a global scale, of the abused but teeming quadrilateral. For the multitude south of Gibraltar and east of Suez, liberation is in their hands. In the end, the map of the quadrilateral is a map of potential freedom.

7

Women

After a year or two of marriage, George Bowling, hero of *Coming Up for Air*, stops wanting to kill his wife, and starts wondering about her:

> Just wondering. For hours, sometimes, on Sunday afternoons or in the evenings when I've come home from work, I've lain on my bed with all my clothes on except my shoes, wondering about women. Why they're like that, how they get like that, whether they're doing it on purpose.*

It seems only fair to have a chapter on women; all the other chapters are about men. What did Orwell know about women and how did he know it? George Bowling is not a portrait of George Orwell, of course, but it is a portrait that suggests the author knew what it was like to be a man for whom women were a problem. Orwell, in turn, has been a problem for many feminists, and has been vigorously attacked as a misogynist and the perpetrator of sexist, objectifying, and demeaning representations of women.* The oriental-imperial theme in Orwell may give us a perspective on both problems.

With an older and a younger sister, Eric Blair's early years were spent in a predominantly female household. His father, absent in India in Eric's early childhood years, seems to have been aloof and not highly communicative, and the two were never close. At the age of 8, however, the boy was sent away to St Cyprian's, and from then until he left Eton, aged 18, he spent most of every year in all-male boarding schools. Less than a year later he started work in the Indian Imperial Police in Burma, remaining there for five years. So apart from his early childhood, he had lived in a predominantly masculine world; there were women, to be sure, but few in his peer group. This experience was not so unusual among privately educated young men of his class; his Eton contemporaries who went on from public school to Oxford or Cambridge, where women undergraduates were few and without the privileges of their male counterparts, exchanged one largely masculine community for another. But from Oxford or Cambridge you could slip down to London for the weekend, or further afield for the vacation. Orwell moved around Burma for the five years of his service there, but never left the country until his return to Europe.

In the early days, there were few white women in British India. In the second half of the nineteenth century, and especially after the opening of the Suez Canal made the journey easier, they started to become a feature of the Raj, radically altering the social life of the British and their relation with local people. For a European woman in the East, life could be luxurious. The father of the future Lord Beveridge was no more than a middle-ranking bureaucrat, but his household in India had thirty-nine servants.* But in Anglo-India there was even less scope for working women than at home. With some exceptions—school-teaching, perhaps, or nursing—the requirements of ethnic prestige would not allow British women to work, even if they wanted to, and social life and perhaps some charity work marked the boundaries for most white women in the empire. Consequently memsahibs had a bad reputation for snobbery, laziness, gossip, bullying the servants, and being ignorant about their surroundings. Orwell himself mentioned his Limouzin grandmother who lived in Burma for forty years and at the end could not speak a word of Burmese—'typical of the ordinary Englishwoman's attitude', he said.* In *A Passage to India*, E. M. Forster was repeating a familiar joke when he wrote of Mrs Turton that she had learned a little Urdu, 'but only to speak to her servants, so she knew none of the politer forms and of the verbs only the imperative mood'.*

The European memsahib gets a bad press from the better male English writers, Somerset Maugham, Forster, Orwell, even (for the most part) Kipling. Undoubtedly some of this reputation was unfair, and indeed sexist. There was literally not much that an Englishwoman in the East could do. There are two of them in *Burmese Days*. Mrs Lackersteen spends her time scolding her husband and trying, without much success, to keep him away from other women and from the bottle. Her niece Elizabeth has come east with the sole intention of finding a husband, settling in the end for the boring Mr Macgregor and the life of a *burra* memsahib. 'Her servants live in terror of her, though she speaks no Burmese.'* When such women came home to England, they brought their trivialities and snobberies and uselessness with them, to judge from the two who come into Gordon Comstock's bookshop in *Keep the Aspidistra Flying*, or the wretched mother-in-law of George Bowling, living in Ealing in reduced circumstances, 'so colourless that she was just like one of the faded photos on the wall.'*

For Englishmen in the East, it was different. Opportunity abounded; power seemed almost unlimited. (*Burmese Days* shows us that the servant's pronoun for the Englishman is 'the god'. 'The god has hurt himself? Shall I carry the god back to the house?')* The masculine conversation in the Club in Kyauktada proves this to be very much a man's world. The lascivious jokes, the swearing, and the boasting are only curtailed by the unwelcome arrival of Mrs Lackersteen, like the headmaster's wife entering a boys' dormitory.* Mrs Lackersteen may be unalluring, but there were other kinds of women in Burma, and when her husband escapes to his jungle camp, he is rumoured to enjoy the company of '[t]arts by the score.'* It seems likely that Orwell's own first sexual experiences were in Burma, with prostitutes, and were therefore both commercial and highly asymmetrical, the man being much the more powerful in gender, ethnic, and economic terms. Local women were no doubt easily available and relatively undemanding: they were poor, and it seemed all they wanted was money. These stanzas are from the draft of a cynical little poem about a brothel, which Orwell probably wrote in Burma:

> The woman oiled her hair of coal,
> She had no other occupation.
> She swore she loved me as her soul,
> She had no other conversation.
>
> The only thing that woman knew
> Was getting money out of men.
> Each time she swore she loved me true
> She struck me for another ten.*

The company of unattractive memsahibs by day and local whores by night was not the best environment in which to nurture a respect for women. It is clear that Orwell patronized prostitutes from time to time after his return from Burma, at one point seeking his wife's permission to visit a Berber girl in Taddert in the Atlas Mountains, and later giving an enthusiastic report to Harold Acton (of all people).* It was a taste formed in Anglo-India before he was 20, and made possible, though perhaps not inevitable, by the conditions there.

The theme recurs in his fiction. In *Keep the Aspidistra Flying*, Gordon Comstock, sexually frustrated with his middle-class girlfriend, gets drunk and picks up a prostitute who takes him to a mean and dreadful room (with an aspidistra).* In *Nineteen Eighty-Four* Winston Smith remembers his own wife's frigidity, and confesses in his diary to visiting a prostitute, only to discover when the light is turned up that she is old and very ugly.* These are fictional scenes, of course, but there is a certain callousness about them. The most egregious example occurs in *Down and Out in Paris and London*, where Orwell devotes a whole chapter to an anecdote told by his young Parisian friend Charlie, who recounts with relish how he paid a thousand francs (stolen from his brother) to rape a young girl in a brothel cellar.* Charlie describes this as the happiest day of his life. The incident, presumably a fantasy, may carry echoes of the extreme asymmetry, and the colonial symbolism, of the congress of a white man and a local woman in Burma:

> She was twenty years old, perhaps; her face was the broad dull face of a stupid child, but it was coated with paint and powder, and her blue, stupid eyes, shining in the red light, wore than shocked, distorted look that one sees nowhere save in the eyes of these women. She was some peasant girl, doubtless, whom her parents had sold into slavery.*

Infantilized, brutalized, powerless, and silenced after crying out for mercy, exotically coated with paint and powder (like a Burmese girl wearing *thanaka* cream on her face), and essentialized ('these women'), this wretched French girl comes in the trappings of Orientalism. Orwell may have forgotten this chapter of his own writing when, in an essay of 1944, he deplored the depiction of rape, cruelty, and sexual perversion in James Hadley Chase's thriller *No Orchids for Miss Blandish*. He diagnosed its theme as the triumph of the strong over the weak: Chase was presenting 'a distilled version of the modern political scene'.* This analysis entitles us to speculate that the rape story in *Down and Out* may present a distilled version of the structures of power in colonial Burma, which Orwell had recently left behind.

In one of the central scenes in *Burmese Days*, there is a meeting, of a kind, in Flory's house between Elizabeth Lackersteen, the blonde English girl recently arrived from Europe, and Ma Hla May, Flory's Burmese mistress. 'No contrast could have been stranger; the one faintly coloured as an apple-blossom, the other dark and garish, with a gleam almost metallic on her cylinder of ebony hair and the salmon-pink silk of her *longyi*.'* Each seems outlandish to the other. Yet they have this in common: both are imprisoned in a demeaning role from which there is no escape. May is a kind of slave, Flory having bought her from her parents for three hundred rupees, two years before. Elizabeth is enslaved in less simple ways. She is small-minded, snobbish, a philistine, and a racist, but her situation is potentially a tragic one too. She has come to Kyauktada to offer herself on the marriage market. Flory himself, Verrall, the military policeman, and Macgregor, are all possible buyers. Elizabeth's aunt, discovering that Verrall is the youngest son of a peer, comes close to pimping her niece out to this excellent prospect, though in the end she will have to settle for Macgregor. Elizabeth's uncle in Burma tries to rape her and her aunt wants rid of her. She has no other family and no money. For Elizabeth, finding an English husband is very nearly a matter of life or death.

Ma Hla May, also a snob, enjoys the prestige of being a white man's mistress although she does not care for Flory. When he decides to dismiss her because he intends to pay court to Elizabeth, he does so in one of the most distressing scenes in Orwell's fiction. She has nowhere to go, for she cannot go back to her father's house to be jeered at by peasants whom she despises. Flory offers her money. To his horror, she bursts into a loud wail and falls to her knees, before creeping, wormlike, right across the floor to his feet. She has become not only abject but ugly. The fact that she never loved him makes it worse. 'If she wept and grovelled it was only for the position she had once had as his mistress, the idle life, the rich clothes and the dominion over servants. There was something pitiful beyond words in that.'* Association with him has debauched and corrupted her utterly: her degradation is both sexual and economic. Though at first he will not face her, and cannot look at her, in the end he has no choice. 'He stood looking down at her with his hands in his pockets, helpless.'* This is what he has done, to her and the 'endless procession of Burmese women' who preceded her, whose names and faces he has forgotten.* Ma Hla May will end her days working in a brothel, but not before taking her revenge on Flory.

One of Orwell's more prominent feminist critics complains that 'discussions of *Burmese Days* typically focus on the issue of imperialism, while ignoring the appearance within the novel of quite another major theme: that of sexual and social identity and the linkage between them.'* This would indeed be a grievous fault. In fact, the sexual and gender theme is not separable from the issue of imperialism in this novel. Flory's mistreatment of Ma Hla May, and his own entrapment in a certain kind of masculine privilege, do not compromise his critique of empire, but thematize and reinforce it. His bad faith as a critic of imperialism, dramatized in this highly painful scene, is obvious even to himself.

A Clergyman's Daughter, his next book after *Burmese Days*, is one of the most surprising turns in Orwell's literary career. His first and only fiction centred on a woman's experience, it suggests there was something still unresolved in his idea of woman's predicament. The whole panoply of English patriarchy—religious, familial, cultural, economic, educational, linguistic, disciplinary—is ranged against Dorothy Hare, the clergyman's daughter. But the focalization of the novel, the way the story is told not by her but through her, opens up an inner life which was not plumbed in the cases of Elizabeth Lackersteen or Ma Hla May. It is a sympathetic picture, but a bleak one. Dorothy makes a literally unconscious escape from her bondage by means of a somewhat implausible attack of amnesia involving loss of identity. She wanders far from her father's house, and church, only to return at the end of the story to identity, father, home, Christianity, and subjection, seemingly no better off than before. Dorothy's escape into narrative was a false one. She is trapped in a dismal repeating cycle of female bondage, its avatar being Mavis Williams, the illiterate child in Dorothy's schoolroom, endlessly filling her exercise book with pothooks, 'page after page of pothooks, looping on and on like the mangrove roots in some tropical swamp'.*

Dorothy is enslaved not by chains but by the appropriately domestic symbols of pins and glue. In the final chapter we see her, back in her father's Knype Hill parish, using these to make the costumes for the coming St George's Day pageant. But a pin, a long glass-headed one, has appeared in the opening chapter, where she uses it to prick her arm until it bleeds, 'her chosen form of self-discipline', a punishment for not concentrating in church.* This self-harm indicates that Dorothy is complicit with her own subjection. Believing she deserves to be punished, she introjects (as Freud might say) and collaborates with the authority of her masters.

But then, it is simply the case that no romantic rebellion is available to free her from her situation. If her experience has not taught her this, it is made clear to her by the goatish and unsavoury Mr Warburton when he asks her to marry him. He spells out the reality that faces her if she refuses, with a sadistic frankness that anticipates O'Brien's domineering of Winston Smith in the Ministry of Love. 'Consider what your future will be like,' he tells her. 'It's the same future that lies before any woman of your class with no husband and no money,' the unrelieved prospect of drudgery and loneliness, a 'slavish, worrying life'.* That paradigm of enslavement, which fitted closely over Ma Hla May and Elizabeth Lackersteen in their different ways, encircles Dorothy Hare too, and will soon be seen to circumscribe the woman whose 'dreadful destiny' is to kneel on the stones of a back yard, trying to unblock a leaden waste-pipe.* This is another way in which the road to Wigan, via Knype Hill, started in Burma.

The plight of women, both local and European, in the East was not only an effect of the imperial set-up. There was no equality for women in traditional Asian societies, and their low status and lack of opportunities were among the aspects of 'oriental' life often deplored by western observers. William Beveridge reported that his liberal mother was 'repelled' by the Indian attitude to women.* At the BBC, Orwell asked the author Naomi Mitchison to take part in a discussion on the emancipation of women, explaining (or mansplaining) that 'this subject is a very important one for India, and one cannot assume that opinion there has moved nearly as far as in Britain'.*

His manners towards women were those of his upbringing. 'He had this ultramasculine attitude to them,' his girlfriend Kay Ekevall remembered, 'so that they were just sort of useful appendages to life rather than people. Mind you, he didn't treat you like that when you met him.'* In Orwell's fiction there are plenty of examples of women who have accepted, more or less willingly, to live a life ancillary to the needs of men. Gordon Comstock's sister Julia (Orwell is strangely economical with names) was given almost no education, while huge sums were wasted on sending her brother to third-rate schools. She works twelve hours a day in a nasty, ladylike little tea-shop, and lives in a bed-sitting room in Earl's Court where Gordon, sworn enemy of the Money-God, comes round from time to time to borrow funds which she cannot afford and he will never repay. He finds her depressing, and leaves as soon as possible. Gordon's girlfriend Rosemary, though much more independent and spirited, also behaves as something of an adjunct to her man. When she becomes pregnant, she is ready to accept that Gordon may abandon her and the baby, and she will not pressure him into accepting the well-paid job that is open to him. 'I want you to feel free,' she tells him.*

It was not all a story of subjection and self-denial. According to Jacinta Buddicom, one or two of Eric Blair's aunts were militant suffragettes, and his mother was 'in sympathy, but not so active'.* His aunt Nellie, to whom he was close in Paris, embraced radical causes all her life.* In his own generation, the semi-bohemian world of intellectuals, artists, and journalists he inhabited was full of independent, well-educated, sexually emancipated modern women. It was a cohort that included his first wife, Eileen O'Shaughnessy, and his second, Sonia Brownell. Partly because of his chronic illnesses, and later as a widower with a small child, Orwell was inclined to depend on women (including his sister Avril). But if he was needy, he was also persistently clumsy with them. From Jacinta onwards, he 'lacked the gentle art of seduction', as Gordon Bowker puts it politely.* He seems to have had a reputation as a pouncer, particularly out of doors. Sexual morality in his circle was not inordinately strict, but contraception was not as easily available as it later became (though he didn't mind assuring women friends that he was sterile).* The result was some awkward and some unpleasant moments.

Traditional patriarchal thinking about gender bequeathed an idea that women, for apparently obvious biological reasons, were specialists in the bodily life, which left the intellectual sphere to men. Women had babies, nursed and fed families, while their menfolk went out into the world to make plans, have careers, and run everything. Not surprisingly, in more recent times the association of women with the body is looked on with suspicion, and the representation of a woman as a sex object in particular is considered demeaning, even a form of violence. If indeed Orwell's early sexual experiences were transactional and asymmetrical, in Burma and perhaps in Paris where he said he lived with 'a little trollop,'* this might have encouraged him to think of women in this way, associated with the life of the body and, in the familiar pattern, deficient in intellectual life.

This degrading way of thinking of women paralleled a similar and contemporary idea of the non-European 'native', and the feminization of the latter is recognized as a recurring Orientalist trope. It is to be glimpsed, for example, in Orwell's enthusiastic description of the 'oriental' body in *The Road to Wigan Pier*, where, he says, 'I felt towards a Burman almost as I felt towards a woman.'* We have already looked at the commodification of Elizabeth Lackersteen's attractions in the marriage market of Anglo-India, and the objectification of Ma Hla May, a possession to be discarded by Flory when the game changes (though when something occurs in a fiction, it is bad reading to assume that it does so with the author's approval). It is now time to consider the woman's body in three more complex examples: Rosemary in *Keep the Aspidistra Flying*, and Julia and the lost mother in *Nineteen Eighty-Four*.

Much of the plot of *Keep the Aspidistra Flying* concerns Gordon Comstock's efforts to get Rosemary into bed. She resists, not wanting to become pregnant, and when she finally consents, this is exactly what happens. Rosemary, you could say, is certainly the object of Gordon's sexual desires, and Gordon is certainly no feminist. But they are also friends, forever discussing and arguing. Described as 'bright and debonair',* she is one of Orwell's most sympathetic depictions; 'the authorial voice is always in awe of Rosemary', according to Loraine Saunders,* though it is a more light-hearted relationship than this may suggest. When Gordon pontificates about women, Rosemary laughs at him.* She seems to offer Gordon the conversation and the fun, the kind of partnership of equals, that Flory so unrealistically dreamed of with Elizabeth Lackersteen.

Gordon's first reaction on hearing of the pregnancy is to panic. Then he goes to a library to look up a book on midwifery. He stares at pictures of a foetus, at first with horror, then with a growing realization that what he is looking at is an image of a life which is literally his responsibility. He decides to marry Rosemary, and go back to the New Albion advertising agency. It is a complex moment. Rosemary has forced him to pay attention to the pragmatics of the body. His inspection of the foetus in the womb is related to other epiphanies of interiority—the bodily functions of the condemned man walking towards death on the scaffold, the thorax of the dying elephant, the inner life of the woman at the drain-pipe—which all bring home to the observer, painfully, his own responsibility. Gordon is now giving up his long and lonely war against the Money-God, to knuckle down to bourgeois respectability and the aspidistra. The warm needs of the body trump the chilly demands of his ideals. And Rosemary and her pregnancy liberate Gordon back into narrative—'once again things were happening in the Comstock family'.*

In one sense this is a disappointing ending to the story of both of them, with Gordon compromised and domesticated, and Rosemary seemingly confirmed as the same sort of woman as Ravelston's girlfriend Hermione, the natural enemy of her lover's ideas and principles. ('She [Hermione] lay quiet, content to argue no longer, her arms round him, like a sleepy siren. The woman-scent breathed out of her, a powerful wordless propaganda against all altruism and all justice.')* On the other hand, Gordon's revolt has been shown to be obtuse, theoretical, and absurd. Some intellectuals, after all, display an 'utter ignorance of the way things actually happen'.* And all Orwell's fiction, almost obsessed as it is with bodily sensations and particularly uncomfortable or painful ones, seems to cry out that the needs and dignity, and indeed the pleasures, of the body are not to be despised. It does not go without saying that the life of the mind should always take precedence over that of the body, even for intellectuals.

Julia in *Nineteen Eighty-Four* looks like powerful evidence in the case against Orwell as sexist. She is sexually promiscuous, and has not the faintest interest in the ramifications of Party doctrine or the principles of Ingsoc. Notoriously, she falls asleep while Winston reads aloud from Goldstein's Book, the Bible of the resistance. When they visit O'Brien to offer themselves to the Brotherhood (an organization whose name suggests its gender assumptions), she takes no part in the conversation. O'Brien ignores her, until she breaks in to say she is not willing to be separated from Winston and never to see him again. A specialist in love, not politics, she is ruled by her emotions. She has been said to represent 'the power of instinctive feeling and the continuity of love'.* Unlike Rosemary in *Keep the Aspidistra Flying*, Julia is bored with ideas and discussion. She has a desirable body but an apparently negligible mind, the male chauvinist's fantasy. Winston tells her she is only a rebel from the waist downwards.* (There is sometimes a coarseness in the way Orwell's men talk to women, and about them.) She dislikes the Party for its puritanism, its hostility to pleasure—for, indeed, the Party has declared war on the body, and its doctrines, expounded by O'Brien, are no less abstract, theoretical, and crazy than Gordon Comstock's.

In all these ways Julia seems an unreconstructed male idealization, conforming to a stereotype of woman (passive, bodily, emotional, etc.) that confirms men as having the opposite qualities (active, intellectual, rational, and so on). But it goes beyond this. Winston Smith is middle-aged, unhealthy, ill-favoured, depressed, and unimportant. Julia is desirable and a free spirit. Yet it is she who, out of the blue and at enormous personal risk, declares her love for this miserable specimen. She then makes the arrangements for their meeting, calls him dear, takes the sexual initiative, talks dirty, gives him chocolate, fixes their next meeting. Improbably, she dotes on him, like Titania with the ass. In a classic realist novel, albeit one set in the future, how credible is all this?

One way of accounting for this implausibility is to suppose that Julia is actually a Party member, set on luring Winston into a honeytrap. This reading has been interestingly canvassed by Richard Lance Keeble.* It would account for Julia's surprising availability to Winston (though it would not let Orwell off the hook of feminist disapproval). However, I don't think it is the solution to the Julia conundrum. Orwell is not the kind of writer to leave such an important theme ambiguous, especially as he goes on to narrate the last meeting and conversation between Julia and Winston, where there is no hint of it. In any case, since Winston is an unimportant and completely ineffectual rebel, and already doomed to arrest and punishment from the moment he begins his diary, as he acknowledges, why should the Party bother with the honeytrap and all the rest?

But then, why does O'Brien, a senior Party official, seemingly keep this insignificant subject under surveillance for years, and then devote months to his one-to-one interrogation in the Ministry of Love? Furthermore, how, not to mention why, does Mr Charrington, a secret policeman, disguise himself as a much older man and potter around in a junk shop in the prole quarter, waiting for some passing dissident to wander in and buy an album with cream-laid pages? In other words, if Julia is an unrealistic fantasy, unrealistic compared with what? To answer these questions, we may need to think carefully about what kind of a book *Nineteen Eighty-Four* is.

The last female figure in *Nineteen Eighty-Four*, the one I call the lost mother, is an actual dream figure, and much more besides. There are not many mothers in Orwell's novels, and they get scant attention. George Bowling gives an affectionate portrait of his mother in *Coming Up for Air*, but says he never remembers her when she wasn't cooking.* Orwell's own mother, Ida Blair, takes up little space in the cumulative index of his *Complete Works*. There is not much of a record of their feelings for each other, and his surviving letters to her are not confidential. Mabel Fierz saw 'absolutely no warmth of contact' among the Blairs,* and Avril, Orwell's sister, remembered that her brother's relations with his family 'had always been detached and one almost might say impersonal.'* In 'Such, Such Were the Joys', he expressed the view that although one can love a child more deeply than an adult, 'it is rash to assume the child feels any love in return.'* Not to expose your true feelings to an adult, he says, seems to be instinctive from the age of 7 or 8 onwards.

This generalization from his own experience is sad. 'Looking back on my childhood, after the infant years were over, I do not believe that I ever felt love for any mature person except my mother, and even her I did not trust, in the sense that shyness made me conceal most of my real feelings from her.'* It looks as if the manners of a Victorian Anglo-Indian household, its demarcated divisions of gender, the stiff reticence about feelings, the long absences at boarding school and later overseas, and his own aptitude for secrecy and suspicion, prevented much closeness between Orwell and his mother. It was something which, in the way of these things, he may have regretted when it was too late (she died in 1943). Certainly an air of poignancy and loss hangs about the haunting figure of the mother in *Nineteen Eighty-Four*.

In the opening chapter of the novel, Winston Smith's first entry in his diary is an account of a visit to the cinema the previous evening, when he watched a war film or newsreel in which a ship full of refugees was bombed somewhere in the Mediterranean. In breathless and barely punctuated prose, he recalls a lifeboat full of children, being attacked by a helicopter:

> *there was a middle-aged woman might have been a jewess sitting up in the bow with a little boy about three years old in her arms. little boy screaming with fright and hiding his head between her breasts as if he was trying to burrow right into her and the woman putting her arms round him and comforting him although she was blue with fright herself, all the time covering him up as much as possible as if she thought her arms could keep the bullets off him.**

Winston does not know why he writes about this incident; he is scarcely aware of what he is setting down on paper. It seems a report straight from the unconscious, rather like the automatic writing practised by the surrealists. The tentative specification of the woman as Jewish is of great interest. Here in any case is the first appearance in the novel of a motif we can call the Madonna-and-child group, and notably it is not only gendered but also orientalized. (Jews were 'oriental'. The state of Israel was founded while *Nineteen Eighty-Four* was being written, and many Jewish refugees were trying to cross the Mediterranean to reach it.)*

The Madonna-and-child group makes its next appearance again through the unconscious, when Winston has a dream in which he sees his own mother 'sitting in some place deep down beneath him, with his young sister in her arms', apparently in the saloon of a sinking ship. The death by water of this Madonna links the dream to the memory of the Jewish woman in the lifeboat, and Winston intuits in his dream that in some way the lives of these female victims have been sacrificed to his own. He now realizes that his mother's death nearly thirty years before had been tragic and sorrowful in a way that was no longer possible, belonging as it did 'to the ancient time, to a time when there was still privacy, love and friendship, and when the members of a family stood by one another without needing to know the reason'.* His own mother's death is associated with the helpless gesture made by the Jewish mother in the lifeboat, to protect her child. In the novel's dream plot, these images are not linked by logic or by narrative, but poetically, by association. It is no accident that these images arrive in oneiric and in cinematic form. Orwell is using the filmic trope of the dissolve, the merging of one frame into another, in such a way that the dream image is *both* the Jewish refugee and Winston's mother.

What is happening here is that, around the image of the mother and child—cinematic, remembered, dreamed about, but always lost—a set of ideas and feelings is being assembled, and these ideas (the private realm, unconditional love, compassion, courage, unselfishness) make up the opposition to tyranny in Winston's mind.* The prole woman who sings, 'It was only an 'opeless fancy' is another mother figure: Winston feels a 'mystical reverence' for her.* (The Madonna-and-child group is later inverted and parodied in the figure of the large drunk woman who sits on Winston's lap in the prison cell in the Ministry of Love.)* They are ideas and feelings that seem doomed to defeat in the face of the power and violence of authority, but are nonetheless worth dying for.

The Madonna-and-child group reappears next in another dream, in which Winston seems to review his whole life, taking place within the glass paperweight he has bought in Charrington's shop. The paperweight itself, containing a scrap of coral which so fascinates Winston, is a little Orient; Charrington tells him it must have come from the Indian Ocean.* Waking, he feels that the whole dream is comprehended by 'a gesture of the arm made by his mother, and made again thirty years later by the Jewish woman he had seen on the news film, trying to shelter the small boy from bullets'.* It becomes clear that in this dream he has been remembering his very last glimpse of his mother, drawing her arm protectively round Winston's baby sister as Winston himself, after stealing chocolate from the small dying girl, flees down the stairs and abandons them:

> The dream was still vivid in his mind, especially the enveloping, protecting gesture of the arm in which its whole meaning seemed to be

contained. His mind went back to another dream of two months ago.
Exactly as his mother had sat on the dingy white-quilted bed, with the
child clinging to her, so she had sat in the sunken ship, far underneath
him and drowning deeper every minute, but still looking up at him
through the darkening water.*

Winston's mother is always absent in the novel. She appears only in displaced or estranged forms, in an image on a screen, a ghostly memory, a
dream. Through the overarching maternal gesture, the mother in the
cheerless apartment is identified with the mother in the sinking ship,
and with the Jewish mother in the lifeboat. Winston's dying sister,
from whom he steals food, is aged 3, the same age as the refugee child
machine-gunned in the lifeboat. The aggressor from whom the mother
ineffectually shields her baby is Winston himself: he has seized his sister's chocolate ration, and then callously abandoned the two females to
their fate, never to see them again. Winston is, in his own mind, the
betrayer and killer of his mother and sister. But if he is the murderer of
his mother, he is also her child, the son of a Jewish mother—Jewish
according to the associative logic of dream—and therefore himself a
Jew. In the same way Winston is both a privileged member of the Party,
and its doomed victim.

An extraordinarily rich and suggestive cluster of feelings adheres to
this image of mother and child: the mother's self-sacrifice and her brave
if useless attempt to shield her child, the child's cruelty and betrayal in
one instance, and helplessness in another, and always looming over the
group the menacing presence of authority and violence bent on the
destruction of human feeling and natural relations. Like a dream, this
tangle of feelings is hard to pin down, and to unpick. But it seems to be
testimony to the unfailing courage and selflessness of a woman, even in
the face of a brutish callousness of which her son himself is a part. 'One
can love a child, but it is rash to assume that the child feels any love in
return.'* For a lifetime of hard-heartedness, Winston Smith, at least,
atones in his dreams.

8

Race

The demographic mix of the United Kingdom today may turn out to be the most lasting legacy of imperial history for the British, but it is the fruit not of empire, but of the end of empire. Substantial immigration from former or current British possessions did not get going until after the Second World War. In George Orwell's lifetime, very large numbers of people living in Britain had next to no contact with people of a different colour, or with foreigners of any kind. The exceptions, of course, were those who had lived and worked in the empire.

What is race? It is likely that Orwell did not know. The term is notoriously hard to define, no doubt because it refers to a phenomenon with no basis in nature, and people of his generation used it quite promiscuously to describe all sorts of large groups of people. The English were a race. Anglo-Saxons were a race, or possibly a mixture of two races. Blacks and whites were different races, as anyone could see. So were Japanese, and Indians. Italians, Spaniards, and the like were the Latin races. The British, according to Winston Churchill, were an island race. The Germans were a race too, but so were the Aryans, and in Hitler's view they were superior to other races, but especially to the Slavs and the Jews, who were inferior races.

It is probably inevitable that racial thinking involves these hopeless tangles, muddling geographical, political, and linguistic groups, 'colours', and often fanciful ideas of heritage. But it is probably inevitable too that it comes with an idea of the inequality of races. Orwell seems to have been happy to use the term loosely. He was equally casual with the word 'nation', and in his great essay 'Notes on Nationalism', he oddly talks about the 'passionate nationalistic feeling' inspired by movements and tendencies like Jewry, Islam, Christendom, the Proletariat, and the White Race, none of which are nations.*

A science (or 'science') of race had come into being in the late nineteenth century, an age of nationalism, imperialism, and Social Darwinism. It considered that a race was a large group of people with shared physical characteristics (biology), and that these were systematically associated with certain kinds of behaviour or character (anthropology); in the end, even the most scientific descriptions of racial difference tended to end up with cultural difference. Race was a heuristic; the difference between races was held to explain, for example, why some groups of people were powerful, rational, and modern, while others were weak, instinctive, and primitive. You can find a kind of allegory of this in the story of the pith helmet, that imperial fetish ridiculed by Orwell:

> You can only rule over a subject race, especially when you are in a small minority, if you honestly believe yourself to be racially superior, and it helps towards this if you can believe that the subject race is *biologically* different. There were quite a number of ways in which Europeans in India used to believe, without any evidence, that Asiatic bodies differed from their own.*

Hence the European 'knowledge' that their skulls were thinner than those of Asiatics, and hence their fantastic belief that their lives depended on wearing a pith helmet in the tropics—but hence also their feeling of a natural superiority that entitled them to rule in the East.

Whether or not race existed, Orwell was very sensitive to it, his race consciousness being as acute as his class consciousness. He observed ethnic differences carefully in his wanderings in the East End: 'The East London women are pretty (it is the mixture of blood, perhaps), and Limehouse was sprinkled with Orientals—Chinamen, Chittagongian lascars, Dravidians selling silk scarves, even a few Sikhs, come goodness knows how.'* There was an assortment of people among the homeless too, with 'all races, even black and white' mixing together in the lodging-house on terms of equality.* Dorothy in *A Clergyman's Daughter* picks hops alongside a family of gypsies, dark as Indians.* It was his imperial experience, and particularly his job in the police, that had sharpened Orwell's eye for human differences. 'A Hanging', for example, is obsessively specific about its cast of characters—the Indian Hindu prisoner, the tall Indian warders, the fat Dravidian, and the young Eurasian jailer, the Burmese magistrate—though once the prisoner has been killed, the rest are bonded in their shared responsibility for his death, having a drink together, 'native and European alike, quite amicably'.*

Burma was multiracial and multilingual. In a population of fourteen million, E. A. Blair had informed his French readers, nine million were Burmese, and there was tension not only between Burmese and British but also between Burmese and Indians, and the descendants of the 'countless Mongol tribes who have emigrated at various periods from the steppes of Central Asia'.* A hundred and twenty different languages and dialects were spoken in Burma. These conditions made it a hard country to police, particularly in a time of anti-colonial unrest. During his training Orwell learned Burmese and Hindustani to a high level of proficiency, and also passed an exam in Shaw-Karen (S'gaw-Karen), a rare language qualification.* No doubt part of his motivation was the thousand-rupee bonus given for each examination passed.

He was sensitive to ethnic diversity in Burma, and the rest of the Empire of India was at least as diverse as Burma. But sometimes that sensitivity was betrayed by a cruder kind of thinking, and by Anglo-Indian habits of speech. 'The whites were up and the blacks were down' in Burma, he explained in *The Road to Wigan Pier*, 'and therefore as a matter of course one's sympathy was with the blacks'.* The sympathy is admirable, while the characterization of the population of Burma as 'blacks' is crude, and unworthy of his own knowledge of the country's different peoples. This was Anglo-Indian lingo. It has been pointed out that the use of 'black' and 'nigger' to describe Asian people 'reveals continuities in racial attitudes and actions across the British empire, from the eighteenth-century slave plantations on Britain's Caribbean colonies to the nineteenth-century British Raj'.*

As we have seen, Orwell said his first sight of Asia had been of a white police sergeant kicking a clumsy coolie. It is an example of what Peter Marks has called Orwell's 'old rhetorical strategy, basing his argument on ... eyewitness experience'.* The story is told as an example of the casual racism of white people in the East.* But the incident, as he tells it, happened after the ship was boarded at Colombo by 'the usual swarm of coolies'—the generic and rather dehumanizing phrase not a very sensitive description of the Ceylonese dock workers. It is not the only time that Orwell seems to participate in a state of mind that he is condemning, the voice of the socialist anti-imperialist haunted by the ghost of a hard-bitten Anglo-Indian.

The whole passage is of great interest. The other passengers, he goes on to say, watched with mild approval. 'They were white, and the coolie was black. In other words he was sub-human, a different kind of animal.' We have returned to the problematic equation of the 'oriental' and the animal. But Orwell has his eye on a different context (he was writing in 1940). 'In Burma I have listened to racial theories which were less brutal than Hitler's theories about the Jews, but certainly not less idiotic.' Racialism, his experience has shown him, has nothing to do with nationalism, which tends to arise among people who do not want to be governed by foreigners. Racialism is something totally different. 'It is the invention not of conquered nations but of conquering nations. It is a way of pushing exploitation beyond the point that is normally possible, by pretending that the exploited *are not human beings*.' His understanding of Hitler in 1940 is framed, explicitly, by his observation on the quayside at Colombo in 1922. Drawing on his experience in the East, this is Orwell at his best, and at his most awkward.

With their conquest of Burma, the British had destroyed the Burmese monarchy and the institutions of what had been a feudal state. 'In general,' says the historian Thant Myint-U:

> the primary cleavage in the new Burma was not to be one of class but of ethnicity, between those seen as 'foreign' and those seen as 'native', and between the 'native races' themselves…The peculiar twentieth-century divide between 'Europeans', 'Indians', the 'Burmese' and the 'minorities' was firmly set.*

Like so much else in Burma, this way of looking at a society was imported from British India. Racial difference, and the racial hierarchy that inevitably went with it, were in large part the creature of imperial policy, and the government actions (early twentieth-century censuses, for example, and the treatment of 'minority' tribes) that followed from it. While the British were used to seeing, and governing, subject peoples in terms of ethnic categories, another part of the theory was that their law was blind to such divisions. 'I have never wavered in a strict and inflexible justice between the two races,' Lord Curzon, Viceroy of India, wrote to Lord George Hamilton in 1903. 'It is the sole justification and the only stable foundation for our rule.'*

But on the ground, and perhaps especially in a backwater like Kyauktada in *Burmese Days*, no such scruples obtained. In Kyauktada, the senior official, Macgregor, is a fair-minded man and fond of 'orientals'. 'Provided they were given no freedom he thought them the most charming people alive.'* The rest of the Europeans, apart from Flory himself, are more or less virulent racists, their venom directed not only at the Burmese but at all non-Europeans, who are referred to as blacks, or worse. ('I dare say it's unfair in some ways and inaccurate in some details,' Orwell said of his novel, 'but much of it is simply reporting of what I have seen.')* The timber merchant Ellis, whose racism is pathological, speaks of the Indian Dr Veraswami in terms I will not quote, but he hates the Burmese just as much. His beating of an insufficiently respectful Burmese student, which causes the boy to go blind, leads to an ineffectual riot. The European Club is besieged, with Ellis screaming for the police to open fire on the protestors and 'slaughter them in bloody heaps'.* The rioters want justice for the injured boy, and their leader, who perhaps has not heard of Lord Curzon, says 'there is no justice for us in your courts'.* The siege of the Club is a kind of paradigm of the British sense of their race: threatened, outnumbered, but superior in arms.

Orwell noted that British soldiers on imperial service, tasked with holding down a hostile population, developed an attitude towards locals which was far more brutal than that of the officials or businessmen. This applied even to their conduct towards the Spanish 'natives' in Gibraltar.* In Burma, Orwell himself had occasionally resorted to violence against subordinates, servants, and coolies, in moments of rage: as he said, 'orientals' could be 'very provoking'.* His association of racism with conquest might be extended to the suggestion that it was the very weakness, the disadvantage of the 'oriental' that provoked overbearing behaviour in the sahib. This may be an explanation for this disturbing passage (which was not intended for later publication) in the manuscript of his

War-Time Diary, discussing the possibility of a post-war Russian takeover of India:

> Wintringham said that even in Spain some of the Russian delegates tended to treat the Spaniards as 'natives', and would no doubt do like-wise in India. It's very hard not to, seeing that in practice the majority of Indians *are* inferior to Europeans and one can't help feeling this and, after a little while, acting accordingly.*

If you know you have a conqueror's power over somebody, the implication seems to be, sooner or later you will 'act accordingly'. Orwell owned up to this overbearing habit of feeling, and the difficulty of unlearning it.

Since race was supposed to be a matter of physical identity and difference, it is not surprising that racial speech is obsessed with the body. The racially different were different in physical appearance, and to some that physical difference was scandalous. Ellis's rage against the Indian Veraswami expresses itself in a compendium of physical insults: he describes the doctor as stinking, pot-bellied, greasy, with sweaty hands and filthy garlic breath, and so on.* These are demeaning terms, but the paradox of racial speech is that its object is thought of as physically contemptible and physically threatening at the same time. Thus, Mrs Lackersteen may abuse her Burmese servants all day long, but she is kept awake at night by 'a picture of herself being raped by a procession of jet-black coolies with rolling white eyeballs'.*

Orwell's own thoughts on the racialized body are remarkable. In the memoir that begins the second part of *The Road to Wigan Pier*, he moves from his experience of England and the question of class to Burma and the question of race, and his first thought is about the Burmese body. He had been taught to shrink from the working class, or the idea of them, on the grounds that they smelt. In Burma, it was different.* 'The essential point was that the "natives", at any rate the Burmese, were not felt to be physically repulsive.'* Even white men who had the most vicious colour prejudice were ready to be physically intimate with them. Orwell himself remembers that he was happy to be dressed and undressed by his servant, for example. 'I felt towards a Burman almost as I felt towards a woman,' he goes on, 'for if one faces facts one must admit that most

Mongolians have much nicer bodies than most white men.'* He warms to the theme, itemizing the firm-knit silken skin of the Burmese, his hair in the appropriate places, his perfect teeth, his beautiful bones and comely shape, his smell that makes your teeth tingle. All these attractions contrasted with the corresponding unhealthy, ugly-looking, repulsive features of white men.

It is an unexpected testimonial. It shows us, incidentally, that when Orwell thinks of 'the Burmese', he is thinking of Burmese men, and in a non-speaking role. It is often remarked that in colonial discourse, colonized people may be described, figuratively, as feminine, or childlike, and that this is a sign of the power relations between colonial observer and colonized subject. Orwell's odd intimacy with the Burmese man or boy—'almost as I felt towards a woman'—looks like an example of this Orientalist trope (and incidentally looks very odd beside the occasional homophobia—'pansy-left circles', and so on*—he expresses elsewhere). But it does have a strange tenderness. The portrait is more erotic, and a lot more innocent, than any description of Ma Hla May in *Burmese Days*. It is perhaps an example of what Orwell called 'benevolent imperialism', which could give the impression that 'the creatures being described are some kind of charming but unreliable animal'.*

This romantic closeness contrasts violently with a different picture of the Burmese body, the description of the *pwe*-dancer whose performance is watched by Flory and Elizabeth in a Kyauktada street, in *Burmese Days*. Here the emphasis is not upon intimacy but alienation, a grotesque and unfathomable difference:

Her face was powdered so thickly that it gleamed in the lamplight like a chalk mask with live eyes behind it. With that dead-white oval face and those wooden gestures she was monstrous, like a demon...Still in that strange bent posture the girl turned round and danced with her buttocks protruded towards the audience. Her silk *longyi* gleamed like metal. With hands and elbows still rotating she wagged her posterior from side to side. Then—astonishing feat, quite visible through the *longyi*—she began to wriggle her two buttocks independently in time with the music.*

This performance, much appreciated by the local audience, embarrasses Flory and is absolutely horrifying to Elizabeth. Here race is an unbridgeable chasm, and the dancer's body seems inorganic, inhuman, frightening, and insulting. Elizabeth gets up and leaves, all her prejudices about the Burmese confirmed. Her own white body has no place among these people:

> What was she doing in this place? Surely it was not right to be sitting among the black people like this, almost touching them, in the scent of their garlic and their sweat? Why was she not back at the Club with the other white people? Why had he [Flory] brought her here, among this horde of natives, to watch this hideous and savage spectacle?*

The two bodies, or rather the observer's reaction to them, represent, perhaps, positive and negative poles of race consciousness as Orwell understood it. Both might be described as Orientalist: the positive one patronizing, the negative hostile. Among many differences, one more can be singled out. Orwell's attractive Burmese man is inactive, and does not speak. The *pwe*-dancer is vigorously expressive, and she makes a gesture—turning her bottom to the observer—which is eloquent in any language.

Still, there was a bodily feature that was even more eloquent. The human face is the most haunting image across all Orwell's writing, and it comes from Burma. There is a strong association between race and face. The disfiguring birthmark on Flory's face is a not very subtle sign of his feelings of guilt as a white man in Burma, but again and again it is the faces of others that pronounce sentence on the imperial enterprise. 'Innumerable remembered faces' haunted Orwell intolerably on his return from Europe, making him conscious, he says, of an immense weight of guilt.* They were the faces of prisoners in the dock, of men waiting in the condemned cells, of subordinates and peasants he had bullied and servants and coolies he had beaten. In Burma, Orwell remembered, the imprisoned thief did not think of himself as a criminal, but as the victim of a foreign conqueror. His face behind the bars of the jail said so clearly. 'And unfortunately I had not trained myself to be indifferent to the expression of the human face.'*

Dark racial faces stare out from all the Burmese writing, usually expressing suffering or accusation. The convicts in 'A Hanging' have grey, cowed faces, but the Indian warders too seem to turn grey as the condemned man's death approaches. In *Burmese Days*, a prisoner interrogated by Westfield, District Superintendent of Police, also has a grey, timorous face. The officer on his way to shoot the elephant is followed by a crowd two thousand strong, 'a sea of yellow faces', waiting to see how he will perform.* When Ma Hla May comes to beg Flory to take her back, it is with downcast face, but Flory is unwilling to face her. She prostrates herself, face hidden, offering to be his slave. But when she returns to denounce him in church in front of the white congregation, she demands that he turn and look at her, a 'grey-faced maniacal creature'.* No modern man, Orwell thought, really believes it is right to conquer and rule another people. It is an unjustifiable tyranny. 'Even the thickest-skinned Anglo-Indian is aware of this. Every "native" face he sees in the street brings home to him his monstrous intrusion.'*

The face of the victim is an image carried over into *Nineteen Eighty-Four*, a book full of faces. The Two Minutes Hate possesses people with a desire 'to smash faces in with a sledge-hammer'.* Their hatred is directed at the Asiatic faces projected on the telescreen, the face of the Jewish renegade Goldstein, which dissolves into that of a Eurasian soldier. In Oceania facecrime is a punishable offence. To dissemble his feelings, Winston has had to learn to control his face, but it is no use. The ultimate violence awaiting him in Room 101, as he knows, is violence to the face, in the shape of a cage of hungry rats attached to a face-mask. The victimized face is even central to the anti-philosophy of the Party, as O'Brien patiently explains. 'If you want a picture of the future, imagine a boot stamping on a human face—for ever,' he tells Winston, and then he adds: 'The face will always be there to be stamped upon.'*

And the Asiatic face? We have seen the way, in the Two Minutes Hate, the Jewish face of Goldstein dissolves into the figure of the Eurasian soldier, both of them the targets of the hysterical hatred of the spectators. Janice Ho has shown how in the novel, 'the totalitarian state employs a regime of racist nationalism and economic scarcity to scapegoat foreigners as threats'.* There is a curiously similar (but opposite) instance later in the story, when Winston and Julia meet in the crowd in Victory Square to plan their next assignation, and a column of trucks carrying prisoners of war is passing.* Both Oceania's global rivals are Asiatic—Eurasia and Eastasia. Party propaganda makes much of the danger they pose, but this danger is never seen (and may be imaginary anyway). 'Foreigners, whether from Eurasia or from Eastasia, were a kind of strange animal. One literally never saw them except in the guise of prisoners, and even as prisoners one never got more than a momentary glimpse of them.'* In a description of some such prisoners, we may get a momentary glimpse of our own, of the memory of the jails in Burma that haunted Eric Blair. In Victory Square, Winston watches the trucks full of squatting prisoners of war, little yellow men with 'sad Mongolian faces' staring incuriously about them. (The squatting posture may recall the Burmese prisoners in the prison yard, noticed at the end of 'A Hanging', and 'the wretched prisoners squatting in the reeking cages' remembered in *The Road to Wigan Pier*).* The face, once again, is a register of helpless victimhood. Here is an explicit racial antagonist, disciplined, and reduced to a figure of abjection.

But are the prisoners Eastasian or Eurasian? Curiously, at this point Orwell blurs the racial face. 'The round Mongol faces had given way to faces of a more European type, dirty, bearded and exhausted.' Citizens of Oceania (and readers of *Nineteen Eighty-Four*) may find it hard to remember whether Oceania is at war with Eastasia and allied with Eurasia, or the other way round. And does it matter? One face in particular strikes Winston: 'In the last truck he could see an aged man, his face a mass of grizzled hair, standing upright with wrists crossed in front of him, as though he were used to having them bound together.'* The upright posture signals resistance, the crossed wrists indicate enslavement. Winston Smith watches this tragic stranger pass in the company of his lover Julia, a free spirit and the only ally of his secret rebellion. In the momentary substitution of one face for another, Julia in turn is orientalized and rendered abject, in a dissolve that seems a prophecy of the punishment that awaits them both: 'With hands locked together, invisible among the press of bodies, they stared steadily in front of them, and instead of the eyes of the girl, the eyes of the aged prisoner gazed mournfully at Winston out of nests of hair.'* It is a moment of no importance to the actual plot of *Nineteen Eighty-Four*. But on a poetic level, this fleeting interchangeability between the faces of the old man and the girl, the prisoner of war and the future political prisoner, is heavy with meaning. Subjection is indivisible. The racial victim and the ideological dissident are on the same side, faced with the same enemy. The image here is a tragic one, but this idea of solidarity across differences was really Orwell's core belief. 'Either we all live in a decent world, or nobody does.'*

It was in the subjection of one race by another that Orwell found the continuity between imperialism and Nazism. It was this that caused him to write belligerently in 1943 that 'the battle against Amery [Leo Amery, Secretary of State for India and Burma] and the battle against Hitler are the same'.* It was rank hypocrisy to bleat about fighting Fascism while bolstering up the 'far vaster injustice' of a racial empire, he had written in a review article originally given the ironic but brutal title 'Not Counting Niggers'.* Perhaps knowledge of his own family's involvement in slavery in the Caribbean brought this hypocrisy home. In 1929, he had written that the Burmese had a relationship with the British Empire, and with European capitalism, which was 'that between slave and master'.* Now, while the British might be having second thoughts about empire, Hitler was bent on enslaving whole racial populations. It was in his belief in racial supremacy, a belief which the British themselves were starting to be ashamed of, that Hitler was 'only the ghost of our own past rising against us'.*

Looking at the world as a whole, Orwell wrote in 1945, 'the drift for many decades has been not towards anarchy but towards the reimposition of slavery'.* All over wartime Europe and North Africa there were forced-labour camps where the conquered—'Poles, Russians, Jews and political prisoners of every race'—worked as slaves.* Slavery was a condition of subjection, but also of silence. Appallingly, the hundreds of millions of slaves in antiquity had left behind them no record whatever. 'In the whole of Greek and Roman history, how many slaves' names are known to you?'*

With Hitler's war, two other racial groups with a history of enslavement start to make their appearance in Orwell's writing: people of African descent, and Jews. African Americans were coming to Britain in numbers in the armed forces. And the peril faced by the Jews in Europe was belatedly becoming public knowledge.

In some parts of American life, the treatment of black people sounded a lot like that faced by subject people in colonized countries:

> In spite of the quite obvious necessities of war, Negroes are still pushed out of skilled jobs, segregated and insulted in the Army, assaulted by white policemen and discriminated against by white magistrates. In a number of the Southern States they are disenfranchised by means of a poll tax.*

In the 1940s, there were still lynchings and race riots in the American South. Orwell saw this as merely a single facet of a world-wide problem of colour, and he felt it could not be solved inside the capitalist system. With a globally differential standard of living—an English worker spending on cigarettes roughly what an Indian peasant earned for a living—solidarity between coloured and white workers was not possible. 'In Asiatic eyes the European class struggle is a sham. The Socialist movement has never gained a real foothold in Asia or Africa, or even among the American Negroes: it is everywhere side-tracked by nationalism and race-hatred.'* There was not much an individual could do 'to mitigate the horrors of the colour war', but Orwell did recommend that writers at least should find out which names are resented by members of other races, and avoid using words like 'native', 'Negro' with a small N, 'Chinaman', and so on: 'one's information about these matters needs to be kept up to date.'* As we have seen, he was busy revising *Burmese Days* for republication with these sensitivities in mind.

Sometimes race operated like class, with certain groups kept in a kind of economic enslavement while others forged ahead. This was the case with the African Americans, but also with most of the population of British India and Burma. In the grip of the landlord and the money-lender, the Indian peasant ekes out a miserable existence 'tilling his tiny patch of soil with the tools and methods of the Bronze Age'.* There were examples nearer to home. Morocco was orientally backward, and so were parts of Spain. In a disused hut near Huesca in 1937, Orwell came upon a primitive implement that produced in him an estranging, virtually physical shock:

I remember my feeling almost of horror when I first came upon one of these things in a derelict hut in no man's land. I had to puzzle over it for a long while before grasping that it was a harrow. It made me sick to think of the work that must go into the making of such a thing, and the poverty that was obliged to use flint in place of steel. I have felt more kindly towards industrialism ever since.*

Even on Jura in Scotland, where economic neglect and the highland clearances had seen the population fall from ten thousand in the eighteenth century to less than three hundred, land was farmed 'in an incredibly primitive way', with the corn sown broadcast, and scythed and bound into sheaves by hand.* This was not exactly Burmese peasant agriculture, and the Hebridean islanders of Jura were neither 'oriental' nor a race. But some would argue that the history of the Scottish highlands and islands, until not so long ago, has been a quasi-colonial one, with its military garrisons, its land set aside for sport hunting, its absentee landlords, and rule from a distant capital. Even in 1947, Orwell felt bound to admit, in some areas, 'Scotland is almost an occupied country.'*

A chapter about race cannot end without attention to the great racial catastrophe of Orwell's lifetime, the fate of European Jewry and the Holocaust. It is dealt with briefly here only because I do not see that it has a close relation to Orwell's oriental experience and vision. He could see that the English culture in which he grew up, and especially its literature, had always had an element of anti-Semitism; he was thinking of Shylock, Fagin, Svengali in *Trilby*, the Jew-baiting of Hilaire Belloc and G.K. Chesterton, but also of a persistent grumbling about Jews in everyday conversation, especially among the London working class. Andrew Palmer is right to say that there are moments in Orwell's earlier writing, especially in *Down and Out*, when he 'unthinkingly repeated the "polite" prejudice of his class' in portraying Jewish characters.* After Hitler's rise to power, this became another part of his cultural heritage that he struggled to renounce. In wartime, however, anti-Jewish prejudice in Britain seemed to be getting worse, partly because of the presence of Jewish refugees from the continent, although in Orwell's view anti-Semitism was still not a respectable opinion in Britain, to be owned up to. It was mild in form—nobody in wartime England was suggesting pogroms or violence against Jews—but quite widespread, and he thought it was dangerous in its way, 'because it causes people to avert their eyes from the whole refugee problem and remain uninterested in the fate of the surviving Jews of Europe'.*

As for that fate, already in 1942, Orwell knew, wrote, and was broadcasting about the emerging facts of the Holocaust. He told his Indian listeners about the systematic massacre of Jews in German-occupied Poland, and the genocidal pronouncements of the Nazi leaders themselves:

> For instance, in March of this year Himmler, the head of the Gestapo, issued a decree calling for the 'liquidation'—remember that in totalitarian language liquidation is a polite name for murder—of 50 per cent of the surviving Polish Jews. It seems as if his programme is being carried out successfully. The Polish Government's figures show that of something over 3 million Jews living in Poland before the war, well over a third—that is, *well over one million human beings*—have been killed in cold blood or died of starvation and general misery. Many thousands of them, men, women and children, have been deported to Russian territory, sealed up in cattle trucks without food or water for journeys that may take weeks, so that when the trucks were opened sometimes half the people inside are dead. This policy, which Hitler himself has proclaimed over and over again as his chosen one in speeches both before and after the war, is carried out wherever the Germans are in control. Already, now that they have taken over the whole of France, they are putting the anti-Jewish laws into operation there and French Jews are being deported to the East.*

This, he reminded his listeners, is 'the nature of Fascism, the thing we are fighting against'. The transportation of trainloads of Jews to extermination camps was described the following year in *Arrival and Departure* by his friend Arthur Koestler, which Orwell, reviewing the book for the *Manchester Evening News*, called 'one of the most shocking descriptions of Nazi terrorism that have ever been written'.*

It could be said that, at least in his writing, Orwell was more interested in anti-Semitism than in the Jews (he shows no curiosity, as far as I can see, about Judaism). A writer had to be careful: 'it is almost impossible to mention Jews in print, either favourably or unfavourably, without getting into trouble.'* But his wartime writing keeps coming back to anti-Semitism. He couldn't understand it; his usual parameters of explanation didn't seem to work on it. It was not enough, obviously, to dismiss it as irrational. There might be a distinction to be drawn between 'true anti-Semitism, an essentially magical doctrine', and 'mere xenophobia and rationalisation of economic grievances'.* 'Clearly the neurosis lies very deep, and just what it is that people hate when they say that they hate a non-existent entity called "the Jews" is still uncertain.'*

The subject needed serious investigation, he said rather helplessly, though this would be hard to do dispassionately in the present circumstances. In April 1945, he contributed an essay about anti-Semitism to the *Contemporary Jewish Record*.* Again he prowls round the subject, but it remains an enigma; he may have felt that prejudice against the Jews did not really fit in his understanding of racialism as the behaviour of a bullying conqueror. 'All I would say with confidence is that anti-Semitism is part of the larger problem of nationalism, which has not yet been seriously examined, and that the Jew is evidently a scapegoat, though *for what* he is a scapegoat we do not yet know.'*

His puzzling about anti-Semitism, then, was the prompt for the wider-ranging essay 'Notes on Nationalism' which followed in October. In that essay, he analyses nationalism as an irrational devotion to a group idea, but he doesn't really get much further in his attempt to understand anti-Jewish prejudice. Still, he finishes with a suggestion. Prejudice is emotional. If you hate a group or an institution or a race, you cannot get rid of those feelings simply by taking thought. 'But you can at least recognise that you have them, and prevent them from contaminating your mental processes. The emotional urges which are inescapable, and are perhaps even necessary to political action, should be able to exist side by side with an acceptance of reality.'* It was a programme he had set himself for dealing with other prejudices of his own, inherited and otherwise. It would not be easy.

Awareness of the Holocaust meant that support for the idea of a Jewish homeland was widespread in the English press during and after the war. In 1944, Orwell was reviewing a book about Jewish settlers in

Palestine, and their achievements in making the desert fertile, written by an American supporter of Zionism. The book deserved to be read, Orwell wrote, 'but with the proviso that applies to all Zionist and pro-Zionist literature—that there is also an Arab viewpoint, and, owing to the fact that the Arabs have little footing in the Press outside their own country, it seldom gets a hearing'.* The silence of the racial other, it seems, had not gone away.

To return finally to Burma, Orwell does not seem to have had any Burmese friends in England, although he was in contact with Burmese groups in London in wartime.* Nor is there evidence that he developed friendships with Burmese people in his five years of service in the country. This might not have been an easy thing for a policeman, but it is notable that in *Burmese Days* Flory's only local friend is Veraswami, an Indian and a government official. One last detail, which can be interpreted in several different ways (see note). At the Police Training School at Mandalay when Blair was there in 1922–23, there was just one officer-probationer who was Burmese. In a now famous group photograph of the intake, this man stands out in a sea of European faces. Because of the date of their appointments, he was senior to Blair. Later Orwell was to give his name, U Po Kyin, to the villain in *Burmese Days*.*

9

Police

In January 1951, a year after George Orwell's death, ten thousand members of the British public were canvassed in an opinion survey by his old friend the social anthropologist Geoffrey Gorer. One set of questions was about the police. Gorer found that the force was popular with all social classes. 'There is extremely little hostility to the police as an institution,' he reported. 'To a great extent, the police represent an ideal model of behaviour and character, an aspect about which many respondents are articulate.'*

It had not always been so, and this probably represented a high-water mark in the relations between the British police and the public. But Orwell's own books about England in the 1930s show that, at least from the point of view of the middle class, the police were regarded as quite benign and trustworthy. Finding herself among the homeless in Trafalgar Square on a bitterly cold night, Dorothy Hare meets a friendly constable who offers to find her a bed for the night. In *Keep the Aspidistra Flying*, Gordon Comstock is arrested for drunkenness and hits a police sergeant, but this does not prevent a sympathetic constable from handling him 'almost like a nurse handling a child'.* The police are not even mentioned in *The Road to Wigan Pier* (almost fifty years before the violent clashes between police and northern workers in the Miners' Strike of 1984–85), while in the world of George Bowling in *Coming Up for Air*, respect for the forces of law is the norm: 'I'm the ordinary middling kind,' says Bowling, 'that moves on when the policeman tells him.'* And in the sleepy tableau of timeless images—'the barges on the miry river, the familiar streets, the posters telling of cricket matches and Royal weddings'—that seem to guarantee the changeless peacefulness of England at the end of *Homage to Catalonia*, we may spot some 'blue policemen'.*

In Britain, the police were not an alarming but a reassuring presence. This is why Orwell thought they were dangerous. Unwittingly, they were agents not of oppression but of complacency. The overwhelming majority of English people had no experience of violence or illegality, a perilous state of ignorance in the age of Hitler and Stalin. 'If you have grown up in that sort of atmosphere it is not at all easy to imagine what a despotic régime is like.'* But Orwell, when he returned from Burma, had no such difficulty.

Eric Blair began his training at the Provincial Police Training School in Mandalay in 1922. The fact that a 19-year-old, not long out of school, entered the Imperial Police as a trainee assistant superintendent was some indication of how the racial hierarchy in the force operated. He was joining a cadre of only ninety senior officers in Burma, in authority over a force of some thirteen thousand civil police. Cadets were instructed in law, languages, police accounts, and procedure. Salary increments depended on passing exams in Burmese, Hindustani, criminal law, drill, and riding. Probationary Assistant Superintendents had to familiarize themselves with the Indian Penal Code, the Criminal Procedure Code, the Police Act, the Indian Evidence Act, and various other laws such as the Opium Act and the Excise Act. Special attention was given to practical police work, 'carrying out searches, taking finger prints, preparing plans of scenes of crime, writing reports and giving evidence', and mock cases were staged, ranging from theft to murder, 'in which cadets were detailed in turn to play various roles'.* (So it is possible that the young Blair may have experienced what it was like to be a Burmese criminal, if only in play.) As part of standard equipment, he was issued with a sword and a revolver.*

In the years after the First World War, civil order was not easy to enforce in Burma. Animosity towards British rule created political unrest and a lack of respect for law and order, and there were also ethnic tensions between the main different demographic groups—the Burmese, the Indians, the Europeans, and minority peoples like the Karens and the Shans. There were violent outbreaks of anti-Indian feeling in 1924 and again in 1931, and anti-Chinese riots in 1931. Besides the civil police, and a substantial garrison of mostly Indian regular troops, the government of Burma maintained a special force of ten battalions of Military Police, about twelve thousand men, none of whom was Burmese, 'acting as an armed reserve for the Indian Army and for dealing with frontier raids and internal disturbances'.* In the 1920s there were no frontier raids.

The numbers of disciplinary forces in the country testify to the government's distrust of the Burmese people. Besides, Burma had a notorious crime rate, the highest in Asia. In the decade up to 1921, the population increased by about 9 per cent, but there was an increase of 31 per cent in cases of murder, and of 109 per cent in robbery and dacoity.* Kyauktada in *Burmese Days* has 'one of those huge durable jails which the English have built everywhere between Gibraltar and Hong Kong'.* But as fast as jails were built, the prison population outgrew the new accommodation, despite measures taken to reduce overcrowding, such as the frequent substitution of whipping for imprisonment.*

'In Moulmein, in Lower Burma, I was hated by large numbers of people,' Orwell was to recall.* This hostility could express itself in minor incidents: provocative fouls committed on the football field, unpunished by the referee; the jeering of Buddhist monks, whose privileges had been severely cut back under British rule; the insolent laughter of the high school boys in *Burmese Days*, which provokes Ellis to lash out with his stick, leading to a riot. This relates to an actual incident at Mission Road station in Rangoon when Blair himself was 'accidentally bumped into' by a school student, causing him to fall down the stairs; he lost his temper and struck out at the boy with his cane.* It was Blair's job to keep the peace, and enforce the law, in an atmosphere of racial animosity and potential violence from which he was not immune. As a policeman in these conditions, he was professionally estranged from the local population.

The British had invented modern Burma in the sense that they mapped it and brought into it hitherto separate jurisdictions. They imposed on a feudal state a model of administration which they had developed for India itself. This was in effect a revolution from outside, involving 'nothing less than a complete dismantling of existing institutions of political authority and the undermining of many established structures of social organization'.* Their Indian experience had meant that the British were used to seeing, and governing, subject peoples in terms of ethnic categories. So British Burma was both heavily policed and racially divided, as we saw in Chapter 8. The machinery of law and order was an instrument not only for controlling and protecting the local population but also for imposing a new economic and cultural order on it, and with it the power of white men. According to J. S. Furnivall— no anti-British radical, but a former officer of the Indian Civil Service (ICS)—popular local self-government was succeeded 'by the machinery of a foreign legal system, unable to control the anti-social forces which it liberated.'* Part of the brief of the Imperial Police was to be (to use Orwell's phrase from a different context) 'the bodyguards of the possessing class.'*

This was the state of affairs when Eric Blair arrived in Burma in 1922. As Maurice Collis, a British magistrate and another ICS man, was to put it, 'nearly all the rich people in the country were foreigners and...the Burmese, from being poor in a poor country, had become the poor in a rich one.'* Some Burmese flourished in these conditions, and the civil police and the magistracy were among the few areas in which local people could rise to any official authority. In the police, Eric Blair reported to a superior officer who was Burmese in three of the five districts to which he was posted, including Katha, on which Kyauktada is modelled, where the Deputy Commissioner also was a Burmese.* But the mass of Burmese people lived under the British oligarchy in a state of comprehensive alienation and powerlessness. In the early days of the occupation of Upper Burma, the Chief Commissioner of Military Police had forbidden all Burmese, on pain of death, to bear arms, a prohibition which helps to explain the mood of the crowd in 'Shooting an Elephant'.

They were powerless in other ways too. Furnivall quotes Sir Reginald Craddock, who governed Burma from 1918 to 1922:

> Her [Burma's] military forces, her military police, are not Burmans, her prison warders, her clerks, her post office, her labour force are largely manned by the Indian races. In her capital, Rangoon, there are 190,000 Indians, or nearly 60%. Her captains of industry and her richest men are almost entirely non-Burmese.*

This was not a recipe for a harmonious society. In 1923, the year after Eric Blair arrived, a system of dyarchy or double government was introduced in implementation of the Government of India Act (1919). But many Burmese grumbled that they were not enjoying even the partial liberties of their neighbours across the border in India, and in Burma the reforms did not make much difference to people's lives. In the 1920s, 'racial tension became more acute, crime increased and dissatisfaction spread'.* Blair returned to England, and resigned, in 1927. In 1928, he described British Burma as 'a latent despotism' which 'hides behind a mask of democracy'.*In 1931, when he was writing *Burmese Days*, the tragic peasant rebellion under Saya San was entering its second year.

It is not surprising that a red thread of violence runs through Orwell's writing about Burma, and specifically the Burma police, and emerges later in what he says about police activities in *Homage to Catalonia*, *Animal Farm*, and *Nineteen Eighty-Four*. (In *Animal Farm* Napoleon's dogs, modelled on Stalin's NKVD, are both police and executioners.) His first-hand experience of policing the empire had given him a differ- ent and rougher picture of the forces of law and order than he might have had if his image of them had been based on the amiable and unarmed blue policeman who walked his beat in the British domestic imagination. Painful encounters punctuate Orwell's description of dis- ciplinary work in Burma, and in every case the point of view is that of the agent of discipline, while the emotional weight of the account falls on the helplessness of its object. There is an uncomfortable identifica- tion of the person who inflicts punishment with the person who suffers it. This replays a pattern set down in his teenage years, when the elite schoolboy felt a commonality with those who were disadvantaged by, or rebelling against, the structures of power and entitlement that sustained his own privileges. Much later he came to understand that 'a natural hatred of authority' was one of the chief reasons why he became a writer.*

'A Hanging' is an example, where the narrator finds himself *ex officio* a member of the disciplinary party doing to death a pathetically outnum- bered and entirely passive prisoner. As we have seen, in the scenario of 'Shooting an Elephant' there is a moving disproportion between the harmlessly grazing and immobile animal, and the officer whose rifle will bring him down, and then pour bullet after bullet into his fallen body. In both these scenes of execution, there is a painful dwelling on the vulnerable body of the victim, while the suffering of the object of violence transfers itself, in the form of guilt, to the person who inflicts and observes it. Orwell's writing is haunted, as he says he himself was, by the memory of violence. As a policeman, he had seen the bodies of numbers of murdered men, and remembered 'the terror, the hatred, the howling relatives, the post-mortems, the blood, the smells'.* While he probably did not kill anyone in Burma, he had certainly taken part in scenes of distress and violence which brought a kind of collateral guilt, which he seems to have experienced as something like a physical pain. He summoned up the memory in *The Road to Wigan Pier*:

> The wretched prisoners squatting in the reeking cages of the lock-ups, the grey cowed faces of the long-term convicts, the scarred buttocks of the men who had been flogged with bamboos, the women and children howling when their menfolk were led away under arrest—things like these are beyond bearing when you are in any way directly responsible for them.*

He adds that he never went into a jail without feeling that his place was on the other side of the bars.

As a police officer, he could not avoid scenes, and feelings, like these. In England, the police were respectable, although, unlike the army and navy, the force was considered somewhat doubtful as a career for a gentleman. But in Burma, Orwell recalled, other Europeans looked down on the police 'because of the brutal work they had to do'.* He illustrates this with an anecdote. He was inspecting a jail, he says, and one of his Burmese sub-inspectors was bullying a suspect. An American missionary saw this squalid scene unfold:

> The American watched it, and then turning to me said thoughtfully, 'I wouldn't care to have your job.' It made me horribly ashamed. So *that* was the kind of job I had! Even an ass of an American missionary, a teetotal cock-virgin from the Middle West, had the right to look down on me and pity me! But I should have felt the same shame even if there had been no one to bring it home to me.*

It is violence perpetrated on the body that causes Orwell to associate police work with dirt—'the dirty work of empire'.* There is a corresponding scene in the fiction of *Burmese Days*, though without the

American observer to frame it. Police Superintendent Westfield watches as a fat sub-inspector interrogates a prisoner suspected of theft, a pathetic figure 'dressed only in a ragged *longyi* kilted to the knee, beneath which his lank, curved shins were speckled with tick-bites'. He is told to bend over:

> The suspect turned his grey face in agony towards Westfield, who looked away. The two constables seized him, twisted him round and bent him over; the Sub-inspector tore off his *longyi*, exposing his buttocks.
>
> 'Look at this, sir!' He pointed to some scars. 'He have been flogged with bamboos. He is an old offender. *Therefore* he stole the ring!'*

The abjection of the prisoner's posture, as well as the injustice whereby the signs of violence on his body are taken as proof of a new guilt, make the scene an especially painful one. The shame of the suspect seems to transfer itself to the police officer. No wonder Westfield turns away from the prisoner's face. But he is obliged to turn back, and is requested, as the man in authority—'Look at this, sir!'—to inspect his bottom. From his grey face to his scarred buttocks, the wretched victim is caught, in a self-fulfilling cycle of recidivism and shame, in what Orwell calls 'the whole machinery of so-called justice'.*

Maung Htin Aung describes something similar when he writes about laws giving powers to the Burma police to arrest a villager who had 'no ostensible means of livelihood', who could then be sent to prison by a magistrate. 'Once imprisoned, the unfortunate villager was considered a criminal, and embittered and emboldened by his prison experiences he actually became a thief or a robber.'* Crime existed, to be sure, in Burma as anywhere else. But the attentions of the police could have the effect of criminalizing the underclass, a phenomenon Orwell was alert to when later he described how the vagrancy laws in England could turn a tramp into a criminal, although 'a tramp is only an Englishman out of work, forced by law to live as a vagabond'.* In the Kyauktada jail, however, it is not only the prisoner who suffers from the law. Though certainly not in a commensurate way, the police officer Westfield too is caught in the machinery of so-called justice, as much as the narrator in 'Shooting an

Elephant', who, in executing a death sentence on the animal, becomes its murderer. Dirty work indeed.

Burmese Days is, in part, a police story, about how a subject population is kept under control in a regime of conquest. Although its central figure is the civilian John Flory, the law-and-order plot and a proliferation of detail mark it as a policeman's novel. Historically, the first of several law-and-order events in the novel is the earliest childhood memory of U Po Kyin, the book's main Burmese character, which is of the entry of the British army of occupation into Mandalay in 1885. In fictional Kyauktada in the1920s, Macgregor the Deputy Commissioner has general responsibility for the district, but law and order is the responsibility of Westfield, District Superintendent of Police. In an emergency, the Deputy Commissioner could amplify the powers of the senior police officer (as, in the Kyauktada riot, Macgregor gives the police the statutory authority to fire on the crowd), but was not competent to give him or his force any orders.

As you might expect, Orwell was sensitive to this separation of powers and the attitudes that tended to come with them. Macgregor embodies government policy, for example, in encouraging the election of a 'native' to the European Club on instructions from his Commissioner. His feelings for the local people are paternalistic, and benign provided they are given no freedom. However, though he has no taste for bloodshed, he shares the view that General Dyer, relieved of his command after ordering the Amritsar massacre in the Punjab in 1919 (in which some 380 Indian civilians were gunned down), was an imperial martyr. The police officer Westfield is a good deal more robust. There is a running joke in the novel that Westfield has never shot a man, or been in the right place at the right time to put down a riot, much to his chagrin. He has a definite nostalgia for martial law with its opportunities for violence, for emergencies warrant extreme measures. 'Can't do anything unless you put your foot down,' he grumbles. 'And how can you, if they haven't the guts to show fight?'*

There are two phases of communal violence in Kyauktada. The first is a rebellion in the jungle neat Thongwa, secretly instigated by U Po Kyin. On getting wind of this threat, Macgregor had asked for a company of (non-Burmese) military police to be sent to Kyauktada, under a British officer, Verrall, who then comes under Westfield's command. But it turns out that this insurrection consists of only seven rebels, who are armed with one stolen shotgun, six home-made and eleven dummy guns, and some Chinese firecrackers. Po Kyin has no difficulty in overpowering them with the help of a police inspector and twelve constables. When Macgregor, Westfield, and the Military Police Lieutenant Verrall arrive with fifty armed sepoys and a force of civil police, they are not needed. One of the rebels is shot and killed, and the rest are sent for trial: two of them to be sentenced to fifteen years' transportation, three to three years' imprisonment and twenty-five lashes, and one to two years' imprisonment. There is meticulous specification—you could even call it police-procedural—in the way the novel reports this incident, from the rebels' miserable weaponry to their harsh punishments.

This pathetic revolt, and its ruthless punishment, anticipate the wretched uprising of Saya San and, more distantly, the doomed resistance of Winston Smith. Orwell's most memorable portrayals of colonial punishment are inflicted on victims extreme in their helplessness—a condemned man in 'A Hanging', and an animal in 'Shooting an Elephant'. But the forces of law and order could command an arsenal that was not confined to physical instruments like the gallows and the gun. The law itself was also a weapon at their disposal; like an act of violence, the interpretations of judges can result in someone suffering bodily pain and being deprived of their freedom, their property, even of their life.

In 1928, the magistrate Maurice Collis was instructed to preside over the trial of the Bengali lawyer and Congress member Jatindra Mohan Sengupta for sedition, under section 124A of the Indian Penal Code. On a visit to Burma, Sengupta had given a couple of mild-seeming speeches, advising the Burmese not to seek separation from India in case this prompted the British to offer them an inferior political settlement. But the sedition law was so generally and broadly framed that 'it left a great discretion to the executive',* and Collis was obliged, against his own better judgement, to find Sengupta guilty.* Reviewing Collis's memoirs of his time as a magistrate in Burma, Orwell was again prompted to think of the image of machinery. 'In theory he is administering an impartial system of justice; in practice he is part of a huge machine which exists to protect British interests, and he has often got to choose between sac-rificing his integrity and damaging his career.'* Orwell and Collis were not alone in their misgivings. Leonard Woolf, a colonial officer and *ex officio* police magistrate in Ceylon, was eventually worn down by the life of 'doing justice to people who thought that my justice was injustice',* for he admitted many years later that they had a point: 'This ambivalence with regard to law and order and justice in an imperialist society,' he continued, 'was one of the principal reasons for my resigning from the [Ceylon] Civil Service.'*

The second police emergency in *Burmese Days* is the riot in the town, provoked by Ellis's striking a Burmese boy in the face with his stick. Westfield is away in the jungle, thus missing another opportunity for punitive violence. Two thousand Burmese (out of Kyauktada's popula-tion of four thousand) besiege the Club in which six Europeans are trapped. The crowd demand mob justice for the boy. They throw stones and make a lot of noise. About a hundred and fifty civil and military police, eventually summoned from their lines by Flory, restore order by firing over the heads of the crowd, who disperse to do a little looting. Next day, all of Kyauktada is quiet. Ellis goes unpunished, and unre-proached, for his attack on the Burmese boy. There is never any sugges-tion, among the British, that he might be held to account for his crime of violence.*

It is Flory, behaving for once like a hero of imperial romance, who escapes from the besieged Club and swims the river, to take charge of the police and quell the riot with the threat of gunfire. We will come back to this moment, where a European civilian gives orders to a body of Asian police. But it is a reminder that, in Flory's own words, in Burma, 'every white man is a cog in the wheels of despotism'.* Police or military, civilian or official, they were all conscripts in the forces of imperial order. Unlike some of his literary contemporaries, Orwell was never seduced by the glamour of violence. But he did seem to think that experience of violence, professional or not, conferred on men a knowledge of the real world which was not available by other means. In a revealing moment, he seems to argue that H. G. Wells had an invincible naivety about Hitler because, Orwell says, he came from 'the non-military middle class'.*

After *Burmese Days*, the Orwell book that has most to say about the police is *Homage to Catalonia*. The Imperial Police in Burma served what was, at least nominally, a rule-of-law regime, even if the law bent to the interests of a racial oligarchy. In Barcelona, in 1937, Orwell was to acquire first-hand experience of what it was like to live in a police state. And here there was none of the uncomfortable complicity of Eric Blair, or John Flory, in the machinery of despotism. In Barcelona, Orwell found himself, as it were, on the other side of the barricades, in serious danger from the police.

In January, he had joined the POUM anarchist militia to fight for the Spanish Republic against Franco, but had also unwittingly become 'a pawn in an enormous struggle that was being fought out between two political theories'.* He cast an ex-professional eye over the disciplinary forces in the city. Under the monarchy, the Spanish police had served the owners of property. 'The Civil Guards, in particular, were a gendarmerie of the ordinary continental type, who for nearly a century past had acted as the bodyguards of the possessing class'.* Briefly, in 1936, the police were driven out of revolutionary Barcelona and replaced by workers' patrols. Now, in April to June 1937, something like a civil war had broken out in Catalonia between the communists, who now virtually controlled the republican government in Valencia and were supported, funded, and directed by Stalin, and the anarchist and trade union forces which included the POUM.*

As the republican side in Barcelona came increasingly under the control of the communists, the workers' patrols were abolished and the prewar police forces, largely reinforced and heavily armed, were seen on the streets again. Bizarrely, as his anarchist comrades continued fighting for the republic in the trenches on the Aragon front, the wounded Orwell returned to Barcelona to find the POUM leaders had been denounced as fascists, and POUM soldiers like himself were being hunted down by the police as traitors. The streets of Barcelona had become as dangerous for him as the trenches of Aragon. As Dorian Lynskey puts it, 'Barcelona during the crackdown was Orwell's first and only taste of the "nightmare atmosphere" that would envelop *Nineteen Eighty-Four*'.* But at least here for the ex-policeman there was none of the ambivalence that had haunted his activities in Burma. 'I have no particular love for the idealized "worker" as he appears in the bourgeois Communist's mind, but when I see a flesh-and-blood worker in conflict with his natural enemy, the policeman, I do not have to ask myself which side I am on.'*

The boot might now be definitely on the other foot, but a similar disproportion of forces prevailed:

> The Valencian Assault Guards had one sub-machine-gun between ten men and an automatic pistol each; we at the front had approximately one machine-gun between fifty men, and as for pistols and revolvers, you could only procure them illegally. As a matter of fact, though I had not noticed it till now, it was the same everywhere. The Civil Guards and the Carabineros, who were not intended for the front at all, were better armed and far better clad than ourselves. I suspect it is the same in all wars—always the same contrast between the sleek police in the rear and the ragged soldiers in the line.*

The ragged militia were duly liquidated by the sleek police, who in this case were the servants of an oligarchy which was not racial but (as in Oceania in *Nineteen Eighty-Four*) political—the Party.

What had happened to the law? In Barcelona, in 1937, the police were not enforcing the law but implementing the policy of the Valencia government which in turn was taking orders from the Soviet Union. In due course, the Communist Party consolidated its power over what was left of the Spanish republic, and that power was reinforced by the armed and disciplinary forces, the Civil Guards, and the Carabineros. In Catalonia, the POUM was suppressed and its members, including wounded men, wives, and in some cases even children, hunted down by the police. 'This was not a round-up of criminals; it was merely a reign of terror.'* The revolution had started to eat its children.

The number of political prisoners swelled into thousands. The POUM, denounced as Trotskyist, stood accused of pro-fascist treachery, an accusation, Orwell says, that rested solely upon unsupported statements in the communist press, encouraged by the Ministry of Propaganda, and the activities of the communist-controlled secret police.* Orwell and his wife went on the run. Neither he, in the trenches, nor Eileen, who worked in the Independent Labour Party office in Barcelona,* had broken the law, but this was irrelevant. They were not guilty of any definite act, but guilty of what they *were*, a predicament foreshadowed in *Burmese Days*: 'In India you are not judged for what you do, but for what you *are*.'* Orwell's membership of the POUM militia was quite enough to get him put in prison. 'It was no use hanging on to the English notion that you are safe so long as you keep the law. Practically, the law was what the police chose to make it.'*

In Burma, the police may have served and protected an unjust political system, but it was a legal force as well as an ideological one. When Superintendent Westfield grumbles that his hands are tied by red tape, he is acknowledging that the police have to obey the law as well as enforce it. In Barcelona, Orwell encountered a situation which was worse, but one for which Burma must have prepared him, which is why *Homage to Catalonia* is an important link back to *Burmese Days* and forward to *Nineteen Eighty-Four*. In Barcelona, in 1937, the police were nothing but an ideological force, and law itself had all but disappeared, remaining only as a threadbare and cynical veil between police and power. The law was what the police chose to make it. What's more, the deadliest arm of the police had gone underground, operating in the dark and spreading 'all the while a hateful feeling that someone hitherto your friend might be denouncing you to the secret police'.* It was a state of affairs not confined to Spain, or the time of civil war. In the middle of 1949, Orwell was to write, 'half the world is ruled by secret police forces'.*

Here, of course, we have the seeds of *Nineteen Eighty-Four*'s Oceania, where the Thought Police are everywhere and there is no law. In a careful contrast, Orwell ends the account of his escape from Spain, 'with the police one jump behind me',* with the story of his return to the cosy safety of home, and with that vision of the smug tranquillity of England, guaranteed by those benign, unarmed, blue policemen.

10

The Law

'The army of unalterable law' is the last line of 'Lucifer in Starlight', a sonnet by George Meredith which Eric Blair came across at school; perhaps he had to memorize it for class. He took it to heart:

> I understood to perfection what it meant to be Lucifer, defeated and justly defeated, with no possibility of revenge. The schoolmasters with their canes, the millionaires with their Scottish castles, the athletes with their curly hair—these were the armies of the unalterable law. It was not easy, at that date, to realise that in fact it *was* alterable. And according to that law I was damned.*

Meredith's words depressed and haunted him; variations on the phrase recur in his writing all the way up to *Animal Farm* and *Nineteen Eighty-Four*. Like all Romantics, he sided with the rebel Lucifer against the armies of the law. But those armies were not just legal, or religious. They were all the circumstances stacked against you. They were the forces of authority and punishment, of property, of popularity (those curly-haired athletes), against which the morose schoolboy felt he was ranged. The army of unalterable law condemned you to failure, preventing you from getting what you wanted. Its forces were, to use Cyril Connolly's phrase, the enemies of promise. They turn up in *Coming Up for Air* in comic, phantasmagorical form, pursuing George Bowling, who only wants to go on holiday. In his mind's eye, he sees a huge army streaming up the road behind him, the massed ranks of the social superego, led by his wife and children and the neighbours:

> And Sir Herbert Crum and the higher-ups of the Flying Salamander in their Rolls-Royces and Hispano-Suizas. And all the chaps at the office, and all the poor down-trodden pen-pushers from Ellesmere Road and

from all such other roads, some of them wheeling prams and mowing-machines and concrete garden-rollers, some of them chugging along in little Austin Sevens. And all the soul-savers and Nosey Parkers, the people whom you've never seen but who rule your destiny all the same, the Home Secretary, Scotland Yard, the Temperance League, the Bank of England, Lord Beaverbrook, Hitler and Stalin on a tandem bicycle, the bench of Bishops, Mussolini, the Pope—they were all of them after me.*

There was the unalterable law of God and of men. And there was also an unwritten law, the inexorable way things were, the inertia in the system, and all the people and institutions that guarded it, and ensured that no individual could escape or change it. This is the law of failure. All through his boyhood Eric Blair had a profound conviction that he was no good, a monster of folly and wickedness and ingratitude—'and all this, it seemed, was inescapable, because I lived among laws which were absolute, like the law of gravity, but which it was not possible for me to keep'.* In 'Why I Write', he speaks of his natural hatred of authority, which was only strengthened by his five years as an imperial police-man.* Emotionally, temperamentally, Orwell rebelled against the law. Culturally and professionally, he accepted and policed it. The child who read about unalterable law in the Meredith poem was both a Romantic schoolboy and a member of the ruling class.

In Burma, there was a quite specific, professional sense in which he was a soldier in the army of unalterable law. Much as he may have loathed it, he was a salaried officer in a police force under the rule of law.* The rule of law was central to the British theory of empire. It was universally agreed to be the special characteristic of Britain's imperial government and its unique justification, as Nasser Hussain explains:

Indeed, by the time of the impeachment of colonial India's first governor-general, Warren Hastings, in the 1780s, government by law was already becoming the privileged basis for the conceptualization of the 'moral legitimacy' of British colonialism. The ideological justifica-tion for the British presence in India drew heavily on a much-vaunted tradition of ancient English liberty and lawfulness.*

We have already seen the Viceroy Lord Curzon arguing in 1903 that the British empire was not a despotism; its application of strict and inflexible justice was 'the sole justification and the only stable foundation for our rule'.* J. S. Furnivall, a former Indian Civil Service (ICS) officer, was highly critical of British rule in Burma, yet he too endorsed this argument for its legitimacy: 'Our government is based on the western principle of the rule of law, and in that respect may justly be claimed as superior to the Burmese system.'* Maurice Collis, serving as District Magistrate in Rangoon, took comfort in the same belief. 'The law of England is admired the world over, and it is on the excellence of its practice that our moral right to be in India is founded.'* Not surprisingly, that loyal Indian imperialist Dr Veraswami in *Burmese Days* shares this faith in 'unswerving British justice and the Pax Britannica'.*

The foundation of British rule upon law was especially vaunted in Asia, where, as western observers from Montesquieu to Marx had agreed, the native forms of government were typically despotic. In British-ruled territories, government was bound by the law, whose rules were applicable to everyone, and its officials acted within legal restraints. Law was the guarantee of order. After Burma, Orwell had gone through a brief period of rebellious anarchism, but he came round to the idea of the need for law, on the grounds that 'it is always necessary to protect peaceful people from violence'.* Even so, he never really shook off the feeling that the punishment always does more harm than the crime.

One implication of the rule of law is that it sets boundaries to police action; the police have to obey the law while enforcing it. Orwell must have had to remind himself of this when, under provocation, he felt that 'the greatest joy in the world would be to drive a bayonet into a Buddhist priest's guts'.* Superintendent Westfield in *Burmese Days* chafes under the same constraint. He is a conscientious officer, proud of his men. He upholds the law. But in the sanctuary of the European Club he expresses his views freely, grumbling about the way his hands are tied by red tape—bureaucratic legality—and affronted that 'the natives know the law better than we do'.*

This was a complaint heard all over British India, and shortly the rest of the empire, with the appearance of the cohort of British-trained lawyers, like Gandhi and Nehru (and Sengupta), who were in the vanguard of anti-British nationalist movements. In *Burmese Days*, the out-and-out racist Ellis, a civilian, urges that the British have got to hang together and say '*We are the masters*', but Westfield responds gloomily that this is impossible. Although in his own mind the agent of British mastery, professionally he is the servant of British law. 'It's all this law and order that's done for us,' says this unlaughing policeman.* Later when Ellis proposes the torture of some villagers to extract information, Westfield again demurs. 'But that won't do nowadays. Got to keep our own bloody silly laws.'*

Westfield's grumbling seems to register accurately a state of mind widespread among long-serving British officials and unofficials alike, that the real business of protecting British interests was annoyingly compromised by British law itself, increasingly irksome with the intro-duction of the dyarchy reforms, which reached Burma in 1923. 'We seem to have no *authority* over the natives nowadays, with all these dreadful reforms,' moans Mrs Lackersteen.* In private, Westfield could not agree more. When he dreams, the policeman dreams of the escape from these constraints which, he feels, would follow a worsening of the situation and the declaration of a state of emergency. The patron saint of this state of mind is General Dyer, relieved of his command after ordering the massacre of hundreds of unarmed protestors at Amritsar in 1919, a martyrdom (Dyer's) spoken of in reverent tones in the Kyauktada Club.

The principle of the rule of law is that governments and their func-tionaries may not act illegally. In ordinary circumstances the law is para-mount in a rule-of-law regime, and applies equally to everybody. But there was an exception. In times of emergency, of war or civil unrest, for example, martial law could be declared, and some of the protections of the law suspended in the name of security. Though it had its source in the common law of England, martial law was never proclaimed in the home country, but only in colonial areas.* It was an apparatus for con-trolling foreigners. Martial law was not declared in Burma while Orwell was there. But, as he certainly knew, the Defence of India Act, enacted in September 1939, effectively declared martial law in India at the start of the Second World War. It gave the Viceroy wide powers to make rules for the safety of British India, and to provide punishments, including death or transportation for life, for anybody assisting His Majesty's enemies. Special courts were set up, where trials could be held in camera, and from whose judgments there was no appeal.* The Japanese were defeated in 1945, but the Act providing these draconian wartime powers was not repealed until 1947, the year of independence.

Martial law was temporary. But in some states, if the government felt that a state of emergency was chronic, martial law might achieve a kind of permanence. This is one way in which the ongoing war against Eurasia (or is it Eastasia?) is useful to the Party in Oceania. In the endless emergency that ensues, the governing power at home can do whatever it wants. The self-appointed oligarchy maintains its control with a licence to do violence to people with no power to resist it. In these quite specific ways as well as more generally, as explored by Firas A. J. Al-Jubouri among others, issues in *Burmese Days* rehearse *Nineteen Eighty-Four*.* And *Homage to Catalonia* too. In an emergency, as Orwell discovered in Barcelona in 1937, it is childish to believe that 'they' cannot arrest you unless you have broken the law.*

Meanwhile, there was another, unwritten law in Burma. This can be illustrated by a favourite anecdote of Macgregor, the senior official in Kyauktada, who remembers jocularly the good old days when, if one's butler was disrespectful, 'one sent him along to the jail with a chit saying "Please give the bearer fifteen lashes"'.* What law is operating here? The letter of the law might be reformed from time to time, as when dyarchy was introduced to Burma in 1923, the year after Blair's arrival. But there was an unwritten law of racial hierarchy which, being inscribed on the skin, seemed unalterable. To many people, the right of white men to rule over others was thought about (when it was thought about) as underwritten by a law of nature. Orwell's later writing may be another story, but *Burmese Days* gives no reason to suppose this situation can ever be changed. Macgregor's action in ordering violence against his employee is, of course, against the law. But it is justified in terms of another law, that of white power. You only had to look at people to know who was protected, and who could be punished, under that jurisdiction. This was the natural order, unalterable, the way things were.

There are plenty of examples, in Orwell's Burmese writing, of this unwritten law trumping the written law. Flory has purchased Ma Hla May from her parents for three hundred rupees, although slave trading had been abolished in the British empire as long ago as 1807. When she displeases him, he threatens to beat her with a bamboo. In the sphere of domestic and bodily intimacy, the natural order, as everyone understood it, could overrule the law. Verrall kicks the club butler: nobody remarks that this is illegal. (Imagine if he had done it in the Athenaeum Club in Pall Mall!) Ellis blinds a Burmese boy: nobody suggests he ought to be arrested, though he has clearly committed a serious crime. For all his own admiration of the Burmese physique, Orwell remembered punching servants and coolies in moments of rage.* It is inconceivable they would have hit him back.

Racial prestige made every Englishman in the East semi-official, and their colour was the visible badge of their conscription in the unofficial 'army of unalterable law'. A conspicuous example is Flory, who finds himself, in the riot outside the Kyauktada Club, in a scrum of military and civil policemen, a body of a hundred and fifty men including a Military Police subahdar (captain) and a Burmese police inspector. 'The sahib will give the order!', says the subahdar, relieved in more than one sense.* Flory, a civilian with no official authority, immediately takes charge, issues orders, and saves the day. Under the unwritten law, accepted as if it were a law of nature, the white man outranks the officer.

Admittedly, the circumstances are unusual. Yet even in what passed for ordinary times, there was not really an opt-out from colonial identity and solidarity, and the obligations and privileges of the racial authority or 'prestige' that went with it. Flory's feelings for local people are a great deal warmer than for his fellow countrymen, all of whom he despises. Yet he has to admit to himself that he is under the unwritten law, 'a creature of the despotism, a pukka sahib, tied tighter than a monk or a savage by an unbreakable system of taboos'.* Dr Veraswami is his only friend, yet he knows that he is bound to betray him. 'There's no law telling us to be beastly to Orientals—quite the contrary. But—it's just that one daren't be loyal to an Oriental when it means going against the others.'* Overriding the law that mandates equality is the pukka sahib's code, which brings enormous privilege, but dictates the actions and opinions of a white man in the East. Under this discursive regime, friendship can hardly exist, and 'Free speech is unthinkable',* although of course, as in *Nineteen Eighty-Four*, there is no law against it. Beneath the institutions of the rule of law, which said that everyone should be treated equally, ran an ideology of racial difference that insisted—anticipating the pigs' amendment to the last Commandment of Animal Farm—that some people were more equal than others.

Animal Farm is a story about law that has absorbed some of these lessons. It would be tiresome to argue that everything Orwell wrote is somehow about Burma. *Animal Farm* is about the Soviet Union. It is a political allegory that follows the pattern of the Russian Revolution, and does so cleverly and in some detail. Nevertheless, Burma had been the site of Orwell's political education, and his first paradigm of unjust rule. It is not surprising that many of the themes of his later political work had made their first appearance in his Oriental writing. One of these is the story of lives under the law that are shadowed by another law, which people (or animals) feel is natural and unalterable, just the way things are, but is actually ideological, like the unwritten law of race.

How is it that Orwell's fiction seems so gloomy? David Dwan's *Liberty, Equality, and Humbug* contains a fascinating study of what he calls 'Orwell's unhappiness with happiness'.* His characters try to be happy, but perhaps they live in unhappy times; in any case, there can be no happy endings (with the outstandingly ambiguous exception of Gordon Comstock's story). This is the way things are. His characters are doomed to fail, as the schoolboy Eric Blair felt himself to be. This is the keynote of all his stories, the sense of an unalterable law of circumstance, stacked against the protagonist. This law has many faces. In *Burmese Days*, it is race and empire, in *A Clergyman's Daughter*, it is class and gender, in *Keep the Aspidistra Flying*, it's the Money-God. It is there at the beginning and end of the story of the animals' misfortunes in *Animal Farm*, where its exponent is the long-suffering donkey, Benjamin. He takes part in the animals' revolution, but his belief that actually nothing changes seems to be borne out by the revolution's eventual failure.

All of Orwell's fictions follow the same unalterable pattern: an attempt, and failure, to escape from a predicament. And yet, taken as a whole, his non-fiction clings stubbornly to a belief that, with a combination of toughness and goodwill, life can actually be made better for very large numbers of people. Here the Orwellian contradiction might be expressed in a different way: the pessimistic imagination that bows to the force of circumstance, the hopeful intellect that defies it. 'I see now where it is that we part company, Dr Swift,' he says in his imaginary conversation with the author of *Gulliver's Travels*. 'I believe that human society, and therefore human nature, can change.'*

In *Animal Farm*, Orwell took the chance to show a political situation as it evolved, unlike unchanging British Burma, or the miserable round of Dorothy Hare's existence (the plot of *A Clergyman's Daughter* describing a complete circle, like that of *Animal Farm*), or even the politically frozen Oceania in *Nineteen Eighty-Four*, clamped in the iron fist of the Party. *Animal Farm* is the story of a history, the development of ideas and institutions and the changing fortunes of a population. It is indeed based on the history of the Soviet Union, but draws also on what Orwell had seen in Burma and Barcelona and the industrial North.

There is a respectable conservative argument that the status quo should be accepted, because it cannot be changed for the better. This is challenged in the first chapter of *Animal Farm*, when the old boar Major summons the farm animals to a meeting. The life of an animal is misery and slavery, he tells them: that is the plain truth:

> But is this simply part of the order of Nature? Is it because this land of ours is so poor that it cannot afford a decent life to those who dwell upon it? No, comrades, a thousand times no!...Man is the only real enemy we have. Remove Man from the scene, and the root cause of hunger and overwork is abolished for ever.*

Old Major is Karl Marx in the allegory of *Animal Farm*, and here he expounds an idea central to Marxism, that of naturalization. Marxists argue that certain economic relations are dressed up, by the work of ideology, as natural, and people accept them as if they were the product of natural laws, and no more open to challenge than the law of gravity. This naturalization has to be unmasked, the argument goes, before people can see that their circumstances are the result of human action and can be altered by human action. There is nothing inevitable about the gap between rich and poor, powerful and powerless. These things are not a law of nature, or of God. But it takes an effort to realize that they are, in fact, alterable. This is because naturalization short-circuits thinking.

It persuades you to accept things with a shrug, not to question whether they can be changed.

Orwell may well have come across the idea of naturalization in the Marxist writings that he read in the 1930s. But as a matter of fact, Anglo-India had already given him a vivid example, as we have already seen. We could call it the Pith Helmet Theory. British rule in the East was justified on the grounds of a natural difference between races that was in fact purely imaginary. The British were not naturally equipped to govern people in Asia, any more than they were naturally more vulnerable to sunstroke. And the animals on Animal Farm were not condemned to hunger and overwork by some law of nature. There was enough for all. Old Major's inspiration leads to revolution and the overthrow of the farmer. But at the end of the story, the animals are back where they were at the start. So was their misery inescapable after all? Is this another victory for the army of unalterable law?

To answer this question, we can follow the law plot in the story. The revolution at Animal Farm is sudden, arbitrary, and violent. But as soon as the tyrant is expelled, the animals set about making law for Animal Farm. The pigs, who are the intellectual class, have already worked out the principles of an ideology, Animalism, and expounded them to the rest of the population of the farm in public meetings. They reduce these principles to Seven Commandments. 'These Seven Commandments would now be inscribed on the wall; they would form an unalterable law by which all the animals on Animal Farm must live for ever after.'* (This is the first appearance of the Meredith phrase 'unalterable law' in *Animal Farm*.) With the two-legged oppressor sent into exile, still affronted by the animals' 'rebelling against the laws of Nature',* something like a post-colonial society is established. Rituals and a bureaucracy are invented. The Seven Commandments are reduced for convenience to a single maxim, 'Four legs good, two legs bad.'* The animals now have their own rule of law, and they have ownership of the law, because they made the law together. Authority develops organically. The pigs emerge as the executive class, making policy, but their decisions have to be ratified by majority vote. What could possibly go wrong?

There are divisions in the leadership, and on Napoleon's orders Snowball is driven out by the dogs, Orwell's unflattering representation of the police. It turns out that the rule of law is no protection if the law is not the possession of the people. Authority goes dark. The pigs abolish the regular democratic Meeting, and announce that a special committee will meet in private and communicate their decisions to the others. Comrade Napoleon is now rarely seen in public, except to read out the orders for the week 'in a gruff soldierly style'.* He rules by propaganda, and his executive decisions are broadcast and explained by his propagandist Squealer, and brutally enforced by his dogs.

At this point, the regime at Animal Farm still claims the legitimacy of the Seven Commandments. But when the pigs move into the farmhouse, the laws start surreptitiously to be altered—'No animal shall sleep in a bed *with sheets*', 'No animal shall kill any other animal *without cause*'.* There are show trials, confessions, executions, like those going forward in the Soviet Union while Orwell was in Spain. Meanwhile the pigs go on accumulating privileges. Natural sanction is claimed for these changes: the pigs are different, in being possessed of brainpower. They are born to lead, so naturally they need extra resources, as Squealer patiently explains. 'You do not imagine, I hope, that we pigs are doing this in a spirit of selfishness and privilege? We pigs are brainworkers. The whole management and organisation of this farm depend on us. Day and night we are watching over your welfare.'* They present their government as a sort of welfare programme, which is how Rudyard Kipling characterized the British Empire in 'The White Man's Burden', a job of dutifully looking after the helpless and ignorant.

For the other farm animals, hardships worsen, and at the same time they begin to forget the past. Benjamin alone has a historical sense. But in another way he is ahistorical, an animal for whom nothing ever changes. 'Only old Benjamin professed to remember every detail of his long life and to know that things never had been, nor ever could be, much better or much worse—hunger, hardship and disappointment being, so he said, the unalterable law of life.'* Meredith's phrase comes back with a freight of irony: hunger and hardship are unalterable laws, but the laws made by the animals are all too alterable. The pigs learn to walk on their hind legs, and the ever-compliant sheep are taught to bleat 'Four legs good, two legs *better*!'. The Seven Commandments on the barn wall have unaccountably become the slogan. 'ALL ANIMALS ARE EQUAL BUT

SOME ANIMALS ARE MORE EQUAL THAN OTHERS'. This is just one step away from the Oceania of *Nineteen Eighty-Four*, where law has disappeared entirely.

When humans are invited to come and inspect the farm, they congratulate the pigs on creating 'a discipline and an orderliness which should be an example to all farmers everywhere'.* Law is dead, order prevails. In the imperial fashion, the farm's resources are commandeered, Napoleon explaining that 'the title deeds, which were in his own possession, were owned by the pigs jointly'.* (Though he hardly needs to, he is still maintaining that his actions are legal.) The other animals have been returned to slavery, and the story comes full circle as the pigs occupying the farmhouse have become indistinguishable from the humans.

From here it is not far at all to *Nineteen Eighty-Four*, with its permanent state of emergency. In Oceania, as in Barcelona in 1937, 'the law was what the police chose to make it'.* Authority can reach into every household and even into the unconscious: Winston's thoroughly orthodox colleague Parsons is arrested for talking mutinously in his sleep. The whole population is the police force, since everyone, even small children, is on the lookout for political deviation and can denounce everyone else. But the boldest development in Orwell's thinking about law is Newspeak.

Newspeak is the only language in the world whose vocabulary gets smaller every year. As Syme explains to Winston, its whole aim is to narrow the range of thought. When Newspeak is perfected, 'thoughtcrime will be literally impossible, because there will be no words to express it'.* Newspeak is not so much a language as a police action, a permanent state of emergency that exists, like O'Brien's reality, inside the human mind. The mad theory is that it will shut down thought, by making unorthodox thinking impossible, because the words for it have been liquidated.* It is designed to work as a giant naturalization, by which every speaker will come to accept the way things are, because there will be no means of thinking that things might be otherwise. Naturalization short-circuits critical thought.

Once the Party is introjected into the language itself, the law will have become internal, unwritten because written in. 'The intention was to make speech, and especially speech on any subject not ideologically neutral, as nearly as possible independent of consciousness... Ultimately it was hoped to make articulate speech issue from the larynx without involving the higher brain centres at all.'* In a way, it will be a humane (if inhuman) jurisdiction, hardly compatible with O'Brien's vision of the future as a boot stamping on a human face forever. With the authority of the Party thoroughly introjected into the language itself, there will be neither written nor unwritten law, but only ever-obedient writing and speech. Law disappears. If there is no possibility of breaking the law, the law is not needed.

Once Newspeak is fully rolled out, its users will lose all knowledge of literature, of the past, and of all values and ideas except those of the Party. They will utterly surrender the capacity for independent action and thought. In fact, Newspeak is designed to end history, by putting an unbreakable clamp on the very possibility of change. It is to be the last unalterable law. But in their moment of triumph, imposing the discipline of Newspeak, the rulers of Oceania will condemn themselves to life imprisonment, repeating the pattern of Orwell's earlier claim that when the white man turns tyrant (in empire), it is his own freedom that he destroys.*

The triumph of Newspeak, however, is destined to remain partial. Syme tells Winston that by the year 2050, not a single human being will be left who could understand such a conversation as the two of them are having now:

> 'Except—' began Winston doubtfully, and then stopped.
>
> It had been on the tip of his tongue to say 'Except the proles,' but he checked himself, not feeling fully certain that this remark was not in some way unorthodox. Syme, however, had divined what he was about to say.
>
> 'The proles are not human beings,' he said carelessly.*

The often neglected point being, of course, that Newspeak is an official language. It is for use by Party members, from the powerful mandarin O'Brien to humble bureaucrats like Winston Smith. Proles will be left to use their indigenous language, Oldspeak, a language in which new and subversive ideas might still emerge. They will not be subject to the control of Newspeak, because of the familiar doubt—which we encountered in earlier chapters—as to whether subject peoples are fully human. Here in the Appendix, 'The Principles of Newspeak', at the end of *Nineteen Eighty-Four*, the oriental paradigm still operates uneasily. Being despised, the proles are beneath suspicion; O'Brien assures Winston they will never revolt in a million years.* They are, as Elinor Taylor has put it, 'a group whose humanity depends on their dehumanization'.*

'The proles are not human beings', in the eyes of the Party; but also, 'Proles and animals are free.'* So while the ruling elite will be lobotomized by Newspeak, reduced to the 'duckspeak' of repeating orthodox phrases, the proles will be left with at least the possibility of independent, creative speech and action. It is an unexpected twist on the adage that there is one law for the powerful and another for the powerless. And it leaves a potentially deadly weapon in the hands of the proles. In the Newspeak future, the ruling class will be forever intellectually enslaved, and the oppressed people apathetic. The difference is that the latter condition is alterable. Winston Smith was right about where the possibility of change, and hope, might lie.

11

Literature

1.

Once there was a British writer, an Englishman who was born in India. He was privately educated in England, did not go to university, returned to the East after leaving school, and lived and worked there for a handful of years. Empire, and the relation between those in authority and those under authority, became one of the principal themes of his writing, both in journalism and fiction. He lived by his pen, and made a name as an author of strong political convictions. Some of his stories and phrases have embedded themselves in the English language and the conscious-ness of its users, even of those who have never actually read his work. Both admired and disliked in his own lifetime, he became a spokesman and a symbol in the great ideological contentions of modern times, and after his death he was considered not only an important writer but also a particular embodiment of the character of his country.

Not once, but twice. George Orwell and Rudyard Kipling are like twinned heraldic animals, the lion and the unicorn of modern British literature. And though our first instinct may be to think of them as opposites, the similarities between them proliferate. Both of them were patriots, though highly critical of their fellow-countrymen and frequently of their government. Both were public intellectuals who used their writing to raise political consciousness. Both loved animals and wrote books about them, and both had a strong feeling for the English countryside.

Both were men of principle, but they were also realists in the sense of a non-theoretical pragmatism. They were both impatient with orthodoxy, theory, and hypocrisy. Orwell's disgust at W. H. Auden's glib phrase about 'the conscious acceptance of guilt in the necessary murder'—'It could only be written,' Orwell said, 'by a person to whom murder is at most a word'*—is complemented by Kipling's contempt for liberals like

'Pagett M.P.', who pontificated about India without bothering to learn about it. Both attitudes, to be sure, have something of the smugness of a man of the world, playing the trump card of experience. Both writers, after all, were Anglo-Indians.

In quite different ways, Anglo-India gave Kipling and Orwell a global vision. Though Orwell at one point was a village shopkeeper, and Kipling for many years impersonated a country gentleman in Sussex, neither was provincial. Kipling travelled all over the empire, and came to think of himself as its bard, and although he was an acute observer of local differences, he also found it everywhere the same. The empire he knew or imagined was a world network of power, hierarchical relationships, security, and welfare. Globally diffused, it had little to do any more with the European island that had given birth to it. Sometimes when he speaks of it, he makes it sound like the United Nations. It was, at its most exalted, a global moral force.

Apart from India, which he left as a baby, Orwell's only geographical experience of the British empire was in Burma, and the home country. But he was a globalist too. The empire he knew was a world system of economic exploitation of the many by the few, an injustice on a global scale mirrored by a similar injustice at home. Justice for India, and justice for the North of England, were interdependent. The road to Wigan Pier began in Mandalay, because, he wrote, 'Britain cannot become a genuinely Socialist country while continuing to plunder Asia and Africa.'* Like Kipling, he had his eye on the big picture.

There were certainly differences, personal and aesthetic as well as ideological. Kipling was brilliant and precocious, doing some of his best work in his twenties. He had his unhappiness, even tragedy, but he never doubted his imaginative and creative powers, a mysterious unconscious force he called his daemon. He would not have understood Orwell's morose statement that writing a book was like a long bout of some painful illness.* Orwell's genius was prosaic, he was a slow starter, diffident, and often clumsy, always disappointed with his own work, the kind of writer for whom every book was doomed to be, in T. S. Eliot's words, a different kind of failure. Kipling, who died in 1936, probably never read anything written by George Orwell. But Orwell knew Kipling's work very well indeed.

Orwell was to pay tribute to 'the story-teller who was so important to my childhood'.* Children of his class and generation grew up with Kipling's books: *The Just So Stories*, the *Jungle Books*, *Puck of Pook's Hill*, *Rewards and Fairies*, *Kim*, *Stalky and Co.*, and then *Barrack-Room Ballads* and *Plain Tales from the Hills* and the rest. Not just a favourite on the nursery bookshelf, Kipling was the author of childhood for the sons (daughters too) of empire in a wider sense. They experienced the world through his eyes, and Kipling's writings helped them to see and relate to the important things in their environment—animals, the natural world, home, parents and other adults, jokes and games, friends, school, and later more abstract issues, like duty, work, country, masculinity, and femininity. When the young Eric Blair, fresh from school, went to Burma to serve in the police, he was going to a place that Kipling had more or less invented for the benefit of his fellow-countrymen: they knew about the Orient, and 'orientals', through him.

Leonard Woolf, who belonged to the generation between Kipling and Orwell, went to work as a colonial officer in Ceylon (Sri Lanka) in 1904, and found the place uncannily familiar. It was Kipling country. Woolf said he couldn't decide whether Kipling had been brilliantly accurate in his description of the British in the East, or whether by now the British in the East modelled themselves on Kipling's characters.* Sir George Younghusband, an Army man, reported that British soldiers thought and talked and expressed themselves exactly as Kipling had taught them in his stories.*

Orwell too must have felt uncomfortably at home in the 'Kipling-haunted little clubs' of British Burma.* Kipling is a ghostly background figure in 'A Hanging' and 'Shooting an Elephant', and above all in *Burmese Days*. The Englishmen lounging in long chairs in the club at Kyauktada are Kipling characters, stripped of the glamour and charm with which Kipling invested them. But Veraswami, the comically pro-British Indian doctor, is a variation on a theme by Kipling too, as is the wily U Po Kyin. As for the central character, Flory, his local mistress, his white fiancée, his enjoyment of the jungle, his sporting activities, his close friendship with an Indian, his moment of heroism during a riot, his disgrace, and his eventual suicide, all have identifiable precedents in Kipling's stories.

'Kipling's books are essentially about British India.'* No wonder he was a sort of household god in Anglo-Indian homes.* His stories and poems are the epic of Anglo-India. The heroes of this epic are the soldiers and civilians who protected and ran British India (Kipling is much less interested in the 'box-wallahs', the European commercial community in the East). These heroes were admirable, sometimes self-sacrificing, but Kipling did not like them to be show-offs; they are stoical and do their duty. They suffer the dangers, the irksome bureaucracy, the recalcitrance of local people, the boredom or loneliness or ill-health of sweltering barracks or isolated postings. One thing you do not find in Kipling, however, is the central theme of *Burmese Days*, an Englishman in the East who has lost his faith in the empire. In all Kipling's work, there is no sympathy for malcontents and subversives.*

No writer was more important to Orwell, as an influence, example, and antagonist. Orwell's whole life was a conversation, or quarrel, with Kipling. He is mentioned, and quoted, frequently all through Orwell's writing. There are two places where he confronts him directly: a short obituary article written in 1936, and a longer essay for *Horizon* in 1942, prompted by the wartime publication of T. S. Eliot's edition of a selection of Kipling's poetry.*

The first article is too personal to be a conventional obituary. It was written fast, and published in *New English Weekly* within a week of Kipling's death. It contains a well-known statement of Orwell's continuing struggle with the older man, the focus of his conflicting feelings about his Anglo-Indian heritage. 'For my own part I worshipped Kipling at thirteen, loathed him at seventeen, enjoyed him at twenty, despised him at twenty-five and now again rather admire him.'* Though this is rather suspiciously neat, it is worth glossing these phases. At 13, Orwell was at prep school, at 17, he was a sixth-former at Eton, at 20, he was an imperial police officer, at 25, he was a bohemian drifter, and 'now', in early 1936, he was a professional author and had written three novels.

Kipling, in the words of a later Orwell essay, 'seems to have been the first English writer to notice, or at any rate to exploit, the picturesqueness of the Indian scene.'* The 1936 article praises the construction and economy of his tales, and concedes that the verse is memorable, if bad. But what is most distasteful in Kipling is his imperialism, though Orwell argues that this was more forgivable when the empire was concerned with more than squabbles over free trade and imperial preference:

> The imperialism of the 'eighties and 'nineties was sentimental, ignor-ant and dangerous, but it was not entirely despicable. The picture then called up by the word 'empire' was a picture of overworked officials and frontier skirmishes, not of Lord Beaverbrook and Australian but-ter. It was still possible to be an imperialist and a gentleman....*

That Kipling's imperialism might be mitigated on the grounds of gentle-manliness is a surprising argument coming from a socialist, less so com-ing from an Anglo-Indian back from the East. Suffering under what has been called the anxiety of influence, younger writers often need to free themselves from the overbearing presence of a strong precursor.* Orwell raises one hand to kill the father, in the classic pattern, but commutes the sentence with the other.

He was not done with Kipling. He would return to these themes, and this ambivalence, in the *Horizon* essay six years later, where his ongoing wrestling match with Kipling gets mixed up with quarrels he was waging on other fronts. First though, the case is stated. 'It is no use pretending that Kipling's view of life, as a whole, can be accepted or even forgiven by any civilised person,' he says. 'Kipling *is* a jingo imperialist, he *is* mor-ally insensitive and aesthetically disgusting.'* But (Orwell goes on) he is not, as it was fashionable to say in 1942, a Fascist. Again, this is because Kipling's imperialism belonged very definitely to the period 1885–1902. The famous poem 'Recessional', if read carefully, is not an orgy of boast-ing, but 'a denunciation of power politics, British as well as German'.* All his life Kipling believed that the law was above naked force, that pride comes before a fall, and that the gods punish *hubris*. Nobody these days believes these things, says Orwell, Fascists least of all:

> No one, in our time, believes in any sanction greater than military power; no one believes that it is possible to overcome force except by greater force. There is no 'law', there is only power. I am not saying that this is a true belief, merely that it is the belief which all modern men do actually hold. Those who pretend otherwise are either intellectual

cowards, or power-worshippers under a thin disguise, or have simply not caught up with the age they are living in.*

But the law for Kipling was something real and strong. It was a kind of religious faith, and the empire was its instrument. In Orwell's view, this faith in an empire of law deserved a measure of respect, even though it was mistaken because the empire was really about money all along ('the "box-wallah" calls the tune').*

As a matter of fact, much of the case Orwell makes for Kipling is simply repeated or elaborated from Eliot's essay. For all Kipling's identification with India and empire, Eliot found in him an unexpected estrangement, a peculiar detachment, even 'a universal foreignness': 'he remains somehow alien and aloof from all with which he identifies himself'.* Eliot defends Kipling from the charge of Fascism (this was 1941, after all), and he argues that with the idea of empire Kipling sought to convey 'an awareness of responsibility'.* In his own essay, Orwell seizes on this. Because Kipling identified with 'the official class' of empire, he had a sense of responsibility which is never shared by the 'enlightened' people who sneer at the empire while continuing to benefit from it (a familiar Orwell theme). His defence of Kipling begins to look like a defence of that official class. 'The nineteenth-century Anglo-Indians, to name the least sympathetic of his idols, were at any rate people who did things.'*

Kipling may have been a vulgar, class-prejudiced imperialist, so that 'one was bound to think of him, after one had grown up, as a kind of enemy, a man of alien and perverted genius'.* But as the chronicler of empire, he was acquainted with reality, unlike many of his detractors, 'the refined people who have sniggered at him'.* He identified himself with the ruling power and not the opposition, an identification that might seem bizarre in a modern writer, but it gave him a certain grip on reality. Unlike the opposition, the powerful have to take responsibility, and do things. Speaking for them, Kipling had to try to imagine what action and responsibility are like; consequently, though he might fall into abysses of folly and snobbery, 'Kipling...is generally talking about things that are of urgent interest',* even if his words may be 'always good for a snigger in pansy-left circles'.*

It is a remarkable argument, and it is wrapped up in Orwell's thinking about T. S. Eliot, the authors who were his own contemporaries, the wartime year 1942 in which it was written, and perhaps about the magazine, *Horizon*, in which it was published. But above all it is yet another of his attempts to come to terms with Anglo-India.

2.

Orwell's early literary tastes were quite conventional, and were formed in the schoolroom for the most part. Two of his great literary heroes, Jonathan Swift and Charles Dickens, belong to that curious group of English heavyweight authors once considered suitable for children (Daniel Defoe and John Bunyan are fellow members, alongside more middleweight choices like Robert Louis Stevenson), and he would have come to them early. Kipling was certainly on the shelves at home, and so was Thackeray's *Vanity Fair*, and Housman's *A Shropshire Lad*. Villon and Maupassant probably came with his French schoolwork; Flaubert and Zola arrived later. As his personality developed, he found some of what he wanted in Thackeray, H. G. Wells, Thomas Hardy, Samuel Butler, George Gissing, and D. H. Lawrence, important models for his early fiction, and in Jack London. T. S. Eliot and James Joyce were more than fashionable enthusiasms, and in due course make their way into his own writing: the world of Gordon Comstock is thoroughly Eliotic, and the Nighttown chapter from *Ulysses* is imitated, with partial success, in *A Clergyman's Daughter*. These authors were important to him. On visits to Rangoon he no doubt hurried, like John Flory, to Smart and Mookerdum's bookshop for 'the new novels out from England';* these might have included Virginia Woolf's *Mrs Dalloway* (1925), but are just as likely to have been by Arnold Bennett or Hugh Walpole, or even the garishly fashionable Michael Arlen. Later, working as a novelist and prolific book reviewer in England, he read very widely across the literary spectrum, from Marcel Proust to *No Orchids for Miss Blandish*, and in all genres from scientific writing to seaside postcards.

'Inside the Whale', along with the later 'Why I Write', constitutes Orwell's literary autobiography. It includes a broadbrush survey of the

English literature of his own time, from the melancholy pastoral of *A Shropshire Lad* to the revolutionary gestures of the 1930s. Orwell gives a respectful account of the post-war authors we now call modernist, the generation of Eliot and Joyce and Pound, of Aldous Huxley and Wyndham Lewis and D. H. Lawrence: technically innovative, culturally pessimistic, and understood to be politically quietist for the most part; in the 1920s, he says, 'every important event in Europe escaped the notice of the English intelligentsia'.* He points out that their reactionary gloom coincided with a time of unprecedented prosperity for the middle classes.

His own aesthetic difference from the modernists has been exaggerated, largely because of his campaign for plain writing, and his remark, in 'Why I Write', that 'good prose is like a window pane',* an unpopular idea among modernists. But it is often overlooked that the context for this phrase is the need for the writer to efface his personality, which is actually a modernist axiom. In any case, as Alex Woloch has shown in his meticulous study of Orwell's non-fictional prose, that famous plain style can be unmasked as often experimental, performative, ironic, displaced, and layered as anything in literary modernism; but in Orwell's case, as Woloch argues, it is a style evolved in the search for democratic socialism.*

'Inside the Whale' sees modernism as essentially a phenomenon of the 1920s. Then with the 1930s, it is all change, and 'anyone sensitive enough to be touched by the *Zeitgeist* was also involved in politics'.* Here come W. H. Auden and his friends, Orwell's own contemporaries, writers who belong mostly to the English rentier class and subscribe to a left-wing orthodoxy. Subject matter is important once more, harnessed to serious purpose. All other codes (such as patriotism, religion, the empire) having been discredited, these writers needed something to believe in, and most of them found it in communism, which meant allegiance to the Soviet Union, 'the patriotism of the deracinated'.* But the softness and security of life in England had left them naïve about the realities of such things as purges, secret police, and summary executions. The Auden crowd, as Orwell saw it, had simply not seen enough; they were in a state of permanent adolescence. But the course of events towards the end of the decade (which included Stalin's pact with Hitler, signed while Orwell was writing this essay) made nonsense of their left-wing orthodoxy, causing much dismay and confusion. 'On the whole the literary history of the 'thirties seems to justify the opinion that a writer does well to keep out of politics.'* Politics, meanwhile, will not keep out of literature. The novel, in particular, was the canary in the political coal-mine, because it could only breathe in an atmosphere of freedom of thought. In the age of totalitarian dictatorships which seemed to be coming, 'literature, in the form in which we know it, must suffer at least a temporary death.'*

'Inside the Whale' is one of Orwell's great essays.* His criticism is inclined to be vehement, and undoubtedly he is unfair to the Auden group, who are caricatured as overgrown schoolboys, playing with fire. Part of the essay's agenda was to measure his distance from his literary contemporaries. Insulated in cosy liberal England (as Orwell sees it), the unchanging England of the final paragraph of *Homage to Catalonia*, Auden and his friends are attacked as childishly naïve. Auden is skewered on his own boast about 'the conscious acceptance of guilt in the necessary murder', which could only be written, Orwell says, by 'a person to whom murder is at most a word'.* And it is this that links 'Inside the Whale' to his partial defence of Kipling two years later. Auden doesn't need to take responsibility for his words because they are merely *words*. But Orwell's part in the ruling of Burma, much as he had hated it, had left him a realist, with a sense of responsibility for his words and actions.

The essay, meanwhile, is autobiographical in setting up a dichotomy (a false one, perhaps, but useful to him) which his own writing had to face: the aesthetic, formalist 1920s, paying no attention to politics, and the activist, content-oriented 1930s, overwhelmed by politics. 'Why I Write' gives his answer to this antithesis, his determination 'to make political writing into an art'.* 'Inside the Whale' had been literally overtaken by the world crisis—war broke out while he was writing it—and Orwell imagined the writer now sitting on a melting iceberg, 'merely an anachronism, a hangover from the bourgeois age, as surely doomed as the hippopotamus'.* 'Seemingly there is nothing left but quietism', he concluded. It was another mistaken prophecy.

But what, meanwhile, was grist to the mill of Orwell the writer about empire? Kipling, as we have just seen, was important to him throughout his life, and it was Kipling who had made the Orient possible as a theme for an English writer. In childhood, there had been the funny or sinister foreigners of school stories and comics, and a raft of imperial exotica of the kind that.Orwell called good bad books, and might have included A. E. W. Mason's *The Four Feathers* (1902), R. Austin Freeman's *The Eye of Osiris* (1911), or—a cut above—the novels of the prolific Anglo-Indian Flora Annie Steel, such as *On the Face of the Waters* (1896).

In general, the quality of literary writing about the East was not high, partly no doubt because the Orient that writers saw was a British possession, or battleground, and they observed it through an ideologically (often racially) coloured lens. There were exceptions. Orwell found something to admire in the China of *The Good Earth*, by the American Pearl Buck.* The novels of Edward Thompson, who had gone to India as a missionary teacher and became a learned orientalist and a friend of Tagore, Gandhi, and Nehru, drew on a profound knowledge of the country. So did the work of Maurice Collis, who had served as a magistrate in Burma while Orwell was there. J. R. Ackerley's comic memoir, *Hindoo Holiday*, was commended for its lack of colour-consciousness; but then Ackerley's experience, like that of E. M. Forster before him, had not been in British India proper, but in one of the nominally independent princely states.*

Forster's *A Passage to India*, published in 1924, was the best novel written about India by an English writer, in Orwell's view. He commends Forster as a patient and shrewd observer, who showed that almost all his characters, British and Indian, were corrupted by imperialism. But he also had the advantage of writing at a time when belief in white superiority had been deflated, so that 'it was possible to think of an Indian not as a picturesque feudal retainer, nor even as a downtrodden victim, but simply as an individual'.* Forster therefore could look at his characters with equanimity, and though he sided with the Indians against the British, he did not feel obliged to represent them as morally or intellectually superior. Although Orwell had almost certainly read Forster's book before he began *Burmese Days*, his own novel does not share this rather bland-sounding liberalism, nor Forster's confidence in exploring the individualism of an 'oriental' character.

Somerset Maugham travelled widely in Asia, a professional writer in search of copy. He is also probably the strongest literary presence

in Orwell's Burmese writing. It is often remarked that 'A Hanging'
interestingly resembles Maugham's sketch 'The Vice-Consul', set in China
and published in 1922.* Maugham is uninterested in making political
judgements, but beady-eyed in his observation of the Anglo-Indians (and
Anglo-Malayans), with what Orwell called 'a kind of stoical resignation,
the stiff upper lip of the pukka sahib somewhere East of Suez, carrying on
with his job without believing in it, like an Antonine Emperor'.* Ideally
suited to be the chronicler of the late-imperial East, Maugham was the
modern writer who influenced Orwell most, chiefly for 'his power of
telling a story straightforwardly and without frills'.* It was a slow lesson:
Burmese Days is not without frills, but 'of late years', Orwell wrote in
1946, 'I have tried to write less picturesquely and more exactly'.*

Finally, Joseph Conrad. Orwell read Conrad throughout his adult life,
mentions nineteen of Conrad's works in his own writing, and was plan-
ning a major critical essay on him in the last year of his life. Again, this
is less a matter of direct stylistic influence than of a kind of critical conversation, as with Kipling. Conrad was one model of what a writer could
be.* Orwell's reaction to him helped him struggle with questions of
theme, attitude, and technique in his own work. Conrad was a favourite
of highbrow modernists like T. S. Eliot and Virginia Woolf, but was also
known as the author of stirring tales of action on land and sea, many of
them set in the Orient which he had travelled as a young seaman. Orwell
was also drawn to 'the excellence of his political novels'.*

In works like *Heart of Darkness* and *Nostromo*, Conrad had written
powerful stories about the cynicism and greed of imperialism and the
material interests it served, and these find an echo in Orwell's own
experience and convictions. Conrad was another estranged artist: Polish
by birth, English by adoption, writing in his third language. He came
from a country that had been wiped off the map, and his family had
suffered under the Romanov autocracy, so he was not subject to the
political naivety of Orwell's contemporaries of the right or left.*

Though it was not his favourite, the Conrad novel that bulks largest in
Orwell's surviving writing is *Lord Jim*, published in book form in 1900.
Orwell complained that the action was unconvincing, and this was
perhaps because Conrad had seen life in the Far East only from a
sailor's angle. In spite of its brilliant passages of description, the story

was unbelievable, said Orwell, a confection of melodramatic adventure about honour lost, topped off with a dusky maiden in a sarong. This is hardly fair to *Lord Jim*, but it shows Orwell struggling with the clichés of Romantic exoticism which he himself had not entirely avoided in *Burmese Days*. How could an English author write a believable, responsible novel about the East?

The question was coming back to Orwell because, with the war ending, his thoughts were turning to a second eastern novel. Ill-health and the awful trials of writing *Nineteen Eighty-Four* postponed this, and he wrote to David Astor at the end of 1948 that he needed to stay alive for a while because he had 'a good idea for a novel'.* He gave it a thoroughly Maughamesque title, *A Smoking-Room Story*.* He courted comparison with Conrad by opening the first scene on board a ship, and promising the story of a young Englishman who has suffered some sort of disgrace in the East. Besides Conrad's *Lord Jim*, Maugham and Kipling are present in the theme of the boy who has 'gone wrong' in the East. *A Smoking-Room Story*, barely begun, remains one of the most intriguing non-existent books in English literature, and especially so in the light of Dorian Lynskey's observation about the achieved confidence of Orwell's mature post-war style, evident in the fact that 'very little of his work betrays signs of strain or haste'.*

We can piece together something of Orwell's plans for this book from his surviving drafts and notes. His protagonist, Curly Johnson, is aged 24 and is sailing back from Burma to England in 1927—at the same age, and in the same year, as Eric Blair made the voyage. The satirical description of the onboard passengers is in the style of Somerset Maugham. Intriguingly, though he had complained that the long passage of oral narration in which Marlow tells the first part of Jim's story in the Conrad novel was not credible, it looks as if Orwell intended that the scandal of Curly Johnson was to be revealed in the identical device of an embedded first-personal spoken narration, the smoking-room story that gives the novella its title. A story of the East told in masculine company was a familiar device in tales by Conrad, Kipling, Maugham, and Leonard Woolf.*

It is not possible to say in any detail what *A Smoking-Room Story* would have been like, but Fredric Warburg reported that the book that was formulated in Orwell's mind was going to be 'a novel of character rather than of ideas, with Burma as background'.* It is poignant that at the end of his life Orwell contemplated turning back to the Orient, to the time of his youth, and to the literary masters of the imperial-oriental tale.

3.

It is wartime. A writer strides along the corridor of the BBC offices at 200 Oxford Street, where he has been recording a programme for the Indian section of the Eastern Service. He could be described as Anglo-Indian. Born in India in the first decade of the century, educated in England, he is an author of progressive, socialist views. He is a determined enemy of British imperialism across the world, and of the social divisions that sustain inequality in his own country. In younger days, he worked for a while in a restaurant, and he has written books about the life of the disadvantaged and oppressed, though he himself comes from a less uncomfortable background. He travelled to Spain to volunteer in the Spanish Civil War. Now he makes a living as a novelist and journalist, trying to reconcile the demands of literature and propaganda. He has a broad acquaintance in the literary world of the wartime capital, both its established figures and its wide bohemian fringe. In that folder under his arm are the notes for a review he is writing about T. S. Eliot's latest book, *A Choice of Kipling's Verse*.

Not George Orwell (though it could be), but Mulk Raj Anand. That review of the Kipling volume makes some of the same critical points as Orwell's, but none of the excuses. Kipling's imperialism could hardly be forgiven 'when each attempt at glorification simply oozes with Hitleresque pride in the domination of so-called inferior people'; as for Kipling's novel *Kim*, in Anand's view it was 'a wonderful piece of naturalistic writing, full of remarkable observation, from the outside', and 'full of the stock characters of any United Services Club conversation of the period, without much reality of their own'.*

Orwell had invited Anand to talk on the BBC, and commissioned from him a set of programmes called 'Meet My Friend'; Anand was also a frequent guest on Orwell's radio poetry magazine, *Voice*. The BBC were always keen to recruit Indian speakers for the Eastern Service, but Orwell was not giving an opportunity to a literary novice: Anand was at least Orwell's equal in standing in the world of English letters. His two best-known novels, *Untouchable* and *Coolie*, had been published in 1935 and 1936 respectively. He had done work for T. S. Eliot's *Criterion* and Leonard and Virginia Woolf's Hogarth Press, and was well connected in the London literary scene, as attested much later by his *Conversations in Bloomsbury* (1981), a sometimes mischievous retrospect on his talks in the 1930s with luminaries such as Clive Bell, Aldous Huxley, and Virginia Woolf. It could be a small world. *Untouchable* had an introduction by E. M. Forster. Anand's *Letters on India* (1942) was published by the Labour Book Service with a reproachful Foreword, disagreeing with some of the book's argument, by his friend the veteran socialist Leonard Woolf in the form of a letter to Anand, which was followed by a published letter from Anand in riposte to Woolf, prompting a review by Orwell in *Tribune* in the form of a letter to Anand, eliciting an irritated letter to the editor from Woolf, published alongside another rejoinder by Anand: and Orwell pursued the matter the following month in a letter to the *Times Literary Supplement*.*

Anand was an anti-imperialist, a socialist, and an Indian nationalist. This was tricky for Orwell, who was highly suspicious of nationalism.* But he defended Anand from charges of being anti-British and unfriendly to Anglo-Indians in his writing.* He was impatient with Anand's politics for the same reason that he disapproved of Congress agitation for Indian independence from Britain while the imperial Japanese army was storming through Asia. But as a literary figure, Orwell had no doubt about Anand's value and importance. In him, Orwell saw the solution to his Kipling problem, which was also his *Lord Jim* problem, and indeed his *Burmese Days* problem: how to decolonize English literature about the Orient.

No one could accuse Anand's portrayal of India, as Anand had accused Kipling's, of being written 'from the outside'. In novels like *Untouchable*, the Indian author could explore Indian lives almost invisible to the best-intentioned foreigner, and an Indian world in which the British played, at best, a marginal part. *Coolie* does have some Anglo-Indian characters, but Munoo, the title character, is semi-literate and non-English-speaking; English is one of the barriers that keep him in his place. In *Untouchable*, the British are largely absent from the story, except in the form of the fetishized objects—clothes, including an old pith helmet—that Bakha covets as a fantasy escape from the miseries of his abject status in the caste system. In Anand's novel, *The Sword and the Sickle* (1942), Orwell noted approvingly, 'European characters barely appear in the story—a reminder that in India only about one person in a thousand is technically white—and of the few that do it cannot be said that they are treated worse than the other characters'.*

Even before independence, here was an India where the British presence, and the British point of view, were not paramount. But it was still hard for Orwell to see India without the prism of empire; because of the language he used, the world of Anand's fiction was still a kind of Anglo-India, and like the rest of his countrymen Orwell seems to have remained largely unaware of Indian writing in Indian languages.* Anand's was still an India in English, even if it was an English made more lively by a certain unEnglish flavour. Anand's English had a quality of strangeness of which Orwell approved. Why were writers like Anand important beyond their literary merit, in 1942?* 'Partly,' Orwell explained, 'because they are interpreting Asia to the West, but more, I think, because they act as a Westernizing influence among their own countrymen', and the English language was 'a funnel for ideas deadly to the Fascist view of life'.* And beyond the immediate context of the war against Fascism, so long as Indians used English 'they are in a species of alliance with us, and an ultimate decent settlement with the Indians whom we have wronged but also helped to awaken remains possible'.* In the educational programmes he made and commissioned for the Eastern Service, Orwell was working to strengthen that alliance in the literary and cultural domain. Meanwhile, as long as Anand and his friends used English, their work maintained a bond with readers of English, in England and around the world. In their hands, Anglo-Indian literature would fade away and Indo-Anglian literature could take its place.

After Indian and Burmese independence were achieved in 1947 and 1948, Orwell, remarkably, wrote nothing about either country. Was this a self-denial? Perhaps this champion of the struggle against empire felt that it was now not for him, but for others, to continue the story. Perhaps he just had nothing more to contribute to it. For his part, he was hoping to return one last time, in *A Smoking-Room Story*, to the Orient and the Anglo-Indian world of his youth. Tuberculosis and *Nineteen Eighty-Four* had exhausted him, however. His last book was never written.

Notes

References to Peter Davison ed. *The Complete Works of George Orwell* (London: Secker and Warburg, 1998) are indicated by volume and page number, e.g. 13:401. The following titles by Orwell are indicated by abbreviations:

ACD: *A Clergyman's Daughter* (*Complete Works*, vol. 3)
AF: *Animal Farm* (*Complete Works*, vol. 8)
BD: *Burmese Days* (*Complete Works*, vol. 2)
CUFA: *Coming Up for Air* (*Complete Works*, vol. 8)
D&O: *Down and Out in Paris and London* (*Complete Works*, vol. 1)
HTC: *Homage to Catalonia* (*Complete Works*, vol. 6)
KAF: *Keep the Aspidistra Flying* (*Complete Works*, vol. 4)
NEF: *Nineteen Eighty-Four* (*Complete Works*, vol. 9)
RWP: *The Road to Wigan Pier* (*Complete Works*, vol. 5)

Page numbering in the Penguin Modern Classics (or Penguin Twentieth-Century Classics) editions corresponds to the pagination of the *Complete Works*.

Chapter 1

p. 1 **Imperialism means India:** 'Review of *Empire* by Louis Fischer', 13 May 1944, 16:186.
'A Nice Cup of Tea': 12 Jan. 1946, 18:33–5.
p. 2 **Sacrificing burnt offerings:** *CUFA*, 30.
not sufficiently aware of the part played by empire in shaping their nation, as many feel: For a good example, see Sathnam Sanghera, *Empireland: How Imperialism Has Shaped Modern Britain* (London: Viking, 2021), 185–206.
p. 3 **Sumatra Tin and United Celanese:** *ACD*, 26.
***Imperialism* (1902):** J. A. Hobson, *Imperialism: A Study* (London: James Nisbet, 1902).
Middle-class domestic space: Anne McClintock, *Imperial Leather: Race, Gender and Sexuality in the Colonial Contest* (New York: Routledge, 1995), 208.
p. 4 **European political and economic dominance of the Middle East and Asia in the age of empire:** See Edward W. Said, *Orientalism* (Harmondsworth: Penguin, [1978] 1985).

the 'false map of the world' people carried in their heads: 'Riding Down from Bangor', 22 Nov. 1946, 18:493.

combination of anti-imperialism and patriotic attachment: Paul Gilroy, *After Empire: Melancholia or Convivial Culture?* (London: Routledge, 2004), 85, 86.

p. 5 applicability to issues and predicaments today: John Rodden is the leading historian of Orwell's reception, influence, and mythologization over the decades, most recently in his John Rodden, *Becoming George Orwell: Life and Letters, Legend and Legacy* (Princeton, NJ: Princeton University Press, 2020) . The contemporaneity of Orwell is the relentless theme of Richard Bradford's biographical study, Richard Bradford, *George Orwell: A Man of Our Time* (London: Bloomsbury, 2020) .

lower-upper-middle class: *RWP*, 113.

p. 6 No Anglo-Indian will ever deny: *BD*, 27.

members of old Anglo-Indian families: George Woodcock, *Who Killed the British Empire?: An Inquest* (London: Jonathan Cape, 1974), 283. The John Strachey mentioned here is the journalist and Labour politician who served in the Attlee government.

England is a wonderful land: Rudyard Kipling to Charles Eliot Norton, 30 Nov. 1902, in Thomas Pinney ed. *The Letters of Rudyard Kipling*, vol. 3: *1900–1910* (Basingstoke: Macmillan, 1996), 113.

the retired Anglo-Indians: Mulk Raj Anand, *Coolie* (London: Penguin, 1945), 254.

p. 7 above all things, he loved gardening: See 'Orwell to Stanley J. Kunitz and Howard Haycraft', 17 April 1940, 12:148.

he insisted on dressing for dinner: See Gordon Bowker, *George Orwell* (London: Little, Brown, 2003), 232.

He determined to put his baby son's name down for his old school: Ibid., 318.

the England I was taught to love: 'My Country Right or Left', Autumn 1940, 12:272.

one who had been trained for duty: V. S. Pritchett, 'An Anecdote of the Blitz', in *Orwell Remembered*, eds. Audrey Coppard and Bernard Crick (New York: Facts on File, 1984), 167.

p. 7–8 a sort of household god: 'Rudyard Kipling', 23 Jan. 1936, 10:409.

it could never achieve true independence: See 'Comment on Robert Duval's "Whitehall's Road to Mandalay"' and 'Correspondence on Nationalism', 2 April 1943, 15:48.

when his first wife died unexpectedly, he was devastated: See Sylvia Topp, *Eileen: The Making of George Orwell* (London: Unbound, 2020), 407–9.

Yes, she was a good old stick: As remembered by Stephen Spender, quoted in Gordon Bowker, *George Orwell*, 328.

'cranks' of all kinds: See *RWP*, 161–2.

their utter ignorance of the way things actually happen: 'Orwell to Jack Common', 12 Oct. 1938, 11:223.

sleek professors: 'Film Review, *The Great Dictator*', 21 Dec. 1940, 12:315.

it is very difficult to escape: *RWP*, 208–9.

a custodian of Englishness: Rosinka Chaudhuri, 'Introduction', in George Orwell, *Burmese Days* (Oxford: Oxford University Press, 2021), viii.

his admiration of Dickens and *A Shropshire Lad*: See Jacinta Buddicom, *Eric & Us*, The Postscript Edition, ed. Dione Venables (Chichester: Finlay, 2006), 171.

p. 9 that knowledge was importantly shaped by his eastern experience: See Henk Vynckier and John Rodden eds. 'Orienting Orwell: Asian and Global Perspectives on George Orwell', *Concentric: Literary and Cultural Studies* 40:1 (2014) .

the first generation of Blairs: Darcy Moore, 'Orwell's Scottish Ancestry and Slavery', *George Orwell Studies* 5:1 (2020), 16.

a "Provincial" Civil Service: Maung Htin Aung, 'Orwell of the Burma Police', *Asian Affairs* (new series) 4:2 (1973), 182.

p. 10 one of the oldest junior officers in the British Army: D. J. Taylor, *Orwell: The Life* (London: Chatto and Windus, 2003), 39.

we have no record of Orwell being embarrassed: Darcy Moore, 'Orwell and the Appeal of Opium', *George Orwell Studies* 3:1 (2018), 83.

p. 11 Nellie, who would play an important part in Orwell's adult life: See Darcy Moore, 'Orwell's Aunt Nellie', *George Orwell Studies*, 4:2 (2020), 30–44.

p. 12 The dirty work of empire: 'Shooting an Elephant', Autumn 1936, 10:501, and *RWP*, 136.

unlike the other Anglo-Indian boys: Sir John Grotrian, quoted in Stephen Wadhams ed. *The Orwell Tapes* (Vancouver: Locarno Press, 2017), 24.

Blair's destiny apparently lay in the East: John Newsinger, *Orwell's Politics* (Basingstoke: Macmillan, 1999), 2.

He wanted to go to the East: 'A Contemporary in College' (Interview with Steven Runciman), in *Orwell Remembered*, eds. Coppard and Crick, 54.

Blair was intent on Burma: Andrew Gow, quoted in Gordon Bowker, *George Orwell*, 70.

In actual fact: Maung Htin Aung, 'Orwell of the Burma Police', 181.

p. 13 by the tang of uncongenial life: Christopher Hollis, *A Study of George Orwell: The Man and his Works* (New York: Racehorse Publishing, 2017), 27.

Possibly as a consequence of his having shot an elephant: See Gordon Bowker, *George Orwell*, 90–2. See also note 2 to 'Shooting an Elephant' (10:506) and Peter Davison ed. *The Lost Orwell* (London: Timewell Press, 2006), 166. Somebody shot an elephant. It is not absolutely certain that it was Eric Blair.

people who knew him in Burma: See D. J. Taylor, *Orwell: The Life*, 76–7.

p. 14 Their country is so rich: 'How a Nation is Exploited', 4 May 1929, 10:145.

p. 15 a clearer idea of political and social conditions in India: 'Orwell to Alec Houghton Joyce', 12 Feb. 1938, 11:121.

Chapter 2

p. 18 most middle-class boys: 'Inside the Whale', 11 March 1940, 12:93.
chair-like teeth: 'Why I Write', Summer 1946, 18:316.
some animal characteristic: See Rosinka Chaudhuri, 'Introduction', xxv–xxvi.

p. 19 So *coarse*-looking; like some kind of animal: *BD*, 122.
he slit open the body of a live snake: See Gordon Bowker, *George Orwell*, 368.
his rebelliousness at St Cyprian's: See Cyril Connolly, 'Enemies of Promise', in *Orwell Remembered*, eds Coppard and Crick, 32–4.
happy, smiling schoolboy: Jacinta Buddicom, *Eric & Us*, 61.
his childhood was unhappy: See 'Such, Such Were the Joys', 1939?: June 1948?, 19:356–87.
Most of the good memories of my childhood: Ibid., 19:368.
I think that by retaining one's childhood love: 'Some Thoughts on the Common Toad', 12 April 1946, 18:238–41.

p. 20 There is the usual photograph: 'Review of *Baltic Roundabout* by Bernard Newman etc.', 2 Dec. 1939, 11:422.

p. 21 They were white: 'Notes on the Way', 30 March and 6 April 1940, 12:121.
Till recently the Europeans in India: 'As I Please' 45, 20 Oct. 1944, 16:435.

p. 22 You can only rule over a subject race: Ibid., 16:435–6.
a familiar trope of exploration narratives: See Mary Louise Pratt, *Imperial Eyes: Travel Writing and Transculturation* (London: Routledge, 1992), Chapters 3, 9.

p. 23 In a tropical landscape: 'Marrakech', Christmas 1939, 11:418.
Firewood was passing: Ibid., 11:419.
People with brown skins: Ibid., 11:420.

p. 24 shy, wide-eyed Negro look: Ibid., 11:420.
But there is one thought: Ibid., 11:420.

p. 25 It was a kind of secret: Ibid., 11:420.
And really it was almost like watching a flock of cattle: Ibid., 11:420
If *plongeurs* thought at all: *D&O*, 117.

p. 26 the animal instinct: *NEF*, 132.
'common' people seemed almost sub-human: *RWP*, 117.
[T]he actual details of the story: 'Preface to the Ukrainian edition of *Animal Farm*', March 1947, 19:88.

p. 27 the Party taught that the proles were natural inferiors: *NEF*, 74.

p. 28 Proles and animals are free: *NEF*, 75.
She had a round pale face: *RWP*, 15.
the characters of *Animal Farm*: This sometimes involves some awkward moves, such as 'If she could have spoken her thoughts, it would have been to say…', or 'If she herself had had any picture of the future, it had been…', and so on (*AF*, 58).

p. 29 passing up a horrible squalid side-alley: 'The Road to Wigan Pier Diary', 15 Feb. 1936, 10:427.
the monstrous scenery: *RWP*, 14–15.

p. 30   **It came bounding among us:** 'A Hanging', August 1931, 10:208.

p. 31   **This man was not dying:** Ibid., 10:208-9.

the same animal: The point about the kinship of animality is entirely secular and humanistic, and makes nonsense of Hollis's egregious claim that the story's position on capital punishment is 'only tenable if man has a destiny beyond this world'. See Hollis, *A Study of George Orwell*, 40. Hollis also reassures his readers that 'the story has nothing particular to do with the imperial system' (39).

There was a clanking noise: 'A Hanging', August 1931, 10:209.

p. 32   **a homely, jolly scene, after the hanging:** Ibid., 10:210.

We all had a drink together: Ibid., 10:210.

In Moulmein, in Lower Burma: 'Shooting an Elephant', Autumn 1936, 10:501.

p. 33   **No one had the guts to raise a riot:** Ibid., 10:501.

I thought that the greatest joy in the world: Ibid., 10:502.

All I knew was that I was stuck: Ibid., 10:501-2.

the real nature of imperialism: Ibid., 10:502.

I perceived in this moment: Ibid., 10:504.

p. 34   **It seemed to me that it would be murder:** Ibid., 10:504.

In the end I could not stand it any longer: Ibid., 10:506.

A sahib has got to act like a sahib: Ibid., 10:504.

p. 35   **In that instant:** Ibid., 10:505.

it put me legally in the right: Ibid., 10:506.

Chapter 3

p. 36   **Words are such feeble things:** *RWP*, 52.

to make you *see*: Joseph Conrad, 'Preface', in *The Nigger of the 'Narcissus'*, (London: J. M. Dent, 1923), iv.

p. 37   **the very concept of objective truth:** 'Looking Back on the Spanish War', 1942?, 13:504.

In all novels about the East: *RWP*, 101.

I find that anything outrageously strange: Ibid., 100-1.

p. 38   **enormous naturalistic novels:** 'Why I Write', Summer 1946, 18:317-18.

p. 39   **These features stand out:** See *BD*, 14-15.

stories in the East are always vague: See 'Shooting an Elephant', 10:502.

p. 40   **pink villas fifty yards apart:** *BD*, 40.

If we add that the Burmese countryside: 'How a Nation is Exploited', 4 May 1929, 10:143.

p. 41   **The clash of colours hurt one's eyes:** *BD*, 16.

p. 42   **The obliteration of culture by the jungle:** See Douglas Kerr, 'Ruins in the Jungle: Nature and Narrative', in *Asian Crossings: Travel Writing on China, Japan and Southeast Asia*, eds. Steve Clark and Paul Smethurst (Hong Kong: Hong Kong University Press, 2008), 131-40.

Human habitations succumb to the jungle: 'The Judgement of Dungara' (1888) is collected in Rudyard Kipling, *Soldiers Three* (London: Macmillan, 1911), 'The King's Ankus' (1895) and 'Letting in the Jungle' (1894) in Rudyard Kipling, *The Second Jungle Book* (London: Macmillan, 1906). Leonard Woolf published *The Village in the Jungle* (London: Edward Arnold, 1913) two years after his return from Ceylon. 'The Skulls in the Forest' is collected in Hugh Clifford, *Malayan Monochromes* (London: John Murray, 1913).

The more you are in jungle: Leonard Woolf, *Growing: An Autobiography of the Years 1904–1911* (London: Hogarth Press, 1961), 212.

Somerset Maugham's disturbing story, 'Neil MacAdam': W. Somerset Maugham, *Ah King and Other Stories* [1933] (Singapore: Oxford University Press, 1986), 269–339.

p. 43   a lonely, hollow sound: *BD*, 56.

There was a stirring high up in the peepul tree: Ibid., 56–7.

p. 44   Alone, alone, the bitterness of being alone!: Ibid., 57.

One does not often see green pigeons: Ibid., 57.

he will later be seen slaughtering green pigeons: See ibid., 171–2.

shooting garden birds in the nesting season: See Jacinta Buddicom, *Eric & Us*, 101.

p. 45   hated to see his master behave differently: *BD*, 60.

p. 46   I remember reading something in a magazine: Ibid., 122.

She uses it for everything in her life that is cheap: See ibid., 92–4.

He did not realize that this constant striving: Ibid., 137.

the first word little Eric Blair learned to say: See Gordon Bowker, *George Orwell*, 15.

p. 47   our beastliness to the natives: *BD*, 37.

What fun they would have together: Ibid., 283.

She could hardly give it up: Ibid., 172.

p. 48   alien yet kindly: Ibid., 283.

p. 49   could justly claim to be called the ugliest town: *RWP*, 98.

I find that anything outrageously strange: Ibid., 100–1.

It is important to remember this: Ibid., 101.

a lost organic community: See the excellent discussion in Philip Bounds, *Orwell and Marxism* (London: I. B. Tauris, 2016), 191–7.

Chapter 4

p. 50   The road from Mandalay to Wigan: *RWP*, 113.

familiar with Marx's major works: Stephen Ingle, *George Orwell: A Political Life* (Manchester: Manchester University Press, 1994), 24.

he was well aware of the work of British communist writers: See Philip Bounds, *Orwell and Marxism*, 6–14.

p. 51   evil despotism: *RWP*, 138.

It was in this way that my thoughts turned: Ibid., 138.

p. 52   The whites were up and the blacks were down: Ibid., 139.

naïve sense of certitude: David Dwan, *Liberty, Equality, and Humbug: Orwell's Political Ideals* (Oxford: Oxford University Press, 2018), 100.

he had an extremely sensitive nose for it: There is an extensive study of Orwell's sense of smell in John Sutherland, *Orwell's Nose: A Pathological Biography* (London: Reaktion, 2016).

p. 53   So, very early: *RWP*, 117.

not of the type who in England would be called "gentlemen": Ibid., 132.

the lost people, the underground people: *KAF*, 227–8.

p. 54   In fact it is very difficult to escape: *RWP*, 208–9.

essentially middle-class notions: Ibid., 149.

it is only when you meet someone of a different culture: Ibid., 153.

Dressed in a tramp's clothes: *D&O*, 130.

You are a gentleman?: 'The Spike', April 1931, 10:198.

Good Beds for Single Men: *D&O*, 130.

[t]his tramp-monster is no truer to life: Ibid., 203.

you do not solve the class problem: *RWP*, 143.

p. 55   the strangeness of being at last down there: Ibid., 142.

might instructively be linked: Gilroy, *After Empire*, 78.

a tramp is only an Englishman out of work: *D&O*, 205.

of every race in Europe: Ibid., 71.

The *plongeur* was like an 'oriental': See ibid., 118–19.

the life of a *plongeur* was 'beastly': Ibid., 74.

a sort of heavy contentment: Ibid., 90.

p. 56   After all, if they thought at all: See ibid., 117.

On the day when there was a full chamber-pot under the breakfast table: *RWP*, 14.

p. 57   a quite different picture of a working-class interior: See ibid., 107–8.

a warm, decent, deeply human atmosphere: Ibid., 108.

Father, in shirt-sleeves: Ibid., 108.

all Orwell's paradises are literary: For example, the lush pastoral of pre-war Lower Binfield in *Coming Up for Air*, or the 'golden country' in *Nineteen Eighty-Four*.

the memory of working-class interiors: *RWP*, 109.

provided that you can be not only in it but sufficiently *of* it to be taken for granted: Ibid., 108.

the filthy kennels in which I have seen Indian coolies living in Burma: Ibid., 56.

p. 58   I find that anything outrageously strange: Ibid., 100–1.

p. 59   More than anyone else: Ibid., 30.

coolie empire: 'Looking Back on the Spanish War', 1942?, 13:510.

political apathy: 'How a Nation is Exploited', 4 May 1929, 10:143.

I was in Barnsley at the time: 'War-time Diary', 15 April 1941, 12:479–80.

p. 60 Bertolt Brecht's dark joke: See Bertolt Brecht, 'Die Lösung' (1953), translated as 'The Solution' in *The Collected Poems of Bertolt Brecht*, trans. and ed. Tom Kuhn and David Constantine (New York: Liveright, 2019), 1013.

got rid of [his] class-prejudice: *RWP*, 134.

also interpenetrated by a sort of shadowy caste-system: Ibid., 114.

at any rate people who did things: 'Rudyard Kipling', Feb. 1942, 13:153.

colonial repatriates: Sathnam Sanghera, *Empireland*, 95.

`p. 61` In such circumstances you have got to cling to your gentility: *RWP*, 116–17.

soldiers, sailors, clergymen: *CUFA*, 137.

The carved teak furniture: Ibid., 138.

I looked on them as my social and intellectual superiors: Ibid., 139.

the poverty-stricken officer class: Ibid., 137.

these decayed throw-outs: Ibid., 139.

for, after all, we have nothing to lose: *RWP*, 215.

`p. 62` the worst advertisement for Socialism: Ibid., 161.

virtually invisible: John Newsinger, *Orwell's Politics*, 34.

book-trained: *RWP*, 169.

all that dreary tribe: Ibid., 169.

inferior people: Ibid., 205.

One day this summer: Ibid., 161–2.

substituting a prejudice for an argument: John Newsinger, *Orwell's Politics*, 34.

`p. 63` the manners and traditions: *RWP*, 208.

their lower-middle-class Nonconformist prejudices: Ibid., 209.

a striking example of much Orwell was attacking: Richard Hoggart, 'Introduction', in *The Road to Wigan Pier* (London: Penguin, 1989), vi.

it does make some creditable points: See Ruth Dudley Edwards, *Victor Gollancz: A Biography* (London: Victor Gollancz, 1987), 246–8.

anyone holding opinions not held by the majority: See Victor Gollancz, 'Foreword', in *The Road to Wigan Pier* (London: Victor Gollancz, Left Book Club edition, 1937), xvi.

the shameful way in which he was brought up: Ibid., xv, xvii–xviii.

These two seemingly hostile types: 'The Lion and the Unicorn: Socialism and the English Genius', 19 Feb. 1941, 12:405.

`p. 64` The Bloomsbury highbrow: Ibid., 12:407.

a family with the wrong members in control: Ibid., 12:401.

`p. 65` She is not being true to herself: Ibid., 12:432.

Chapter 5

`p. 66` these dreadful Reforms: *BD*, 26.

civilising us, elevating us to their level: Ibid., 39.

p. 67   **black skin:** Ibid., 46.

trying to purge his own language: See 'Orwell to Production Department, Penguin Books', 21 Nov. 1943, 15:338. 'When the book was written a dozen years ago "native" and "Chinaman" were not considered offensive, but nearly all Orientals now object to these terms, and one does not want to hurt anyone's feelings.' This sentence illustrates the problem it describes.

belonged to an inferior and degenerate race: *BD*, 38.

the slimy white man's burden humbug: Ibid., 37.

if you honestly believe yourself to be racially superior: 'As I Please' 45, 20 Oct. 1944, 16:435.

The official holds the Burman down: *BD*, 38.

the British government turned a blind eye: See *Hansard*, House of Commons debate, 27 June 1921, 143:1809. https://api.parliament.uk/historic-hansard/commons/1921/jun/27/rice-burma (accessed 27 July 2021).

p. 68   **Now, after we've been in India:** *BD*, 39.

forests, villages, monasteries, pagodas: Ibid., 40.

when he was living in Paris: 'How a Nation is Exploited', 4 May 1929, 10:142–7.

the territories of empire were not routinely or uniformly profitable: Sathnam Sanghera, *Empireland*, 132. This powerful book is not always reliable about Orwell, however, claiming that he 'hated being sent away from Burma so much that he recalled his experiences in his essay "Such, Such Were the Joys"' (95).

p. 69   **one of the richest in the world:** 'How a Nation is Exploited', 4 May 1929, 10:143.

in the whole book there is just one paragraph: See *BD*, 207–8.

p. 70   **He had a vision of London:** *KAF*, 166–7.

the highest stage of capitalism: See V. I. Lenin, *Imperialism, the Highest Stage of Capitalism* (London: Lawrence, [1917] 1934).

both Flowery Orange and Pekoe Points: *KAF*, 65.

One of the mainstays of civilization: 'A Nice Cup of Tea', 12 Jan. 1946, 18:33–5.

p. 71   **numberless other remote and dimly imagined companies:** *ACD*, 26.

Blifil-Gordon and the Empire: Ibid., 35–6.

Them and their far-flung Empire!: *CUFA*, 45.

Under the capitalist system: *RWP*, 148.

We all live by robbing Asiatic coolies: 'Rudyard Kipling', Feb. 1942, 13:153.

What we always forget: 'Review of *Union Now* by Clarence K. Streit', July 1939, 11:360.

p. 72   **the coloured working class:** 'Orwell to Jack Common', 26 Dec. 1938, 11:260.

the working class in England: See 'The Lion and the Unicorn', 19 Feb. 1941, 12:396.

the only large scale decent action: 'Gandhi in Mayfair. Review of *Beggar My Neighbour* by Lionel Fielden', Sept. 1943, 15:213.

nearly everyone does these things in the East: *RWP*, 138.

every Anglo-Indian is haunted by a secret sense of guilt: See ibid., 135.

it is a corrupting thing to live one's real life in secret: *BD*, 70.

p. 73   **no one capable of describing the atmosphere there:** See 'Review of *Zest for Life* by Johann Wöller etc.', 17 Oct. 1936, 10:508.

in the haggard morning light: *RWP*, 135.

p. 74   **the actual machinery of despotism:** Ibid., 136.

a huge machine which exists to protect British interests: 'Anonymous Review of *Trials in Burma* by Maurice Collis', 9 March 1938, 11:125.

This too looks forward to *Nineteen Eighty-Four*: Surprisingly, however, Dorian Lynskey's otherwise comprehensive account of the roots of *Nineteen Eighty-Four* begins in 1936. Dorian Lynskey, *The Ministry of Truth: A Biography of George Orwell's 1984* (London: Picador, 2019).

The distinctive feature of Orwell's analysis: Philip Bounds, *Orwell and Marxism*, 17.

I perceived in that moment: 'Shooting an Elephant', Autumn 1936, 10:504.

Classical critics: Jürgen Osterhammel, *The Transformation of the World: A Global History of the Nineteenth Century*, trans. Patrick Camiller (Princeton, NJ: Princeton University Press, 2014), 461.

p. 75   **great beef-fed men:** *BD*, 1–2.

Philip Bounds has made the argument: Philip Bounds, *Orwell and Marxism*, 178.

it is not made credibly by local people: Recent research has opened the possibility that Orwell may have met prominent anti-colonial intellectuals in Rangoon through his friendship with Eric Seeley. See Darcy Moore, 'Orwell in Burma: The Two Erics', *George Orwell Studies* 5:2 (2021), 6–24.

p. 76   **There is no mention of this episode:** I cannot find evidence for Stephen Keck's claim that 'the novel is set around 1930, with the Saya San rebellion in the background'. Stephen L. Keck, 'Text and Context: Another Look at *Burmese Days*', *SOAS Bulletin of Burma Research*, 3:1 (Spring 2005), 28.

And after all: 'How a Nation is Exploited', 4 May 1929, 10:144.

nationalism, which was unacceptable too: See 'Notes on Nationalism', Oct. 1945, 17:141–55.

dull and stodgy beyond all measure: 'Orwell to Jack Common', 26 Dec. 1938, 11:260.

at least they had less colour-prejudice: See 'Orwell to Charles Doran', 26 Nov. 1938, 11:239.

p. 77   **utterly debauched by the tourist racket:** 'Orwell to Cyril Connolly', 14 Dec. 1938, 11:253.

they treated their Arab subjects atrociously: See 'Orwell to Jack Common', 26 Dec. 1938, 11:260.

When a subject population rises in revolt: 'Review of *Zest for Life* by Johann Wöller etc.', 17 Oct. 1936, 10:508.

a horrible brainless empire: 'Review of *Mein Kampf* by Adolf Hitler', 21 March 1940, 12:117.

Hitler is only the ghost of our own past rising against us: 'Notes on the Way', 30 March and 6 April 1940, 12:123.

applied to Europe colonialist procedures: Aimé Césaire, *Discourse on Colonialism* [*Discours sur le Colonialisme*], trans. Joan Pinkham (New York: Monthly Review Press, [1950] 1972), 14.

Either we all live in a decent world, or nobody does: 'Review of *Letters on India* by Mulk Raj Anand', 19 March 1943, 15:33.

p. 78 Why else did we go to war this time?: 'Review of *The Road to Serfdom* by F. A. Hayek and *The Mirror of the Past* by K. Zilliacus', 9 April 1944, 16:152.

Britain could not become a genuinely socialist country: See 'The British General Election', Nov. 1945, 17:340.

every revolutionary opinion draws part of its strength: *RWP*, 146.

a member for about a year in 1938–39: See 'Why I Join the I.L.P.', 24 June 1938, 11:167–9.

the British political party most committed to the abolition of empire: See Priyamvada Gopal, *Insurgent Empire* (London: Verso, 2019).

p. 79 James Maxton and Fenner Brockway: See the discussion in Peter Marks, *George Orwell the Essayist: Literature, Politics and the Periodical Culture* (London: Continuum, 2011), 75–7.

Once check that stream of dividends: '*The Lion and the Unicorn*', 19 Feb. 1941, 12:425.

the average woman in the fish queue: 'Do Our Colonies Pay?', 8 March 1946, 18:144.

he would never have predicted Gandhi's success: See 'Orwell to Dwight Macdonald', 2 May 1948, 19:328.

p. 80 the Jews, the Balts, the Indonesians: 'As I Please' 72, 7 Feb. 1947, 19:41.

empire's structure of government: Robert J. C. Young, 'Postcolonial Remains', *New Literary History* 43:1 (Winter 2012), 31.

The fact is: 'As I Please', 72, 7 Feb. 1947, 19:41.

Chapter 6

p. 81 poem about a tiger with chair-like teeth: See 'Why I Write', Summer 1946, 18:316.

The books one reads in childhood: 'Riding Down from Bangor', 22 Nov. 1946, 18:493.

The Elephant is a sagacious beast: *ACD*, 212.

p. 82 J for the Junk: 'As I Please', 75A, 27 Feb. 1947, 19:50.

The ice cupboard in the Hotel X: *D&O*, 60.

From Greenland's icy mountains: Reginald Heber, 'From Greenland's icy mountains ' (1819), https://victorianweb.org/religion/hymns/heber1.html (accessed 24 July 2021).

p. 83 The Orient could also be the site of glamorous adventure: See Martin Green, *Dreams of Adventure, Deeds of Empire* (London: Routledge and Kegan Paul, 1980).

Among other 'good bad books': 'Good Bad Books', 2 Nov. 1945, 17:348.

The East is a career: Benjamin Disraeli, *Tancred or the New Crusade* (London: Longmans, Green, [1847] 1919), 141.

p. 84   If we add that the Burmese countryside: 'How a Nation is Exploited', 4 May 1929, 10:143.

When nationalism first became a religion: *RWP*, 103.

p. 85   sly, cowardly and licentious: Ibid., 104.

The Myth of the Lazy Native: Syed Hussein Alatas, *The Myth of the Lazy Native* (London: Frank Cass, 1977).

World history travels from East to West: G. W. F. Hegel, *Lectures on the Philosophy of World History* (New York: Cambridge University Press, 1975), 179.

p. 86   *nothing ever happened* in the Comstock family: *KAF*, 41, 66.

sleeping the deep, deep sleep of England: *HTC*, 187.

anywhere south of Gibraltar or east of Suez: 'Marrakech', Christmas 1939, 11:418.

veritable hordes of Indians: 'How a Nation is Exploited', 4 May 1929, 10:146.

We Anglo-Indians: *BD*, 37.

p. 87   incapable of believing that anything would ever change: See 'Orwell to Herbert Read', 4 Jan. 1939, 11:313.

but there wasn't much news: *CUFA*, 9.

p. 88   Every broadcast script was vetted: For the BBC in wartime, see Asa Briggs, *The History of Broadcasting in the United Kingdom*, vol. 3, *The War of Words* (London: Oxford University Press, 1970).

in fact have contained very little that I would not sign: 'To Eastern Service Director', 15 Oct. 1942, 14:101.

to "put across" the British view: Quoted in C. Fleay and M. L. Sanders, 'Looking into the Abyss: George Orwell at the BBC', *Journal of Contemporary History*, 24:3 (1989), 508.

our rule in India: 'Orwell to Geoffrey Gorer', 15 Sept. 1937, 11:80.

p. 89   an anti-fascist rather than imperialist standpoint: 'To Eastern Service Director', 15 Oct. 1942, 14:101.

Indians should decide their own future: Orwell's views can be usefully read alongside Mulk Raj Anand, *Letters on India* (London: Labour Book Service, 1942), supposedly addressed to a young English factory worker.

But in order to follow the events of this war: 'Weekly News Review 4', 3 Jan. 1942, 13:115.

p. 90   in its true perspective: 'News Review 38', 5 Sept. 1942, 14:6.

the ambition of regimes of colonial representation: James B. Ryan, *Picturing Empire: Photography and the Visualization of the British Empire* (London: Reaktion, 1997), 144.

the picture of a war of Asia against Europe: 'Weekly News Review 6', 17 Jan. 1942, 13:126.

When we look at the history of this war: 'Weekly News Review 22', 16 May
1942, 13:324.
p. 91 Willy-nilly, India is already in the struggle: Ibid., 13:324.
immensely more important: 'Newsletter 10', 14 Feb. 1942, 13:180.
p. 92 The thing that will defeat them: 'Weekly News Review 22', 16 May 1942, 327.
our broadcasts are utterly useless: 'War-Time Diary', 5 Oct. 1942, 14:76. See
'Laurence Brander's Report on Indian Programmes', 11 Jan. 1943, 15:343–61.
the defences of India: 'Weekly News Review 56', 16 Jan. 1943, 14:315. Like so many
of his predictions, this was wrong. In March 1944, Japanese forces, supported
by the troops of Subhas Chandra Bose's Indian National Army, attempted an
invasion of Manipur state in northeast India, but were eventually repulsed.
the sordid bargain: 'As I Please 56', 26 Jan. 1945, 17:30.
More and more obviously: 'You and the Atom Bomb', 19 Oct. 1945, 17:320.
p. 93 moving towards a common form of tyranny: See John Newsinger, *Hope Lies in the
Proles: George Orwell and the Left* (London: Pluto Press, 2018), 61–3.
East Asia, dominated by China: 'You and the Atom Bomb', 19 Oct. 1945, 17:320.
anywhere south of Gibraltar or east of Suez: 'Marrakech', Christmas 1939, 11:418.
p. 94 Proles and animals are free: *NEF*, 75.
If there was hope, it *must* lie in the proles: Ibid., 72.

Chapter 7

p. 95 Just wondering: *CUFA*, 140.
many feminists: See for example Daphne Patai, *The Orwell Mystique* (Boston:
University of Massachusetts Press, 1984), Deirdre Beddoe, 'Hindrances and
Help-Meets: Women in the Writings of George Orwell', in *Inside the Myth:
Orwell: Views from the Left*, ed. Christopher Norris (London: Lawrence and
Wishart, 1984), 139–54, Beatrix Campbell, 'Orwell: Paterfamilias or Big Brother?',
in *Inside the Myth*, ed. Christopher Norris (London: Lawrence and Wishart,
1984), 128–36, Leslie Tentler, '"I'm Not Literary Dear": George Orwell on Women
and Family', in *The Future of Nineteen Eighty-Four*, ed. Ejner Jensen (Ann Arbor:
University of Michigan Press, 1984), 47–65, Ben Clarke, *Orwell in Context:
Communities, Myths, Values* (Basingstoke: Palgrave Macmillan, 2007), Ivett
Csaszar, 'Orwell and Women's Issues: a Shadow over the Champion of Decency',
Eger Journal of English Studies X (2010), 39–56, Kristin Bluemel, 'The Intimate
Orwell: Women's Productions, Feminist Consumption', in *Orwell Today*, ed.
Richard Lance Keeble (Bury St Edmunds: Abramis, 2012), 15–29, Ensieh
Shabanirad and Seyyed Mohammad Marandi, 'Edward Said's *Orientalism* and
the Representation of Oriental Women in George Orwell's *Burmese Days*',
International Letters of Social and Humanistic Sciences 60 (2015), 22–33.

p. 96   **The father of the future Lord Beveridge:** See 'Review of *India Called Them* by Lord
         Beveridge', 1 Feb. 1948, 19:262.
         typical of the ordinary Englishwoman's attitude: 'Orwell to F. Tennyson Jesse', 14
         March 1946, 18:128.
         but only to speak to her servants: E. M. Forster, *A Passage to India* (London: Edward
         Arnold, 1924), 40.

p. 97   **Her servants live in terror of her:** *BD*, 300.
         so colourless that she was just like one of the faded photos on the wall: *CUFA*, 139.
         The god has hurt himself?: *BD*, 196.
         the unwelcome arrival of Mrs Lackersteen: See ibid., 26.
         [t]arts by the score: Ibid., 240.
         The woman oiled her hair of coal: From 'The Lesser Evil', 1922–27?, 10:93.

p. 98   **Orwell patronized prostitutes from time to time:** See Sylvia Topp, *Eileen*, 251. The
         Berber girl may not have been a prostitute.
         gets drunk and picks up a prostitute: *KAF*, 196–7.
         Winston Smith remembers his own wife's frigidity: *NEF*, 68–72.
         an anecdote told by his young Parisian friend Charlie: See *D&O*, 6–11.
         She was twenty years old, perhaps: Ibid., 10.

p. 99   **a distilled version of the modern political scene:** 'Raffles and Miss Blandish', 28
         Aug. 1944, 16:355.
         No contrast could have been stranger: *BD*, 88–9.
         If she wept and grovelled: Ibid., 161.

p. 100   **He stood looking down at her:** Ibid., 160.
         endless procession of Burmese women: Ibid., 203.
         discussions of *Burmese Days*: Daphne Patai, *The Orwell Mystique*, 21–2.
         page after page of pothooks: *ACD*, 210.

p. 101   **her chosen form of self-discipline:** Ibid., 8.
         Consider what your future will be like: Ibid., 280.
         dreadful destiny: *RWP*, 15.
         repelled: 'Review of *India Called Them* by Lord Beveridge', 1 Feb. 1948, 19:261.
         this subject is a very important one: 'Orwell to Naomi Mitchison', 4 Aug.
         1942, 13:451.
         He had this ultramasculine attitude: Kay Ekevall, quoted in *The Orwell Tapes*, ed.
         Stephen Wadhams, 83.

p. 102   **I want you to feel free:** *KAF*, 256.
         in sympathy, but not so active: Jacinta Buddicom, *Eric & Us*, 14.
         His aunt Nellie: See Darcy Moore, 'Orwell's Aunt Nellie'.
         lacked the gentle art of seduction: Gordon Bowker, *George Orwell*, 366.
         assuring women friends that he was sterile: See 'Orwell to Anne Popham', 18 April
         1946, 18:249.

p. 103   **a little trollop:** Quoted in Gordon Bowker, *George Orwell*, 112.
         I felt towards a Burman almost as I felt towards a woman: *RWP*, 132.
         bright and debonair: *KAF*, 138.

the authorial voice is always in awe of Rosemary: Loraine Saunders, *The Unsung Mastery of George Orwell* (Aldershot: Ashgate, 2008), 96.

Rosemary laughs at him: See *KAF*, 127.

p. 104 once again things were happening in the Comstock family: Ibid., 277.

She [Hermione] lay quiet: Ibid., 109.

utter ignorance of the way things actually happen: 'Orwell to Jack Common', 12 Oct. 1938, 11:223.

p. 105 the power of instinctive feeling and the continuity of love: Jeffrey Meyers, *Orwell: Wintry Conscience of a Generation* (New York: Norton, 2000), 284.

a rebel from the waist downwards: *NEF*, 163.

This reading has been interestingly canvassed by Richard Lance Keeble: See Richard Lance Keeble, *George Orwell, the Secret State and the Making of Nineteen Eighty-Four* (Bury St Edmunds: Abramis, 2020), 12–25.

p. 106 George Bowling gives an affectionate portrait of his mother: *CUFA*, 48–56.

absolutely no warmth of contact: 'A Great Feeling for Nature' (Interview with Mabel Fierz), in *Orwell Remembered*, eds. Coppard and Crick, 94.

had always been detached: Avril Dunn, 'My Brother, George Orwell', in *Orwell Remembered*, eds. Coppard and Crick, 29.

it is rash to assume: 'Such, Such Were the Joys', 1939?: June 1948?, 19:384.

Looking back on my childhood: Ibid., 19:384.

p. 107 *there was a middle-aged woman*: *NEF*, 10.

many Jewish refugees were trying to cross the Mediterranean: See Fritz Liebreich, *Britain's Naval and Political Reaction to the Illegal Immigration of Jews to Palestine 1945–48* (London: Routledge, 2005). See also Janice Ho, 'Europe, Refugees, and *Nineteen Eighty-Four*', in *The Cambridge Companion to Nineteen Eighty-Four*, ed. Nathan Waddell (Cambridge: Cambridge University Press, 2020), 141–54.

p. 108 to the ancient time: *NEF*, 32.

the private realm: For a good discussion of 'the private realm', see Stephen Ingle, *George Orwell: A Political Life*, 98–102.

The prole woman who sings: See *NEF*, 227–9.

the large drunk woman who sits on Winston's lap: See ibid., 239–40.

it must have come from the Indian Ocean: See ibid., 99.

a gesture of the arm made by his mother: Ibid., 167.

The dream was still vivid in his mind: Ibid., 171.

p. 109 One can love a child: 'Such, Such Were the Joys', 1939?: June 1948?, 384.

Chapter 8

p. 110 passionate nationalistic feeling: 'Notes on Nationalism', Oct. 1945, 17:142. It is arguable that Jewry is an exception in this list of 'non-nations'. In the Bible, the Jews are described as a nation.

p. 111 You can only rule over a subject race: 'As I Please' 45, 20 Oct. 1944, 16:435.

The East London women are pretty: *D&O*, 136.

all races, even black and white: Ibid., 170.

gypsies, dark as Indians: See *ACD*, 111.

p. 112 native and European alike, quite amicably: 'A Hanging', Aug. 1931, 10:210.

countless Mongol tribes: 'How a Nation is Exploited', 4 May 1929, 10:143.

passed an exam in Shaw-Karen: See Maung Htin Aung, 'Orwell of the Burma Police', 185.

The whites were up and the blacks were down: *RWP*, 139.

reveals continuities in racial attitudes: Elizabeth Kolsky, *Colonial Justice in British India* (Cambridge: Cambridge University Press, 2010), 232–3.

old rhetorical strategy: Peter Marks, *George Orwell the Essayist*, 146.

The story is told: 'Notes on the Way', 30 March and 6 April 1940, 12:121–2.

p. 113 In general: Thant Myint-U, *The Making of Modern Burma* (Cambridge: Cambridge University Press, 2001), 243–4.

p. 114 I have never wavered: Quoted in David Gilmour, *Curzon: Imperial Statesman* (New York: Farrar, Strauss and Giroux, 2003), 166.

Provided they were given no freedom: *BD*, 28.

I dare say it's unfair in some ways: 'Orwell to F. Tennyson Jesse', 4 March 1946, 18:126.

slaughter them in bloody heaps: *BD*, 259.

there is no justice for us in your courts: Ibid., 257.

This applied even to their conduct: See 'Democracy in the British Army', Sept. 1939, 11:406.

orientals could be very provoking: See *RWP*, 138.

p. 115 Wintringham said that even in Spain: 'War-Time Diary', 18 April 1942, 13:276.

he describes the doctor as stinking: See *BD*, 21.

a picture of herself being raped: ibid., 142.

In Burma, it was different: For Burma and smell, see John Sutherland, *Orwell's Nose*, 88–107.

The essential point was: *BD*, 132.

I felt towards a Burman: Ibid., 132, 133.

p. 116 pansy-left circles: 'Rudyard Kipling', Feb. 1942, 13:151.

benevolent imperialism: 'Review of *The Story of Burma* by F. Tennyson Jesse; *Burma Pamphlets No. 7, The Burman: an Appreciation* by C. J. Richards; *Burma Pamphlets No. 8, The Karens of Burma* by Harry I. Marshall', 24 Feb. 1946, 18:125.

Her face was powdered so thickly: *BD*, 108–9.

p. 117 What was she doing in this place?: Ibid., 108.

Innumerable remembered faces: *RWP*, 138.

And unfortunately I had not trained myself: Ibid., 137.

p. 118 a sea of yellow faces: 'Shooting an Elephant', Autumn 1936, 503.

grey-faced maniacal creature: *BD*, 286.

Even the thickest-skinned Anglo-Indian: *RWP*, 134.

to smash faces in with a sledge-hammer: *NEF*, 16.

If you want a picture of the future: Ibid., 280.

the totalitarian state: Janice Ho, 'Europe, Refugees, and *Nineteen Eighty-Four*', 142.

Winston and Julia meet in the crowd: See *NEF*, 120–3.

p. 119 Foreigners, whether from Eurasia or from Eastasia: Ibid., 122.

the wretched prisoners: *RWP*, 136.

In the last truck: *NEF*, 122.

With hands locked together: Ibid., 123.

p. 120 Either we all live in a decent world, or nobody does: 'Review of *Letters on India* by Mulk Raj Anand', 19 March 1943, 15:33.

The battle against Amery: Ibid., 15:33.

far vaster injustice: 'Review of *Union Now* by Clarence K. Streit', July 1939, 11:360.

that between slave and master: 'How a Nation is Exploited', 4 May 1929, 10:147.

only the ghost of our own past rising against us: 'Notes on the Way', 30 March and 6 April 1940, 12:123.

the drift for many decades: 'You and the Atom Bomb', 19 Oct. 1945, 17:321.

Poles, Russians, Jews and political prisoners of every race: 'Looking Back on the Spanish War', [1942?], 13:505.

In the whole of Greek and Roman history: Ibid., 13:505.

p. 121 In spite of the quite obvious necessities of war: 'As I Please' 2, 10 Dec. 1943, 16:23.

In Asiatic eyes: Ibid., 16:23. Here is another instance of Orwell's reluctance to give credit to the international socialist movement.

one's information about these matters: Ibid., 16:24.

tilling his tiny patch of soil: 'Review of *Subject India* by Henry Noel Brailsford', 20 Nov. 1943, 15:332.

p. 122 I remember my feeling almost of horror: *HTC*, 56.

in an incredibly primitive way: 'Orwell to George Woodcock', 2 Sept. 1946, 18:385.

Scotland is almost an occupied country: 'As I Please' 73, 14 Feb. 1947, 19:44.

unthinkingly repeated the 'polite' prejudice of his class: Andrew Palmer, 'Orwell and Antisemitism', *Jewish Quarterly*, 45:4 (1998), 41. See also Richard Bradford, *Orwell: A Man of Our Time*, 65–82.

p. 123 because it causes people to avert their eyes: 'London Letter', July–Aug. 1943, 15:111.

For instance, in March of this year Himmler: 'English News Commentary 51', 12 Dec. 1942, 14:234.

one of the most shocking descriptions of Nazi terrorism: 'Review of *Arrival and Departure* by Arthur Koestler, and *Jordan's Tunis Diary* by Philip Jordan', 9 Dec. 1943, 16:20. An extract from Koestler's book, about the deportation of Jews from Poland, was published in *Horizon*, and may have been the first news of the Holocaust to reach some readers.

p. 124 it is almost impossible to mention Jews in print: 'Orwell to Roy Fuller', 7 March 1944, 16:116.

true anti-Semitism: 'Review of *The Devil and the Jews* by Joshua Trachtenberg and *Why I Am a Jew* by Edmond Fleg, translated by Victor Gollancz', 30 Jan. 1944, 16:83.

Clearly the neurosis lies very deep: 'As I Please 11', 1 Feb. 1944, 16:92.

an essay about anti-Semitism: 'Anti-Semitism in Britain', April 1945, 17:64-70. This was published in the month when Richard Dimbleby made his famous broadcast report from the liberation of the concentration camp at Belsen, though Orwell's essay was written in February.

All I would say with confidence: Ibid., 17:69.

But you can at least recognise: 'Notes on Nationalism', Oct. 1945, 155.

p. 125   but with the proviso: 'Review of *Last Essays* by J. A. Spender; *Palestine, Land of Promise* by Walter Clay Lowdermilk; *Selected Writing* by Reginald Moore', 23 Nov. 1944, 16:470.

he was in contact with Burmese groups: See 'Diary', 18 April 1948, 19:320.

the villain in *Burmese Days*: 'Perhaps he was protecting himself from the possibility of a libel action, as the real U Po Kyin was a young man, not a magistrate, slim of figure, and had an absolutely clean service record. Or was the choice of the name an indication of a hidden resentment against a Burmese officer who always remained senior to him by two places? The existence of such a hidden resentment would explain why Blair did not attempt to become friendly with U Po Kyin, as it was Blair's nature to champion the outcast, the misfit, the odd man in any section of society.' Maung Htin Aung, 'Orwell of the Burma Police', 185.

Chapter 9

p. 126   There is extremely little hostility: Geoffrey Gorer, *Exploring English Character* (London: Cresset Press, 1955), 213.

almost like a nurse handling a child: *KAF*, 201.

I'm the ordinary middling kind: *CUFA*, 174.

the barges on the miry river: *HTC*, 187.

p. 127   If you have grown up in that sort of atmosphere: 'Inside the Whale', 11 March 1940, 12:103.

carrying out searches: Burma Police Department, *The Burma Police Training School Manual* (Rangoon: Government Printing and Stationery, Burma, 1939), 22-4.

As part of standard equipment: See Burma Police Department, *Police Supply and Clothing Manual for Burma* (Rangoon: Government Printing and Stationery, Burma, 1925) .

acting as an armed reserve: J. S. Furnivall, *Colonial Policy and Practice: A Comparative Study of Burma and Netherlands India* (New York: New York University Press, 1956), 178.

p. 128 In the decade up to 1921: Ibid., 139. Dacoity is gang robbery with violence.
one of those huge durable jails: *BD*, 15.
the prison population outgrew them: See J. S. Furnivall, *Colonial Policy and Practice*, 139.
In Moulmein, in Lower Burma: 'Shooting an Elephant', Autumn 1936, 10:501.
This relates to an actual incident: See Maung Htin Aung, 'George Orwell in Burma', in *The World of George Orwell*, ed. Miriam Gross (London: Weidenfeld and Nicolson, 1972), 24–5.
nothing less than a complete dismantling of existing institutions: Thant Myint-U, *The Making of Modern Burma*, 2–3.

p. 129 by the machinery of a foreign legal system: J. S. Furnivall, *Colonial Policy and Practice*, 144.
the bodyguards of the possessing class: *HTC*, 98.
nearly all the rich people in the country: Maurice Collis, *Trials in Burma* (London: Faber and Faber, 1938), 223.
In the police: See Michael Shelden, *Orwell: The Authorised Biography* (London: Minerva, 1992), 101, 119–20.
Her [Burma's] military forces: Sir Reginald Craddock, *The Dilemma in India*, quoted by J. S. Furnivall, *Colonial Policy and Practice*, 158.

p. 130 racial tension became more acute: J. S. Furnivall, *Colonial Policy and Practice*, 165. See also Maurice Collis, *Into Hidden Burma: An Autobiography* (London: Faber and Faber, 1953).
a latent despotism: 'How a Nation is Exploited', 4 May 1929, 10:144.
a natural hatred of authority: 'Why I Write', 18:319.

p. 131 the terror, the hatred, the howling relatives: 'Inside the Whale', 11 March 1940, 12:103.
The wretched prisoners: *RWP*, 136.
because of the brutal work they had to do: Ibid., 136.
The American watched it: Ibid., 136.
the dirty work of empire: 'Shooting an Elephant', Autumn 1936, 10:501, and *RWP*, 136.

p. 132 The suspect turned his grey face: *BD*, 75.
the whole machinery of so-called justice: *RWP*, 136.
Once imprisoned: Maung Htin Aung, *A History of Burma* (New York: Columbia University Press, 1967), 275.
a tramp is only an Englishman out of work: *D&O*, 205.

p. 133 Can't do anything unless you put your foot down: *BD*, 30.

p. 134 it left a great discretion to the executive: Maurice Collis, *Trials in Burma*, 88. Collis quotes the relevant section of the law: 'Whoever by words, either spoken or written, or by signs, or by visible representation, or otherwise brings or attempts to bring into hatred or contempt, or excites or attempts to excite disaffection towards His Majesty or the Government established by law in British India, shall be punished, etc'. Ibid., 88.

to find Sengupta guilty: Sengupta's anti-British activities led to frequent arrests. He was to die in prison in India in 1933.

In theory he is administering an impartial system of justice: 'Review of Maurice Collis, *Trials in Burma*', 9 March 1938, 11:125.

p. 135   doing justice to people: Leonard Woolf, *The Journey Not the Arrival Matters: An Autobiography of the Years 1939–1969* (London: Hogarth Press, 1969), 208, 207.

his crime of violence: *Prima facie* Ellis has voluntarily caused grievous hurt to the boy, an action punishable with imprisonment of up to ten years, and a fine. See *The Abridged Law Manual for Sub-Inspectors of Police Burma* (Rangoon: Government Printing and Stationery, Burma, 1926), 73.

every white man is a cog: *BD*, 69.

the non-military middle class: 'Wells, Hitler and the World State', Aug. 1941, 12:538.

p. 136   a pawn in an enormous struggle: *HTC*, 189.

The Civil Guards: Ibid., 98.

Now, in April to June 1937: A fascinating sidelight on these events is given in Marc Wildemeersch, *George Orwell's Commander in Spain: The Enigma of Georges Kopp* (London: Thames River Press, 2013), 31–61.

Barcelona during the crackdown: Dorian Lynskey, *The Ministry of Truth*, 17–18.

I have no particular love: *HTC*, 104.

p. 137   The Valencian Assault Guards: Ibid., 125.

This was not a round-up of criminals: Ibid., 165.

unsupported statements in the communist press: See ibid., 238–42.

Eileen, who worked in the Independent Labour Party office: See Sylvia Topp, *Eileen*, 163–88.

p. 138   In India you are not judged for what you do: *BD*, 139.

It was no use hanging on to the English notion: *HTC*, 165.

all the while a hateful feeling: Ibid., 128.

half the world is ruled by secret police forces: 'As I Please' 63, 29 Nov. 1946, 18:504.

with the police one jump behind me: *HTC*, 189.

Chapter 10

p. 139   I understood to perfection: 'Such, Such Were the Joys', 1939?: June 1948, 19:379. He misremembered the line as 'The armies of unalterable law'.

And Sir Herbert Crum: *CUFA*, 182–3.

p. 140   and all this, it seemed: 'Such, Such Were the Joys', 19:366.

his natural hatred of authority: See 'Why I Write', Summer 1946, 18:319.

Much as he may have loathed it: See Orwell to Brenda Salkeld, late June 1931 (unpublished), quoted in Gordon Bowker, *George Orwell*, 127.

Indeed, by the time of the impeachment: Nasser Hussain, *The Jurisprudence of Emergency: Colonialism and the Rule of Law* (Ann Arbor: University of Michigan Press, 2003), 3.

p. 141   the sole justification: Quoted in David Gilmour, *Curzon: Imperial Statesman*, 166.
Our government is based: J. S. Furnivall, *Colonial Policy and Practice*, 175.
The law of England is admired: Maurice Collis, *Trials in Burma*, 135.
unswerving British justice: *BD*, 40.
it is always necessary: *RWP*, 137.
the greatest joy in the world: 'Shooting an Elephant', 10:502.
the natives know the law: *BD*, 30.

p. 142   It's all this law and order: Ibid., 29, 30.
But that won't do nowadays: Ibid., 250.
We seem to have no *authority*: Ibid., 26.
martial law was never proclaimed in the home country: See Nasser Hussain, *The Jurisprudence of Emergency*, 99–132.

p. 143   Special courts were set up: This is the legal background for the central incident in Paul Scott's novels of the Raj, Paul Scott, *The Jewel in the Crown* (London: Pan Macmillan, [1966] 1988) and Paul Scott, *The Day of the Scorpion* (London: Pan, [1968] 1988) .
issues in *Burmese Days* rehearse *Nineteen Eighty-Four*: See Firas A. J. Al-Jubouri, 'The End was Contained in the Beginning', *George Orwell Studies* 1:1 (2016), 73–88.
'they' cannot arrest you: *HTC*, 181.
one sent him along to the jail: *BD*, 27.

p. 144   Orwell remembered punching servants: *RWP*, 138.
The sahib will give the order!: *BD*, 263.
a creature of the despotism: Ibid., 70.
There's no law telling us to be beastly: Ibid., 151.
Free speech is unthinkable: Ibid., 69.

p. 145   Orwell's unhappiness with happiness: David Dwan, *Liberty, Equality, and Humbug*, 171.

p. 146   I see now where it is that we part company: 'Imaginary Interview: George Orwell and Jonathan Swift', 2 Nov. 1942, 14:160.
But is this simply part of the order of Nature?: *AF*, 3–4.

p. 147   These Seven Commandments: Ibid., 15.
rebelling against the laws of Nature: Ibid., 25.
Four legs good: Ibid., 21.

p. 148   in a gruff soldierly style: Ibid., 38.
No animal shall sleep in a bed *with sheets*: Ibid,, 45, 61.
You do not imagine: Ibid., 23.
Only old Benjamin: Ibid., 87.

p. 149   a discipline and an orderliness: Ibid., 92.
the title deeds: Ibid., 93.
the law was what the police chose to make it: *HTC*, 165.
thoughtcrime will be literally impossible: *NEF*, 55.
The mad theory: John E. Joseph explains why the theory of Newspeak is mad from a linguistic point of view, in John E. Joseph, 'Orwell on Language and Politics', in

Landmarks in Linguistic Thought II: The Western Tradition in the Twentieth Century, eds. John E. Joseph, Nigel Love, and Talbot J. Taylor (London: Routledge, 2001), 29–42.

The intention was to make speech: *NEF*, 321, 322.

p. 150 **when the white man turns tyrant:** See 'Shooting an Elephant', Autumn 1936, 10:504.

'Except—': *NEF*, 55–6.

p. 151 **they will never revolt in a million years:** See ibid., 274.

a group whose humanity depends on their dehumanization: Elinor Taylor, 'The Problem of Hope: Orwell's Workers', in *The Cambridge Companion to Nineteen Eighty-Four*, ed. Nathan Waddell (Cambridge: Cambridge University Press, 2020), 167. This essay is a very good recent discussion of Orwell's representation of the proles.

Proles and animals are free: *NEF*, 75.

Chapter 11

p. 152 **It could only be written:** 'Inside the Whale', 11 March 1940, 12:103. Auden's phrase occurs in the poem 'Spain 1937'.

p. 153 **Britain cannot become a genuinely Socialist country:** 'The British General Election', Nov. 1945, 17:340.

like a long bout of some painful illness: See 'Why I Write', Summer 1946, 18:320.

p. 154 **the story-teller who was so important to my childhood:** 'Rudyard Kipling', 23 Jan. 1936, 10:410.

Woolf said he couldn't decide: See Leonard Woolf, *Growing: An Autobiography of the Years 1904–1911*, 46.

Sir George Younghusband: See editor's note 13 to 'Rudyard Kipling', Feb. 1942, 13:161.

Kipling-haunted little clubs: *BD*, 69.

p. 155 **Kipling's books are essentially about British India:** 'They Throw New Light on India', 9 Aug. 1945, 17:243.

a sort of household god: See 'Rudyard Kipling', 23 Jan. 1936, 10:409.

no sympathy for malcontents and subversives: Even a rare figure like McIntosh Jellaludin in the tale 'To be Filed for Reference', an Oxford man who has 'gone native' in India, has detached himself entirely from the imperial project but is neither a malcontent nor a subversive.

T. S. Eliot's edition of a selection of Kipling's poetry: T.S. Eliot, ed., *A Choice of Kipling's Verse* (London: Faber, 1941).

For my own part I worshipped Kipling at thirteen: 'Rudyard Kipling', 23 Jan. 1936, 10:409.

seems to have been the first English writer to notice: 'They Throw New Light on India', 9 Aug. 1945, 17:243.

p. 156   The imperialism of the 'eighties and 'nineties: 'Rudyard Kipling', 23 Jan. 1936, 10:410. Lord Beaverbrook was the founder of the Empire Free Trade Crusade which campaigned for the Empire to become a free trade bloc.

the anxiety of influence: See Harold Bloom, *The Anxiety of Influence*, 2nd edition (Oxford: Oxford University Press, 1997).

It is no use pretending: 'Rudyard Kipling', Feb. 1942, 13:151.

a denunciation of power politics: Ibid., 13:151.

No one, in our time: Ibid., 13:152.

p. 157   the "box-wallah" calls the tune: Ibid., 13:153.

a universal foreignness: 'Preface', in T. S. Eliot, *A Choice of Kipling's Verse*, 23.

an awareness of responsibility: Ibid., 25.

The nineteenth-century Anglo-Indians: 'Rudyard Kipling', Feb. 1942, 13:153.

one was bound to think of him: 'Rudyard Kipling', 23 Jan. 1936, 10:410.

the refined people who have sniggered at him: 'Rudyard Kipling', Feb. 1942, 13:151.

Kipling...is generally talking about things that are of urgent interest: Ibid., 13:157.

always good for a snigger: Ibid., 13:151.

p. 158   the new novels out from England: *BD*, 66.

p. 159   every important event in Europe: 'Inside the Whale', 11 March 1940, 12:97. Orwell places Somerset Maugham and Lytton Strachey in this group of 1920s writers, but does not include Virginia Woolf among them.

good prose is like a window pane: 'Why I Write', Summer 1946, 320.

as Alex Woloch has shown: See Alex Woloch, *Or Orwell: Writing and Democratic Socialism* (Cambridge, MA: Harvard University Press, 2016).

anyone sensitive enough to be touched by the *Zeitgeist*: 'Inside the Whale', 11 March 1940, 12:105.

the patriotism of the deracinated: Ibid., 12:103.

p. 160   On the whole the literary history of the 'thirties: Ibid., 12:105.

literature, in the form in which we know it: Ibid., 12:110.

one of Orwell's great essays: For fuller discussion, see Peter Marks, *George Orwell the Essayist*, 94–8. Also essential reading is Philip Bounds, *Orwell and Marxism*, 105–16.

a person to whom murder is at most a word: 'Inside the Whale', 11 March 1940, 12:103. Auden's phrase occurs in the poem 'Spain 1937', which he later suppressed.

to make political writing into an art: 'Why I Write', Summer 1946, 18:319.

merely an anachronism: 'Inside the Whale', 11 March 1940, 110–11.

p. 161   Pearl Buck: See 'Review of *The Good Earth* by Pearl S. Buck', June 1931, 10:205–6.

J. R. Ackerley's comic memoir: Forster, Thompson, Collis, and Ackerley are discussed in 'They Throw New Light on India', 9 Aug. 1945, 17:242–4.

it was possible to think of an Indian: Ibid., 17:243.

p. 162   'The Vice-Consul': W. Somerset Maugham, *On a Chinese Screen* (Oxford: Oxford University Press, [1922] 1985), 225–30.

a kind of stoical resignation: 'Inside the Whale', 11 March 1940, 12:97.

his power of telling a story straightforwardly: 'Orwell to Stanley J. Kunitz and Howard Haycraft', 17 April 1940, 12:148.

of late years: 'Why I Write', Summer 1946, 18:320.

Conrad was one model of what a writer could be: See Douglas Kerr, 'George Orwell's Conrad', *George Orwell Studies* 1 (2016), 21–36.

the excellence of his political novels: 'Review of *The Great Tradition* by F. R. Leavis', 6 Feb. 1949, 20:37.

He came from a country that had been wiped off the map: See 'Review of *The Nigger of the Narcissus* etc.', 28 June 1945, 17:196.

p. 163   a good idea for a novel: 'Orwell to David Astor', 21 Dec. 1948, 19:485.

A Smoking-Room Story: See the drafts and notes for this book in 'Unfinished Projects', 20:188–200.

very little of his work betrays signs of strain or haste: Dorian Lynskey, *The Ministry of Truth*, 146.

A story of the East told in masculine company: Kipling didn't write smoking-room stories of this kind, but belongs here on the strength of tales narrated by Private Mulvaney off duty to his friends Learoyd and Ortheris with 'I' listening in, in *Plain Tales from the Hills* ('With the Main Guard'), *Soldiers Three* and *Life's Handicap*. (I am very grateful to Janet Montefiore for pointing this out in lockdown correspondence.)

p. 164   a novel of character rather than of ideas: 'Fredric Warburg's Report on His Visit to Orwell', 15 June 1949, 20:132. See also the discussion in Douglas Kerr, 'George Orwell's Conrad', 26–34.

when each attempt at glorification: Mulk Raj Anand, 'Mr. Eliot's Kipling', *Life and Letters* 32 (March 1942), 169, 170.

p. 165   a review by Orwell in *Tribune*: 'Review of *Letters on India* by Mulk Raj Anand', March 1943, 15:32–5.

This was tricky for Orwell: See Kristin Bluemel, *George Orwell and the Radical Eccentrics* (London: Palgrave, 2004), 87, and David Dwan, *Liberty, Equality, and Humbug: Orwell's Political Ideals*, 134–5.

But he defended Anand: See 'Orwell to the Editor, *The Times Literary Supplement*', 23 May 1942, 13:337–8.

p. 166   European characters barely appear: 'Review of *The Sword and the Sickle* by Mulk Raj Anand', July 1942, 13:380.

largely unaware of Indian writing in Indian languages: Not entirely unaware. 'First Jasmines', a poem by Rabindranath Tagore, was read in English, seemingly at Anand's suggestion, as part of Orwell's monthly BBC radio magazine programme about literature. See 'Voice', 3: A Magazine Programme', 6 Oct. 1942, 14:78–9. The Indian Service also commissioned in 1943 the broadcast of a play, *The King of the Dark Chamber*, written and translated by Tagore. See 'Orwell to B. H. Alexander', 1 June 1943, 15:120.

Why were writers like Anand important: Orwell grouped Anand with Ahmed Ali, Iqbal Singh, Narayana Menon, and the Eurasian novelist Cedric Dover. See 'They Throw New Light on India', 9 Aug. 1945, 17:242. He would include Dover ('Main emphasis anti-white but reliably pro-Russian on all major issues') in his later notorious list of writers who could not be relied on to represent British interests in the propaganda war against the Soviet Union. See 'Orwell's List of Crypto-Communists and Fellow-Travellers', [April 1949], 20:246.

Partly because they are interpreting Asia to the West: 'Review of *The Sword and the Sickle* by Mulk Raj Anand', July 1942, 13:381.

they are in a species of alliance with us: Ibid., 13:381.

Bibliography

Abridged Law Manual for Sub-Inspectors of Police Burma, The (Rangoon: Government Printing and Stationery, Burma, 1926).

Alatas, Syed Hussein. *The Myth of the Lazy Native* (London: Frank Cass, 1977).

Al-Jubouri, Firas A. J. 'The End was Contained in the Beginning', *George Orwell Studies* 1:1 (2016), 73–88.

Anand, Mulk Raj. *Untouchable* (London: Penguin, [1935] 2014).

Anand, Mulk Raj. 'Mr. Eliot's Kipling', *Life and Letters* 32 (March 1942), 167–70.

Anand, Mulk Raj. *Letters on India* (London: Labour Book Service, 1942).

Anand, Mulk Raj. *The Sword and the Sickle* (London: Jonathan Cape, 1942).

Anand, Mulk Raj. *Coolie* [1936] (London: Penguin, 1945).

Anand, Mulk Raj. *Conversations in Bloomsbury* (London: Wildwood House, 1981).

Beddoe, Deirdre. 'Hindrances and Help-Meets: Women in the Writings of George Orwell', *Inside the Myth: Orwell: Views from the Left*, ed. Christopher Norris (London: Lawrence and Wishart, 1984), 139–54.

Bloom, Harold. *The Anxiety of Influence*, 2nd edition (Oxford: Oxford University Press, 1997).

Bluemel, Kristin. *George Orwell and the Radical Eccentrics* (London: Palgrave, 2004).

Bluemel, Kristin. 'The Intimate Orwell: Women's Productions, Feminist Consumption', *Orwell Today*, ed. Richard Lance Keeble (Suffolk: Abramis, 2012), 15–29.

Bounds, Philip. *Orwell and Marxism* (London: I. B. Tauris, 2016).

Bowker, Gordon. *George Orwell* (London: Little, Brown, 2003).

Bradford, Richard. *George Orwell: A Man of Our Time* (London: Bloomsbury, 2020).

Brecht, Bertolt. *The Collected Poems of Bertolt Brecht*, trans. and ed. Tom Kuhn and David Constantine (New York: Liveright, 2019), 1013.

Briggs, Asa. *The History of Broadcasting in the United Kingdom,* vol. 3, *The War of Words* (London: Oxford University Press, 1970).

Buddicom, Jacinta. *Eric & Us*, the Postscript Edition, ed. Dione Venables (Chichester: Finlay, 2006).

Burma Police Department. *Police Supply and Clothing Manual for Burma* (Rangoon: Government Printing and Stationery, Burma, 1925).

Burma Police Department. *The Burma Police Training School Manual.* (Rangoon: Government Printing and Stationery, Burma, 1939).

Campbell, Beatrix. 'Orwell: Paterfamilias or Big Brother?', *Inside the Myth: Orwell: Views from the Left*, ed. Christopher Norris (London: Lawrence and Wishart, 1984), 128–36.

Césaire, Aimé. *Discourse on Colonialism* [*Discours sur le Colonialisme*, 1950], trans. Joan Pinkham (New York: Monthly Review Press, 1972).

Chaudhuri, Rosinka. 'Introduction', George Orwell, *Burmese Days* (Oxford: Oxford University Press, 2021).

Clarke, Ben. *Orwell in Context: Communities, Myths, Values* (Basingstoke: Palgrave Macmillan, 2007).

Clifford, Hugh. *Malayan Monochromes* (London: John Murray, 1913).

Collis, Maurice. *Trials in Burma* (London: Faber and Faber, 1938).

Collis, Maurice. *Into Hidden Burma: An Autobiography* (London: Faber and Faber, 1953).

Conrad, Joseph. *The Nigger of the 'Narcissus'* (London: J. M. Dent, 1923).

Coppard, Audrey and Bernard Crick eds. *Orwell Remembered* (New York: Facts on File, 1984).

Csaszar, Ivett. 'Orwell and Women's Issues – a Shadow over the Champion of Decency', *Eger Journal of English Studies* X (2010), 39–56.

Disraeli, Benjamin. *Tancred or the New Crusade* [1847] (London: Longmans, Green, 1919).

Dwan, David. *Liberty, Equality, and Humbug: Orwell's Political Ideals* (Oxford: Oxford University Press, 2018).

Edwards, Ruth Dudley. *Victor Gollancz: A Biography* (London: Victor Gollancz, 1987).

Eliot, T. S. 'Preface', in *A Choice of Kipling's Verse*, ed. T. S. Eliot (London: Faber and Faber, 1941), v–xxxvi.

Eliot, T. S. ed. *A Choice of Kipling's Verse* (London: Faber and Faber, 1941).

Fleay, C. and M. L. Sanders, 'Looking into the Abyss: George Orwell at the BBC', *Journal of Contemporary History* 24:3 (July 1989), 503–18.

Forster, E. M. *A Passage to India* (London: Edward Arnold, 1924).

Furnivall, J. S. *Colonial Policy and Practice: A Comparative Study of Burma and Netherlands India* (New York: New York University Press, 1956).

Gilmour, David. *Curzon: Imperial Statesman* (New York: Farrar, Strauss and Giroux, 2003).

Gilroy, Paul. *After Empire: Melancholia or Convivial Culture?* (London: Routledge, 2004).

Gollancz, Victor. 'Foreword' to George Orwell, *The Road to Wigan Pier* (London: Victor Gollancz, Left Book Club edition, 1937), xi–xxiv.

Gopal, Priyamvada. *Insurgent Empire* (London: Verso, 2019).

Gorer, Geoffrey. *Exploring English Character* (London: Cresset Press, 1955).

Green, Martin. *Dreams of Adventure, Deeds of Empire* (London: Routledge and Kegan Paul, 1980).

Heber, Reginald. 'From Greenland's icy mountains' (1819), https://victorianweb.org/religion/hymns/heber1.html (accessed 24 July 2021).

Hegel, G. W. F. *Lectures on the Philosophy of World History* (New York: Cambridge University Press, 1975).

Ho, Janice. 'Europe, Refugees, and *Nineteen Eighty-Four*', *The Cambridge Companion to Nineteen Eighty-Four*, ed. Nathan Waddell (Cambridge: Cambridge University Press, 2020), 141–54.

Hobson, J. A. *Imperialism: A Study* (London: James Nisbet, 1902).

Hoggart, Richard. 'Introduction', in George Orwell, *The Road to Wigan Pier* (London: Penguin, 1989).

Hollis, Christopher. *A Study of George Orwell: The Man and his Works* (New York: Racehorse Publishing, 2017).

Hussain, Nasser. *The Jurisprudence of Emergency: Colonialism and the Rule of Law* (Ann Arbor: U of Michigan Press, 2003).

Ingle, Stephen. *George Orwell: A Political Life* (Manchester: Manchester University Press, 1994).

Joseph, John E. 'Orwell on Language and Politics', *Landmarks in Linguistic Thought II: The Western Tradition in the Twentieth Century*, eds. John E. Joseph, Nigel Love, and Talbot J. Taylor (London: Routledge, 2001), 29–42.

Keck, Stephen L. 'Text and Context: Another Look at *Burmese Days*', *SOAS Bulletin of Burma Research* 3:1 (Spring 2005), 27–40.

Keeble, Richard Lance ed. *Orwell Today* (Bury St Edmunds: Abramis, 2012).

Keeble, Richard Lance. *George Orwell, The Secret State and the Making of Nineteen Eighty-Four* (Bury St Edmunds: Abramis, 2020).

Kerr, Douglas. 'Ruins in the Jungle: Nature and Narrative', in *Asian Crossings: Travel Writing on China, Japan and Southeast Asia*, eds. Steve Clark and Paul Smethurst (Hong Kong: Hong Kong University Press, 2008), 131–40.

Kerr, Douglas. 'George Orwell's Conrad', *George Orwell Studies* 1:1 (2016), 21–36.

Kipling, Rudyard. *The Second Jungle Book* (London: Macmillan, 1906).

Kipling, Rudyard. *Soldiers Three* (London: Macmillan, 1911).

Kipling, Rudyard. *The Letters of Rudyard Kipling*, vol. 3: *1900–1910*, ed. Thomas Pinney (Basingstoke: Macmillan, 1996).

Kolsky, Elizabeth. *Colonial Justice in British India* (Cambridge: Cambridge University Press, 2010).

Lenin, V. I. *Imperialism, the Highest Stage of Capitalism* [1917] (London: Lawrence, 1934).

Liebreich, Fritz. *Britain's Naval and Political Reaction to the Illegal Immigration of Jews to Palestine 1945–48* (London: Routledge, 2005).

Lynskey, Dorian. *The Ministry of Truth: A Biography of George Orwell's 1984* (London: Picador, 2019).

Marks, Peter. *George Orwell the Essayist: Literature, Politics and the Periodical Culture* (London: Continuum, 2011).

Maugham, W. Somerset. *On a Chinese Screen* (Oxford: Oxford University Press, [1922] 1985).

Maugham, W. Somerset. *Ah King and Other Stories* (Singapore: Oxford University Press, [1933] 1986).

Maung Htin Aung, *A History of Burma* (New York: Columbia University Press, 1967).

Maung Htin Aung, 'George Orwell in Burma', in *The World of George Orwell*, ed. Miriam Gross (London: Weidenfeld and Nicolson, 1972), 19–30.

Maung Htin Aung, 'Orwell of the Burma Police', *Asian Affairs* (new series) 4:2 (1973), 181–86.

McClintock, Anne. *Imperial Leather: Race, Gender and Sexuality in the Colonial Contest* (New York: Routledge, 1995).

Meyers, Jeffrey. *Orwell: Wintry Conscience of a Generation* (New York: Norton, 2000).

Moore, Darcy. 'Orwell and the Appeal of Opium', *George Orwell Studies* 3:1 (2018), 83–102.

Moore, Darcy. 'Orwell's Aunt Nellie', *George Orwell Studies*, 4:2 (2020), 30–44.

Moore, Darcy. 'Orwell's Scottish Ancestry and Slavery', *George Orwell Studies* 5:1 (2020), 6–19.

Moore, Darcy. 'Orwell in Burma: The Two Erics', *George Orwell Studies* 5:2 (2021), 6–24.

Newsinger, John. *Orwell's Politics* (Basingstoke: Macmillan, 1999).

Newsinger, John. *Hope Lies in the Proles: George Orwell and the Left* (London: Pluto Press, 2018).

Norris, Christopher ed. *Inside the Myth: Orwell: Views from the Left* (London: Lawrence and Wishart, 1984).

Orwell, George. *The Complete Works of George Orwell*, 20 vols, ed. Peter Davison (London: Secker and Warburg, 1998).

Orwell, George. *The Lost Orwell*, ed. Peter Davison (London: Timewell Press, 2006).

Osterhammel, Jürgen. *The Transformation of the World: A Global History of the Nineteenth Century*, trans. Patrick Camiller (Princeton, NJ: Princeton University Press, 2014).

Palmer, Andrew. 'Orwell and Antisemitism', *Jewish Quarterly* 45:4 (1998), 41–5.

Patai, Daphne. *The Orwell Mystique* (Boston: University of Massachusetts Press, 1984).

Pratt, Mary Louise. *Imperial Eyes: Travel Writing and Transculturation* (London: Routledge, 1992).

Rodden, John. *Becoming George Orwell: Life and Letters, Legend and Legacy* (Princeton, NJ: Princeton University Press, 2020).

Ryan, James B. *Picturing Empire: Photography and the Visualization of the British Empire* (London: Reaktion, 1997).

Said, Edward W. *Orientalism* [1978] (Harmondsworth: Penguin, 1985).

Sanghera, Sathnam. *Empireland: How Imperialism Has Shaped Modern Britain* (London: Viking, 2021).

Saunders, Loraine. *The Unsung Mastery of George Orwell* (Aldershot: Ashgate, 2008).

Scott, Paul. *The Jewel in the Crown* (London: Pan Macmillan, [1966] 1988).

Scott, Paul. *The Day of the Scorpion* (London: Pan Macmillan, [1968] 1988).

Shabanirad, Ensieh and Seyyed Mohammad Marandi. 'Edward Said's *Orientalism* and the Representation of Oriental Women in George Orwell's *Burmese Days*', *International Letters of Social and Humanistic Sciences* 60 (2015), 22–33.

Shelden, Michael. *Orwell: The Authorised Biography* (London: Minerva, 1992).

Sutherland, John. *Orwell's Nose: A Pathological Biography* (London: Reaktion, 2016).

Taylor, D. J. *Orwell: The Life* (London: Chatto and Windus, 2003).

Taylor, Elinor. 'The Problem of Hope: Orwell's Workers', *The Cambridge Companion to Nineteen Eighty-Four*, ed. Nathan Waddell (Cambridge: Cambridge University Press, 2020), 155–67.

Tentler, Leslie. '"I'm Not Literary Dear": George Orwell on Women and Family', *The Future of Nineteen Eighty-Four*, ed. Ejner Jensen (Ann Arbor: U of Michigan Press, 1984), 47–65.

Thant Myint-U. *The Making of Modern Burma* (Cambridge: Cambridge University Press, 2001).

Topp, Sylvia. *Eileen: The Making of George Orwell* (London: Unbound, 2020).

Vynckier, Henk and John Rodden eds. 'Orienting Orwell: Asian and Global Perspectives on George Orwell', *Concentric: Literary and Cultural Studies* 40:1 (2014).

Waddell, Nathan ed. *The Cambridge Companion to Nineteen Eighty-Four* (Cambridge: Cambridge University Press, 2020).

Wadhams, Stephen ed. *The Orwell Tapes* (Vancouver: Locarno Press, 2017).

Wildemeersch, Marc. *George Orwell's Commander in Spain: The Enigma of Georges Kopp* (London: Thames River Press, 2013).

Woloch, Alex. *Or Orwell: Writing and Democratic Socialism* (Cambridge, Mass.: Harvard University Press, 2016).

Woodcock, George. *Who Killed the British Empire?: An Inquest* (London: Jonathan Cape, 1974).

Woolf, Leonard. *The Village in the Jungle* (London: Edward Arnold, 1913).

Woolf, Leonard. *Growing: An Autobiography of the Years 1904–1911* (London: Hogarth Press, 1961).

Woolf, Leonard. *The Journey Not the Arrival Matters: An Autobiography of the Years 1939–1969* (London: Hogarth Press, 1969).

Young, Robert J. C. 'Postcolonial Remains', *New Literary History* 43:1 (Winter 2012), 19–42.

Index

For the benefit of digital users, indexed terms that span two pages (e.g., 52–53) may, on occasion, appear on only one of those pages.